P9-CPY-086

ENCOUNTER

WITH

SPURGEON

HELMUT THIELICKE

*Let us save men by every means under the sun;
let us prevent men from going to hell.*

*A mouthful of sea air, or a stiff walk in the
wind's face, would not give grace to the soul, but
it would yield oxygen to the body, which is next
best.*

CHARLES H. SPURGEON

Translated by
JOHN W. DOBERSTEIN

FORTRESS PRESS, PHILADELPHIA

Translated from *Vom geistlichen Reden: Begegnung mit Spurgeon* by Helmut Thielicke, published 1961 by Quell-Verlag, Stuttgart, Germany

Library of Congress Card Number 63-12536

Printed in U. S. A.   UB932

Contents

19677

Translator's Preface

This book gives us a great preacher's best thinking about preaching, but in an unusual context; for here Helmut Thielicke, whose reputation as a theologian and preacher is now world-wide, develops his homiletics against the foil of a nineteenth-century preacher's sermons and lectures on preaching, and brings us straight to the center and secret of Christian proclamation. How piquant, how wonderful, how "ecumenical" that Helmut Thielicke, the highly educated German university professor and Lutheran theologian, should find such deep and warm kinship with Charles Haddon Spurgeon, the self-educated, Victorian Baptist preacher, who to this day remains a "prince among preachers" in the English and American tradition! How strange that a man so widely separated in time and culture should rediscover these lectures on preaching which have influenced a whole line of books on homiletics for fifty years or more! And, after reading of his encounter with Spurgeon and rereading Spurgeon's sermons and his lectures to his students, we are grateful to Thielicke for bringing him again into the stream of our homiletical thinking.

The selection and abbreviation of Spurgeon's lectures and the two sermons were done by Dr. Thielicke. The text of the lectures has been taken from *Lectures to My Students, A Selection from Addresses to the Students of the Pastors' College, Metropolitan Tabernacle, London, First Series* (New York: American Tract Society, n.d.), and *Second Series of Lectures to My Students: Being Addresses Delivered to the Students of the Pastors' College, Metropolitan Tabernacle* (New York: Robert Carter & Bros., 1889). The text of the two sermons is taken from *Sermons of Rev. C. H. Spurgeon of London* (New York: Funk & Wagnalls, n.d.), Vol. VII. Omissions are indicated by ellipsis marks. Spurgeon's spelling has been retained.

In a few instances where Dr. Thielicke quotes from Spurgeon materials other than the lectures and sermons reprinted in this book, the translator, having been unable to locate the original English passages, has had to resort to the unsatisfactory procedure of retranslating from the German.

JOHN W. DOBERSTEIN

ENCOUNTER WITH SPURGEON

by Helmut Thielicke

In the midst of the theologically discredited nineteenth century there was a preacher who had at least six thousand people in his congregation every Sunday, whose sermons for many years were cabled to New York every Monday and reprinted in the leading newspapers of the country, and who occupied the same pulpit for almost forty years without any diminishment in the flowing abundance of his preaching and without ever repeating himself or preaching himself dry. The fire he thus kindled, and turned into a beacon that shone across the seas and down through the generations, was no mere brush fire of sensationalism, but an inexhaustible blaze that glowed and burned on solid hearths and was fed by the wells of the eternal Word. Here was the miracle of a bush that burned with fire and yet was not consumed (Exod. 3:2).

In no way was he like the managers of a modern evangelistic campaign, who manipulate souls with all the techniques of mass-suggestion, acting like salvation engineers. Charles Haddon Spurgeon—it is he of whom we are speaking—was still unaware of the wiles of propaganda, and completely ignorant of the subliminal influence that operates by appealing to secret images, wish-dreams, and anxiety complexes—and hence begins with the results of psychoanalytical tests. He worked only through the power of the Word which created its own hearers and changed souls.

Now this was not *his* word, the product of his own rhetorical skills. It was rather a word which he himself had "merely" heard. He put himself at its disposal, as a mere echo, and it brought to him the Spirit over whom he did not himself dispose. His message never ran dry because he was never anything but a recipient.

1

Nor did he live spiritually beyond his means. For he gave out only what flowed into him in never ceasing supply from the channels of Holy Scripture. With pails and buckets he went up even the remotest rills and tributaries of this stream to bring water to the thirsty, and to make fruitful the land of barren souls.

It would be well for a time like ours to learn from this man. For our preaching is, to be sure, largely correct, exegetically "legitimate," workmanlike and tidy; but it is also remarkably dead and lacking in infectious power. Very often it strikes us as an unreal phantom that hovers above and is isolated from what people feel are the actual realities of their life and what they talk about in their language. There can be no doubt that for many preachers it is simply an escape when, in the face of this failure to get returns in the area of preaching, they take flight into the cultivation of liturgical ceremonial and even make a virtue of the vice of wanting to ignore the times and live in some timeless, spiritual world.

In this desperate situation which threatens to break down even the best of men—for it is a desperate thing to feel the burden of souls committed to our charge and not to be able to do anything about it—everything depends upon our gaining some standards for that which is "Theme Number One"* of the church—our preaching.

There is certainly value in attempting to formulate these standards in theoretical terms, but this still does not meet the need. For, since preaching encompasses a tremendously broad complex of procedures—ranging from prayer for the miracle of the Spirit through study of the text itself and the structuring of a sermon outline to the workmanlike mastery of effective speech—real standards can be found only in living examples. Only in such examples does one find that ordered whole in which these multiple procedures have taken on concrete form, and which can therefore perform for the inquisitive observer the function of a blueprint.

---

*See chapter 27 of Thielicke's *Christ and the Meaning of Life* (New York: Harper & Bros., 1962), pp. 173-180.—TRANS.

One must therefore read sermons like Spurgeon's in order to learn what a sermon can be and what it can give. One must study his commentaries—the greatest of them, a commentary on the Psalms *(The Treasury of David),* comprises seven large volumes—in order to appreciate what careful, painstaking Bible study can be in the hands of a receptive listener, and what a secondary matter it is that this charismatic listener was no great philologist and could call himself only an amateur in theology. (While we realize that the trained theologian dare not bypass the work involved in modern methods of interpretation, still we would be merely pedantically captious and stupid if we were no longer to appreciate this gift of charismatic hearing, this inimitable immediacy which the specially chosen one has to his text. It would only indicate that we had been driven mad by the art of hermeneutics if we were no longer capable of accepting and valuing, as a corrective of our perfect exegesis, the childlike candor of a preacher who could "listen like a disciple."*

It is evidence of the substance and also of the excellence of form in Spurgeon's sermons that—removed from the situation in which they were originally preached, and also from the magnetism of Spurgeon's personality!—they lose very little in print. Not for a moment do they give the impression that we are reading merely historical testimonies to which we no longer have any immediate access and which come alive only in the act of reinterpretation. Even for us they are still a bubbling spring whose water needs no filtering or treatment. And I venture to ask: Of what other preacher of the nineteenth century could this be said? I would not know of a single one, even among the greatest (to speak of German preachers), not Schleiermacher, nor Johann Tobias Beck, nor even Ludwig Hofacker. Indeed, which sermons of the years before World War I—what am I saying: which sermons of the twenties and thirties could we still read today without the additional incentive of a historical interest,

---

*The allusion is to Luther's translation of Isa. 50:4: "He wakens my ear that I may hear like a disciple."—TRANS.

and without feeling it was less ourselves who were being addressed than the fathers and brethren of days gone by?

But this bush from old London still burns and shows no signs of being consumed. Here Christians dare to speak of miracle.

Having in addition the good fortune to possess a book by this man in which he interprets himself and instructs his students on how they can do such preaching themselves—and, what is more, tells them what they must first *become* in order to be capable of it—we can only regard all this as a wonderful gift and look forward to the joy of a new discovery. At least one man who has known the burden—and the joyous privilege—of having to preach finds himself unable to keep silent now that he has begun to surmise what a preacher like Spurgeon could mean for our generation.

It is for this reason that in the second part of this book we undertake to recover and present some of these sunken treasures.

Charles Haddon Spurgeon was born in 1834 and died in 1892. His early years were filled with inner conflict and painful searching until the age of fifteen when, under the influence of a stirring address delivered by a lay preacher in a small Primitive Methodist chapel, he found his way to faith. For the rest of his life he remembered January 6, 1850, as the day of his conversion and new birth. The notation of the exact time when his life as a "new man" began may remind us of certain of the conventionalities of Pietism which are also familiar to us. Such an association is in fact suggested by the Puritan and Methodist tradition to which he was related through his family and his own development. Yet we shall see that with respect to both his personal inclinations and his spiritual attitude he cannot be adequately characterized by that label; he was far too original—and hence too unique—to be easily classified in terms of the history of theology.

He was only sixteen years old, a junior schoolteacher, when by chance he had to preach his first impromptu sermon to a few farmers gathered in a cottage. When it turned out to be successful and his listeners were moved, he continued his preaching activity. This event attracted the attention of many devout people and in 1851—at the age of seventeen—he was called by the little Baptist congregation in the village of Waterbeach to be their preacher. In a short time the young "boy-preacher," as he was called, created a sensation and people flocked from great distances to hear him. Even at that time men recognized that it was not only a matter of his youthful exuberant eloquence evoking excitement, and of curiosity drawing people to this spiritual child prodigy, but that he was endowed with the power of the effectual Word: people were actually changed, and moral laxity was replaced by order and peace.

It is a testimony to the extraordinary maturity and self-insight of the "boy preacher" that success did not delude him. Instead he became aware of his lack of theological preparation and repeatedly and energetically sought admission to a theological seminary. By a strange providence he did not succeed in this but was obliged to remain an autodidact, a self-taught man.

While this set severe limitations on his training in theology, his self-education became all the more unusual in the form that it took. He did not exhaust himself in an indiscriminate, chaotic, book-devouring hunger for education, but rather gave evidence even at that time of a disciplined and purposeful system of study which, undergirded by intellectual power and determination and an astonishing memory, also disclosed itself later in his ability to organize his literary work on a large and well planned scale. During the course of his life he gathered about him a considerable group of assistants who aided him in his twenty years of work on the commentary on the Psalms, exploring for him the rich source materials in the British Museum, providing him with excerpts, and combing through the works of the Puritan fathers for him. The tremendous number of book reviews which he published in *The Sword and the Trowel,* a monthly magazine established later, indicates further how widely and critically and systematically he read for himself and educated himself. After a number of intermediate posts in which the churches were always too small to accommodate the crowds of people and in which he frequently preached in the open air, in vacant barns, once even from the gable of a house, he moved in 1861 to the famous Metropolitan Tabernacle in London. Here until his death he preached Sunday after Sunday to some six thousand people. His largest meeting drew an audience of twenty-four thousand persons in the Crystal Palace on Fast Day in 1857. Even in a time when loudspeakers were unknown, he had no difficulty with his clear, resonant, and penetrating voice in making himself heard in the farthest corner.

When he preached for the first time in the large Surrey Gardens Music Hall, crowded with nearly ten thousand people, a few mischief-makers cried out "Fire! Fire!" Though Spurgeon remained calm in the pulpit and endeavored to restore quiet, he was unable to stop the panic. For the rest of his life he could never forget the horrible spectacle in which seven persons were trampled to death and twenty-eight injured. In his mind it became a symbol of the "darkness" that can befall the very people of God, a good example of the trials and perplexities that make them give heed to the Word.

The nightmare of this horrible scene shadowed his life for a long time afterward and first began to retreat when he thought of the words, "Therefore God has highly exalted him" (cf. Phil. 2:9).

"The fact that Jesus still remains exalted even though his servants lie never so low upon the ground, led me finally . . . back to peace."

So for him joy and pain, success and discouragement again and again became spiritual visitations with which he sought to cope by spiritual means. For him nothing was to be interpreted merely in terms of its immanental context in time; he saw everything in the light of eternity.

It is characteristic of the nature of his preaching ministry that, despite the turbulence of a successful life in which he was surrounded by crowds of people, he did not allow himself to become swamped with externals and consumed with busyness. Instead he immersed himself in the quietness of prayer and meditation, receptively filling his mind and soul, and then went forth recreated from these quiet hours to pour himself out without reserve. Hence the temptation of becoming the star preacher and enjoying the respect and adulation of men held no attraction for him. Neither did he become a "soloist." Instead, as a serving member of the church, he sought out the "ensemble" in which to work. It was there that he radiated his spirit, in order to impart not only the effects of his gifts but also the gifts themselves, and not in order merely to attach people to the greatness of his own personality.

The most important result of his labors was the founding of the Pastors' College (1857), in which with the help of his co-workers he trained nearly seven hundred preachers and evangelists. Out of this work came *Lectures to My Students,* extracts from which are given in the second part of this book. These lectures are distinguished by the fact that they give to the reader far more than technical rules for the art of preaching. They are an inexhaustible store of stimulating material.

Of course, the lectures do provide training in the formal side of preaching as well. The technical aspects of rhetoric and oratory, including the use of the voice, gestures, and facial expression, and the structuring of a sermon, are important enough to be the subject of all-round training; for "the solemn task of preaching the gospel demands everything that a man can give, the very best." For this reason we are responsible not only for what we say, but equally for *how* we say it. Our tools too must be kept sharp. Not only our spiritual knowledge but also the means of its communication are entrusted talents, meant to be used for service. Spurgeon is well aware that many preachers stand in their own way because uncontrolled mannerisms—some defect of speech, a monotonous delivery, a repulsive facial expression, a constantly clenched fist or a continually pointed finger—curb the congregation's willingness to listen, or produce a deadly—and spiritually deadening!—boredom.

While dilating at length upon this catalogue of rhetorical vices, Spurgeon does not make the paradoxical mistake of talking about that which is boring and tedious in a dull and prosy way. One will find few instances in literature where something that is conducive to boredom is discussed in such a sprightly and amusing fashion. The technique Spurgeon employs in this connection is that of caricature and humor. He can picture before their eyes marvellously comic pulpit figures, and make his hearers vow spontaneously never to become such a dreadful preacher as that.

His delight in caricature is applied not only to external behavior but also to the mentality of certain clerical coxcombs, culture-struck abbés, and fashionable gentlemen preachers. The ridicule to which he subjects these figures—and ridicule kills!—becomes for Spurgeon as it were a function of the judging and condemning law. And yet, in that he describes all this from a vantage point of security and is aware of that discipline of the Holy Spirit which drives these infirmities from our hearts, he can say all this with a smile and a twinkle in his eye and turn even destructive criticism into a means of edification. "I commend cheerfulness to all who would win souls." And why should not this cheerfulness be effective already in the training of the soul-winners themselves?

Important as is this formal, outward, "fleshly" aspect for those who would minister the Word of God made flesh, it is only a small sector of the whole circle of seminary instruction. The circle itself can be described only in terms of the effort to give preachers a comprehensive education.

First, it was a matter of education because Spurgeon's influence upon his seminarians was not limited merely to the communication of knowledge and techniques; he sought rather to ground and build them as persons and to make them capable instruments for the task committed to them. Second, this education was comprehensive, because it permeated all dimensions of life and nothing was allowed to go unexposed to the magnetic field of this commitment.

In this kind of education, work upon the spiritual dimension of existence came first. It took the form of pastoral care given to future pastors. It was a matter not merely of exhortation to a life lived in constant association with the Holy Scriptures—lest that life be regarded as a burdensome yoke of the law—but rather in every word of actually bringing that life into being by making the ubiquity of the Scriptures a real and living fact.

When Spurgeon speaks, it is as if the figures of the patriarchs and prophets and apostles were in the auditorium—sitting upon a raised tribune!—looking down upon the listeners. You hear the rush of the Jordan and the murmuring of the brooks of Siloam; you see the cedars of Lebanon swaying in the wind, hear the clash and tumult of battle between the children of Israel and the Philistines, sense the safety and security of Noah's ark, suffer the agonies of soul endured by Job and Jeremiah, hear the creak of oars as the disciples strain against the contrary winds, and feel the dread of the terrors of the apocalypse. The Bible is so close that you not only hear its messages but breathe its very atmosphere. The heart is so full of Scripture that it leavens the consciousness, peoples the imagination with its images, and determines the landscape of the soul by its climate. And because it has what might be called a total presence, the Bible as the Word of God is really concentrated life that enters every pore and teaches us not only to see and hear but also to taste and smell the wealth of reality that is spread out before us here.

Those who listened to these lectures of Spurgeon lived, even "according to the flesh" (*kata sarka*), in the atmosphere of the Bible. They no longer needed to be exhorted to take the Bible seriously; it penetrated into what the psychologists call the "image level" of their unconscious. Even the admonition to prayer was hardly needed, for the words that reached the hearer were spoken by one who himself had come out of the stillness of eternal communion with God, and what he said to the hearer had first been talked about with the Father in heaven.

For Spurgeon the really determinative foundation of the education of preachers was naturally this work on the spiritual man. The education of preachers must not be directly pragmatic; it must not be immediately directed to preaching as its *goal*. Otherwise the process of education becomes an act of mere training, the teaching of technical skills. The preacher must read the Bible without asking in the back of his mind how he can capitalize homiletically upon the texts he studies. He must first read it as nourishment for his own soul. For the light which we are to let shine before men is borrowed light, a mere reflection. He who will not go out into the sun in order to play the humble role of a mirror, reflecting the sun's light, has to try to produce his own light, and thus gives the lie to his message by his vanity and egocentric presumption. Besides becoming unworthy of being believed, he is condemned to consume his own substance and expend his capital to the point of bankruptcy. Because he is not a recipient, he must himself produce and seek to overcome the empty silence within him by means of noisy gongs and clanging cymbals. Thus he ends in the paralysis of emptiness, and his empty, droning rhetoric merely covers up the burned-out slag beneath.

The fact that Spurgeon thus works first upon the souls of these prospective preachers and repeatedly challenges them to work upon their own souls, however, is based not merely upon the desire to achieve a sensible balance between income and outgo, but ultimately upon a basic fact of faith, which is that the arm of the Lord is stretched out over the earth without any help on our part, and therefore that it is not *we* activists who have to take him by the hand and drag him over the continents and the farthest islands of the sea. God is Lord even apart from the instrumentality that we put at his disposal with our talents. His kingdom comes even without our efforts.

Therefore the disciple can take the long view and persevere.

He who is co-ordinated with eternity dare not allow himself to be harassed and hounded by time. Thus Spurgeon makes many comments which are comparable to Luther's calm statement that while he quietly sat and drank his little mug of Wittenberg beer the gospel ran its course. Nervousness is sinful. It is, so to speak, the psychopathological form of unbelief, which takes over too much responsibility itself and to the same degree loses its confidence that God reigns and is looking after his cause.

"It was for this reason," says Spurgeon, "that Jesus, full of wisdom and compassion, said to his disciples, 'Let us go into the desert and rest awhile.'" And then he goes on to say, "What! When the people are fainting? When they are like sheep without a shepherd? How can Jesus talk of rest? When the scribes and Pharisees, like wolves, are rending the flock, how can he take his followers on an excursion into a quiet resting place?" When the decisive battle is beginning and the enemy is breaking through on every side, can one retreat to rest quarters? But, says Spurgeon:

> The Lord Jesus knows better. He will not exhaust the strength of his servants prematurely and quench the light of Israel. Rest time is not waste. It is economy to gather fresh strength. Look at the mower in the summer's day, with so much to cut down ere the sun sets. He pauses in his labour—is he a sluggard? He looks for his stone, and begins to draw it up and down his scythe, with *rink-a-tink, rink-a-tink, rink-a-tink*. Is that idle music—is he wasting precious moments? How much he might have mowed while he has been ringing out those notes on his scythe! But he is sharpening his tool, and he will do far more when once again he gives his strength to those long sweeps which lay the grass prostrate in rows before him.

Nor can the fisherman be always fishing; he must mend his nets. So even our vacation can be one of the duties laid upon us by the kingdom of God.

Reading this, one can think only in sorrow—or in anger!—of the many different practical forms of education in the church today. Whereas Spurgeon enjoins us to remember that preachers must not think too highly of themselves as instruments but in faith accept the fact that they are dispensable, we hound our young vicars—not everybody does this, I know, but many do!—chasing them from examinations into the bustling business of pastoral services in the big cities, from funerals to marriage, and from the pulpit to doorbell-ringing, opening the pores of the body of Christ to all the bacilli against which, after all, we should be mobilizing the antibiotic of our message of peace. We keep killing flowers in the bud, because we are no longer capable of letting things grow. And we can no longer let things grow because down underneath we have forgotten how to pray "Thy kingdom come," and in its place have put our "manager's faith," our belief that everything can be produced and organized. We preach "Do not be anxious!"—and at the same time worry ourselves to death about whether everybody will hear this. We say, "God reigns"—and still we run about madly keeping the ecclesiastical machinery going. We proclaim man's passive righteousness (the righteousness that comes from God)—and still we behave like activists. We preach eternity; but when Jesus asks us, "Did you have enough of everything?" we will have to reply, "Oh, no; we didn't have enough time." This is why we preach peace and radiate restlessness. This is why we give stones instead of bread, and men do not believe us. The faith is refuted by the incredibility of those who proclaim it.

In the period of rationalism—and therefore in times long since past—it may have been true that knowledge seemed to be a refutation of faith; the attack upon faith came from the "world," which supposedly was in possession of knowledge. Today the judgment has begun at the house of God itself: we deter faith by our own incredibility.

So before we fall upon Spurgeon to analyze him homiletically as a purveyor of model sermons, we should first allow ourselves to be led to the place where such model sermons become possible, namely, the place of spiritual calm and sovereign laisser faire. The children of God can afford to dwell there precisely because they are the children of *God*.

Spiritual processes cannot be described without emphasis upon the *place* where they can occur. The man who does not work at the art of preaching without ulterior purpose, but who is always thinking of how the article will sell and perhaps also of how he can keep the market going, becomes a *routinier;* he becomes a servant, not of the kingdom of God, but of the task of perfecting the preaching machinery. What he says may be "legitimate"; the manner in which he says it may be "pleasing"; and the way he puts it may be a masterpiece of ecclesiastical "strategy." And yet what comes out will be a paradoxical self-refutation of the message, because his own existence testifies against it. What then takes place—all very correctly and in accord with the rules of the art— is the mere threshing of empty straw. The well-oiled machine no longer serves; it makes propaganda for an institution which, after all, should itself be only a servant. What the church then does is simply an act of self-assertion on the part of one institution engaged in competition with other institutions.

The result of all this may be some kind of success, but it is not the fruit of the Spirit. It may be quite possible to register certain influences that the church has exerted upon public life, but they are not the salt that preserves from decay nor the leaven that determines the taste of the bread. The grain of wheat of the messenger and the grain of wheat of the church as institution must first be hidden in the earth, in quietness and calm passivity; it must first die if it is to be able to spring up and bear fruit. Yet we work feverishly, pushing things along with artificial fertilizers; we are perpetual "producers," worshipping the gods of production. That is why the valley of dry bones spreads all around us. We are pragmatists, awed by the art of influencing people; we have forgotten the lesson of the grain of wheat about dying in order to be. Only he who dies and rises again with Christ can credibly bear witness to the death and resurrection of the Lord. But because we do not live in the magnetic field of Good Friday and Easter we merely act "as if" he had risen again. That is why the handy formulas and well-aimed addresses help us not a bit. The enemy who goes about at night, sowing his weeds among the grains of wheat which we have ostensibly scattered in the name of Jesus Christ, is the Grand Inquisitor who comes from our own midst and organizes the Christian enterprise with a view to success. He who has ears to hear, let him hear!

"Theme Number One" in the message of Spurgeon is the news about *where* spiritual existence becomes possible: the news that the straight line is precisely not the shortest connection between two points—between the theological seminary and preaching in the pulpit—but that a detour is needed. The most out-of-the-way point on this detour is quiet stillness. Not only the heart must rest, but also our legs. It is not only grace that cries out for stillness, but nature as well. The higher the top of a tree reaches, the more securely must it be grounded in the earth in order that storms may not uproot it.

The storm that Spurgeon is thinking of primarily is the turmoil and temptation of success. For success exposes a man to the pressure of people and thus tempts him to hold on to his gains by means of "fleshly" methods and practices, and to let himself be ruled wholly by the dictatorial demands of incessant expansion. Success can go to my head, and will unless I remember that it is God who accomplishes his work, that he can continue to do so without my help, and that he will be able to make out with other means whenever he "cuts me down to size."

So behind everything a man does in the vineyard we can detect the spiritual attitudes that constitute his true colors. Humility, calmness, and trust are what really do the job—and tell the story! We cannot understand the work of Spurgeon unless we take his integrity into account. We cannot duplicate his work unless we take our place with him at the same point of spiritual existence. As with all great men the example of what he is has greater significance than the example of what he does.

But the spiritual quality we are concerned with here is not something that can be understood as an isolated sector of life.

The resulting picture would then be only that caricature of a man, the "spiritualist." The self of the spiritual man, like that of any other man, is an indivisible whole. And therefore it cannot be divorced from the nature in which it has been incorporated by the will of the Creator. Though the idea of an *analogia entis,* a ladder from nature to grace, appears nowhere in Spurgeon's writings as far as I can see, the two are nevertheless related to each other. But, of course, this vocation of preaching cannot be expressed by ontological means but only with reference to him who as Father, Son, and Holy Spirit is the *one* God and therefore unites all the dimensions of our existence into one.

This is doubtless the reason why in Spurgeon our bodily existence can repeatedly be spoken of as a kind of substructure of the spiritual life, without however allowing—as the Marxist doctrine of substructure and superstructure might suggest allowing —the physical-natural part of our being to assume the determinate role. It cannot assume that role, if for no other reason than this, that in God himself the Creator does not have precedence of the Redeemer; the first article of the Creed does not have pre-eminence over the second.

Spurgeon wishes to tell us that our body too—just like our "heart"—is ordained to be a servant; and because it is to be the instrument of him whom we preach, it must also serve the preaching. Our spirit and soul and body together (cf. I Thess. 5:23) constitute the totality of the spiritual self, and therefore all of them together are entrusted to the supervision and training of those who in the name of the Word made flesh are charged with the education of ministers of the Word.

So even the physical side of speech, including voice culture and gestures, is not merely a matter of the rules and techniques of rhetoric. It is a part of the service which the speaker must render to the Word and its utterance, the service which he is supposed to perform in love for that neighbor to whom he owes this Word.

This does not mean that we scorn the techniques of rhetoric;

they are only put in their proper relative place, their spiritual place. Apart from this place they degenerate into the principle of art for art's sake, a means of striving for psychological effect. It was precisely the masses that Spurgeon had to speak to, plus his own susceptibility to the appeal of the atmosphere they generated and his masterly ability to play upon the instrument of an enthusiastic crowd, that compelled him to exercise special self-control in order to avoid the threat of rhetorical excess. For "if there is anything that is likely to add more fuel to the flames of human vanity than the success of an actor, it is the success of a preacher" (Bruce Marshall).

He obtained this self-control, not from the discipline of the law, but rather from the recollection of what God had bestowed upon him and of the stewardship he had to render as a servant. Just as exegesis is philology in service and dogmatics is diaconic thinking, so rhetoric becomes an *ars instrumentalis* and thus a province of theology. It is, so to speak, taken over from the faculty of arts into the faculty of theology. Just as philology in service does not contribute something less than philology proper to exegesis (but rather employs all the rules of textual and literary criticism as well as interpretation), and just as diaconic thought is not something less than disciplined thinking (but rather respects the laws of logic and by no means practices intellectual glossolalia or devotes itself to the Dadaist cult of the paradox), so spiritual rhetoric in Spurgeon is not something less than good rhetoric and workmanlike skill, but is rather a matter of strenuous training, employing what was known in his time of the physiology of the larynx and the psychology of the listener. *Except* that this heathen rhetoric is baptized and made a part of the activity of the community of Jesus Christ.

Here again Spurgeon subjects our present-day preaching to some critical questions. Have we not taken the perfectly proper recognition that it is not we but the Word itself that creates a hearing for itself and made of that recognition a "pretext for evil," an excuse for slovenly neglect of rhetoric? Is it not a misconception of the doctrine of justification when we allow "by faith alone" to become an abstention from works, including the work of rhetoric? When a man preaches the pure Word of God and the pews are empty or those attending go to sleep in church, we are all too ready to make a virtue of our lack of success and talk about the offense that must necessarily accompany the preaching of the gospel. We have a great talent for persuading ourselves that it is not only the stones which can cry out but that the empty pews too will testify for us. And yet it may have been due only to the miserable structure of our sermons that people who value intellectual order were unable to follow them without torturously abusing their minds, and finally giving it up. Perhaps it was also our poorly used voice that caused people to indulge in church rather than at home their desire for sleep. Or we stood like stock-fish in the pulpit, or we revolved our arms like paddle wheels, or we kept threatening with our fists, or rattling our dentures—in short, we did not pay enough attention to, we did not cultivate, the instrumental factor. We did not *grieve* over the poorly fired, porous "earthen vessels" of our disorderly sermon outlines and our miserable rhetoric. On the contrary—what a strange perversion!—we were pleased with them because, after all, the wretchedness of the vessel seemed only to enhance the treasure it contained.

The church as an institution and the professional theologians often betray the curious tendency to regard everything that once was filled with pagan meaning as being forever doomed to be a bogy; they make it the cause of fondly and anxiously cultivated complexes. For a long time natural science was such a bogy for us, simply because philosophically it once insisted that nature is a self-contained economy of forces, and by so insisting set up the doctrine of "self-sufficient finitude" and hence engaged in polemics against any kind of incursion from the Beyond, such as "supernatural" miracle. But ever since then, we have not been content to repudiate this philosophical misuse of science, but have continued to make science itself an object of distrust, attaching our anxiety complexes to it. Then finally we found that it was no

longer possible to recover our loss of intellectual integrity in this
way when science showed that it could no longer be ignored and
wrung from us a belated, though still rather sour, acceptance.

In exactly the same way sacred rhetoric has become this kind
of a bogy for us, merely because it was practiced by Demosthenes,
Seneca, and other pagans and *(horribile dictu!)* by the Catholics.
The latter instance seems to compromise it especially, for in this
case—particularly among the Jesuits—does not fondly cultivated
oratory clearly show that rhetoric is cursed with the concept of
coöperatio (the idea that man co-operates as a partner in his
salvation) and thus with a heretical doctrine of justification? Are
not these people admittedly failing to allow the Word *alone*
(solum!) to do its work? Are they not coming to the aid of the
Word by means of human initiative, oratorical effort, sensationalism, mesmerism, and techniques of persuasion?

It is instructive and thought-provoking that it is possible to
reply to all these critical objections with exactly the same re-
joinders that were employed by Paul in the Letter to the Romans
against the libertine misusers of his doctrine of justification
and by Luther against the Antinomians: "What then? Are we
to sin"—are we to be sloppy rhetoricians!—"because we are not
under law but under grace? By no means! Do you not know
that if you yield yourselves to any one as obedient slaves, you
are slaves of the one whom you obey. . . ?" (Rom. 6:15-16).
This means, after all, that you belong to him with all you have
and are and are capable of, including your rhetorical resources.
Freedom in Christ is no soft spot for the lazy. And the grace
that does not enlist a man to serve but is misused as a license
for Christian sloppiness and dilettante slovenliness degenerates
from costly to cheap grace.

By the way in which Spurgeon, who was thoroughly grounded
spiritually and certainly not out to create an effect, takes rhetoric
seriously, he compels us to rethink this problem theologically.
It is not sufficient that a theological faculty should, somewhat

shamefacedly, hand over this job of rhetoric to some retired actor. To have theology in one classroom and a rumpus in the adjoining room is certainly one way not to see nature and grace together!

The physical nature of man, however, has still other relationships to his spiritual existence. While it is true that man's physical nature ultimately expresses itself in rhetoric—in the form of voice, facial expression, and gesture—as a kind of final phase in its process of expression, it is also true conversely that man's physical nature has its proper place in those antechambers which must be traversed if anything like spiritual health is even to exist. In other words, because a man is *totally* claimed by his service, the natural, physical side of his person must also be directed toward service. We never gain spiritual health just by continually praying or meditating or consuming ourselves in blind and furious devotion to service, but only by giving to the creaturely side of our life too its proper due; by daring, so to speak, to be men who are not merely "reborn," but also and in the first place simply "born."

> To sit long in one posture, poring over a book, or driving a quill, is in itself a taxing of nature; but add to this a badly ventilated chamber, a body which has long been without muscular exercise, and a heart burdened with many cares, and we have all the elements for preparing a seething cauldron of despair, especially in the dim months of fog—
>> "When a blanket wraps the day,
>> When the rotten woodland drips,
>> And the leaf is stamped in clay."

Thus does our study become "a prison" instead of a place of service, Spurgeon continues, and our books become "the warders of a gaol" instead of helpers of our joy. "A mouthful of sea air, or a stiff walk in the wind's face, would not give grace to the soul, but it would yield oxygen to the body, which is next best." *This* is the co-ordination of nature and soul, as Spurgeon sees it!

Oxygen and grace. It requires a certain sovereign independence of theological thought patterns to juxtapose so unguardedly two such heterogeneous things. And yet it is the very thing which to theological thinking may seem to be a breach between the first and the second articles of the Creed, but which we nevertheless apprehend in faith as a unity before we begin to think at all. There do not exist in God's world any vacuums which are simply left to themselves; he would not allow it. The *horror vacui* so familiar in nature is only an adumbration of God's passion to fill up the void and let his Spirit move upon the deep—upon *all* the deeps! Our nature dare not remain void and be left to itself, but must praise him and be bound to him in order to be a temple of the Holy Spirit and an instrument to perform his deeds.

In this sense, then, it would be almost blasphemous to flee into the sanctuary in order to escape the assaults of hypochondria, the carnal libido, the complexes and traumata of life, and to cling to the horns of the altar in *this* form of "praying without ceasing." This would be to leave nature void and to overleap the stages of creation. Here too we must go by indirect ways and detours, insofar as we are not minded to misuse grace to protect ourselves against the vengeance of that nature which we have contemptuously consigned to disgrace. We should not be too quick to say that God is mighty in the weak, that "he gives power to the faint, and to him who has no might he increases strength" (Isa. 40:29). We should rather seek power and might and strength among "the ferns and the rabbits, the streams and the trout, the fir trees and the squirrels, the primroses and the violets, the farmyard, the new-mown hay, and the fragrant hops." For these are all indirect means of the same grace, to which, of course, we also have direct access through our prayers and groanings. But the sorrowful groaning itself does not entitle us to this direct reception of grace if at the same time we do not ask ourselves whether our groanings are not merely the result of lack of circulation, congestion of our body fluids, a cramped and musty soul. In the Salvation Army they say that anyone who has cold feet and an empty stomach finds it hard to listen to the gospel. So they gather unfortunate waifs and tramps around a warm stove and give them hot soup. Moreover, our Lord himself bound up with the soaring petition for the great cosmic coming of the kingdom of God the simple petition for our daily ration of bread.

And this is the connection that Spurgeon sees too: feet, stomach, and all the juices of the body—today we would say, the whole system of endocrine glands—should praise God and be kept in good running order for his service, that we may not allow sheer zeal for the house of the Lord to turn us into visionary fanatics estranged from nature, that our body may not be allowed to become—paradoxically, *ad maiorem Dei gloriam*—a stagnant swamp emitting gas bubbles of melancholy while we, instead of cultivating this wilderness, blindly and like bigots implore the Spirit of God to be so kind as to move upon even *these* muddy waters!

Hence it is certainly part of the task of the preacher, and of the teacher of preachers, to fight against stiffness in spiritual life, for with Christians it is a sign that they are still existing in an unresolved pressure belt between nature and grace, that they have not made the connection between the first and the second articles of the Creed. The fact that they have not yet settled this question *theologically* is not really the heart of the affliction, for the reflective form of our faith may well limp along a little behind the faith itself; as a matter of fact it does just that time and again.

The affliction of Israel lies rather in this very fracture of spiritual existence itself. You will have to *look!* more redeemed if we are to believe the message of redemption, said Nietzsche. But this redeemed look—and, mind you, we are not here trying to develop a science of Christian physiognomy!—would certainly imply that first there must be a relaxation of stiffness and tension. And what we said about the relation of nature and grace also applies here, namely, that our relationship to nature must be set in order. The hypochrondriac, the person who is stiff and inhibited, cannot really demonstrate "the freedom of the Christian man," even if he goes about among his congregation with an eternally smiling ministerial face. On the other hand, the man who has to overcome an inhibition in order to utter the name of Jesus cannot demonstrate this freedom either, even if he reels off all the christological statements and appellations. So the threat to our convincingness and credibility can come from above *and* from below.

Here again it does not help much just to *say* the right thing about nature and grace; what counts more is *how* we say it. Our task is not just to preach about overcoming the world; the way we speak must itself be a mode of overcoming the world. Otherwise we shall be like the man who, instead of leading people to paradise, merely gave them a lecture about paradise.

So when we talk about the "how" of preaching in Spurgeon, it would again be quite wrong simply to call attention to his brilliant application of exemplary rules and techniques and then appeal to preachers to imitate him. It is true that what Spurgeon gives us is really a brilliant didactic treatment of the question: "How can I say this to my children?" or "How can I get *to* people?" Yet the real secret of the how of preaching lies far deeper. For him who does not share this secret—that is, who does not exist at the place where this secret is to be found—the application of these rules remains out of reach, for even the how of this kind of speech is in itself nothing less than a demonstration of redemption. Tell me, not only what, but how you speak, and I will tell you whether you are sharing in redemption.

It would follow from this that the how of preaching is only a kind of by-product of spiritual existence; you cannot have it by itself, and therefore you cannot get it by simply having someone prescribe it for you in the form of rules of rhetoric. "Seek first his kingdom and his righteousness, and all these things shall be yours as well"—including the right way to speak. It would of course be indicative of a wrong co-ordination of Law and Gospel, if one were to conclude from this that the development of the how of preaching is merely an automatic process that requires no supervision. This would put us right back with the lazy people Paul addresses in Romans, chapter 6, who imagined they were exalting grace by sitting back with their hands folded. Here too the indicative "You are redeemed" is co-ordinated with the imperative "Now see to it that your speech is a *mode* of this redemption." The oneness of God's comforting assurance and the plurality of his claims—represented in the commandments and a multiplicity of admonitions—are explained by the fact that now the renovated heart is supposed to pump the blood into all the members of the body, and that *all* areas of our existence are to be included in this circulatory system.

We would therefore do better to rephrase the classical question concerning the relation between faith and works, and speak instead of redeemed and unredeemed areas in ourselves. For the pluralistic structure of modern life—which claims us very largely, though never fully—consists in the schizophrenia of our consciousness, or more precisely, in the spiritual self-contradiction of our existence. In one area of life, say that of the church, we are Christians; in another, say the economic one, we leave room for unregulated autonomy. Here the co-ordination of indicative and imperative becomes something very practical and immediate, not as a matter of principle, to be sure, but with respect to the formal structure which it assumes, since it contains within it the challenge to see the *whole* man as the object of redemption and therefore to watch over the individual dimensions of our existence in order to bring them into this redemption.

Among these areas is the area of testimony. "Out of the abundance of the heart the mouth speaks." True! But it can happen that the man who simply trusts that he has a full heart and relies upon this automatic "overflow" will be found speaking colorlessly about colors, tonelessly about tones, and odorlessly about fragrances. How many a preacher, whose personal testimony may be a living reality in private, acts like a living corpse as soon as he enters the pulpit. Here we have a demonstration of the danger that the area of preaching has not been incorporated in the cir-

culatory system of the new creation and that there is a breakdown
in the co-ordination of imperative and indicative.

This may illustrate both the extent to which the how of our
preaching is part of the living out of our spiritual existence, and
the fact that it is not only the "what" but also this "how" of our
preaching that bears testimony or hardens people against it, opens
hearts or closes them, makes the message convincing or blocks
the way to faith.

The "how" of our preaching as a mode of redemption—this
would sound very revolutionary if it were not merely an abstract
formulation of what we find in Spurgeon as a living manifestation.
This how of preaching, which in itself is a mode of redemption,
is determined by two characteristics: its cheerfulness and its worldliness.

Because it is cheerful and humorous, it accomplishes the relaxation of stiffness we spoke of above. Here cheerfulness is not
an extra, placed like a *donum superadditum* at the disposal of
grace by a happy mental constitution. Rather this cheerfulness
is something like a manifestation of grace itself. For it is a sign
of that detachment and overcoming of the world which grace
bestows. So Spurgeon's cheerfulness is not evidence of his having
the natural charism of "a good sense of humor"; his humor rather
bears witness to the grace that is at work in him.

Naturally, this humor is also a gift of nature, which grace presses
into service as the sphere of its secondary causes. (The reader
may forgive me if for the moment I speak in such Catholic-
scholastic terms of the *causae secundae*.) But it is precisely service
into which this nature is pressed! We have the opposite example
in those preachers who, though they likewise have at their disposal in their natural constitution a "sunny humor," let it come
out only at a cocktail party or a merry wedding celebration; whereas in the pulpit all they have to operate with is the sound-effects
of thunder and the gloomy hues of apocalypticism. The natural
gift of humor is still no testimony in itself; at most it is, to use

a variation of Spurgeon's earlier example, oxygen, but not pure grace. Later the secularized wedding company may say very sympathetically, "Too bad he became a minister; after all he has such a good sense of humor!"

Spurgeon's humor is a mode of redemption because it is sanctified—because it grows out of an overcoming of the world and therefore itself represents this overcoming of the world in process. So here it is representative of the extent to which the how of our preaching can be a witness. No wonder, therefore, that he took this humor into the pulpit and that the congregation—as in the blessed seasons of "Easter laughter" in the church, the so-called *risus paschalis!*—joined resoundingly in the laughter. But no wonder either that many people took offense when he broke through the accustomed solemn rites of the high church—for many of them came from that background—and suddenly the kingdom of God popped up not only in men's hearts but also in their diaphragms, laying hold upon even this part of nature. In other words, the Word became utterly and radically flesh; and if I may speak somewhat boldly I would say: even in *this* region of the anatomy. Only he to whom nothing is alien can credibly proclaim the incarnation of God. For when I am compelled to laugh I can no longer maintain the aesthetic attitude, the attitude which always remains a possibility where there is an excess of liturgical ceremony. I may laugh swinishly, or I may be lifted by laughter to the realm of angels; but I cannot remain indifferent. Laughter is always a form of engagement—of one type or another. If by nature I am a cheerful person but there is not a sparkle of such cheerfulness in my preaching, it would amount to a dubious sign that in an essential part of my temperament I am still not really engaged by what I am saying.

When Spurgeon was cheerful and humorous in the pulpit, he was putting himself into his preaching; he was entering into the sermon with his whole nature. He who wants the interest of his hearers and wants them to be "in it" must first be in it himself.

Only he who is himself engaged attracts others into engagement. The being-in-it-oneself is the essential evidence of that credibility that is empowered to call others to faith. And this is precisely why the "how" of preaching is itself preaching.

Should we not then, Spurgeon would probably ask in the face of the deadly seriousness with which the business of the church is pursued today, should we not see that lines of laughter about the eyes are just as much marks of faith as are the lines of care and seriousness? Is it only earnestness that is baptized; is laughter pagan? We have already allowed too much that is good to be lost to the church, and cast many pearls before swine. A church is in a bad way when it banishes laughter from the sanctuary and leaves it to cabaret, the night club, and the toast-masters.

As important as humor in the how of preaching is having something interesting to say. Interestingness can be interpreted—quite legitimately as to its etymology—to mean "being in" a thing just as humor draws us in. So interpreted, it loses all smack of the artificial and of a device for attracting attention. For then it issues from an inner kinship with or "interest" in the thing itself. Once the element of interest is recognized as having this vital connection with the thing itself and this faculty of compelling attention, the effort to cultivate it by means of studied rhetorical techniques is not a mere trick of method, but grows right out of the relation between indicative and imperative described above. It was for this reason that Spurgeon gave thematic titles to his sermons that challenge our curiosity and interest, such as "The Golden Muzzle" (on Acts 4:14) or the mysterious-sounding "Perhaps" (on Zeph. 2:3).

And yet it would be totally wrong to charge him with preaching the so-called "topical" sermon, which scants the depth and fullness of the text and merely uses it as an illustration or—worse still!—as a refrain for the pulpit presentation. For him the title was a mere catchword or cue that pointed to some main emphasis of the text, nothing more. Its only purpose was to be a

bell that would call the people together. They would wonder
what it meant, but not be able from the bell alone to tell what
was hidden in the text and what they would therefore hear
as they listened to the sermon.

The first sentences of his sermons too are extremely pointed,
and in his earlier days they were often rather odd and crude.
They are like a chord or dissonance struck by a pianist at the
beginning of a concert in order to produce silence.

He had no inhibitions whatsoever about being blunt and
downright. There was no color, soft and subdued or shrill and
strident, which he did not have on his palette. Is not the Word
of God a hammer which breaks the rock in pieces (cf. Jer.
23:29), and is it not also in the still small voice (cf. I Kings
19:12)? And he had all kinds of people in his congregation:
the thick-skinned and the thin-skinned, the self-confident and
the downcast, the sharp-witted intellectuals and the people who
think in terms of simple, primitive images. He had to be able to
strike the Aeolian harp and to swing the sledge hammer, to present careful, subtle argumentation and at the same time to paint
in broad, clear strokes.

It would certainly be doing Spurgeon an injustice to regard
this merely as a device, a bow to the maxim "Something for
everybody." In this matter of seeking to reach everyone in his
own way, it was *love* that filled his palette with colors. And
here again it was certainly his colorful, many-sided nature that
furnished his mind with imagery and illustrations. Had he not
clothed himself in his message with all that he was and all his
abilities, he might perhaps have become a great storyteller with
an unreal profusion of scenery and figures, but his preaching
would have been dry and didactic, and merely artificially enriched
with a few plums gathered from the best known "treasuries
of Christian illustrations." I set up this monstrous picture of a de-
generated Spurgeon in order at this point to call attention once
more to the ambivalence of nature and its gifts. Spurgeon's
natural gift of imagination too was baptized. The similes came

pouring out, not because he had gathered them together ad hoc, imposing upon himself the labor of providing illustrations, but rather because he was constantly seeing life in the categories and with the eyes of a vital, living Christian. For his ad hoc preparation he needed only to select from the store of things which had become transparent as he saw them from Monday to Saturday. In other words, he did not consciously set out to capture his hearers at the "image level" of their consciousness in order to impress something unforgettably on their minds, but simply put into words what the image level of his own mind had ingested.

The second characteristic of the "how" of Spurgeon's preaching is its worldliness. And this occurs at a great many different levels.

The listeners who came from the background of the customary liturgical forms of worship must have experienced something of the shock produced by the change from a hot shower to a cold one. Today we might speak of the alienating effect that is produced when the message is divested of its sacral dress and one is compelled to face it in its everyday clothes.

This impression would begin with the interior architecture of the Metropolitan Tabernacle and what went on there. It was an enormous secular hall without any ecclesiastical embellishments: no marble columns, no candles, and no churchly trimmings. The preacher appeared in a simple black robe, with no suggestion of letting the clothes speak for the man. In his later years Spurgeon even rejected the white bands.

We mention this not with the intention of indicating that it is exemplary and surreptitiously stirring up a bit of iconoclasm. We are concerned only to bring out a side of preaching which has possibly tended to disappear among us, but which I believe might well have its place within the framework of a Lutheran service of worship which, of course, is not *overly* "rich" and *overly* proud of tradition. The intent of this worldliness in architecture and worship was certainly to indicate symbolically that the listen-

ers did not need to soar out of this world but simply to become
a part of an oasis of stillness *in the midst of this world*. The room
was an architectural demonstration of the message that the Word
has become flesh and come into the midst of this world. And because it came through with such exceeding clarity, it was necessarily difficult for men who had received it in the very midst of
this world to shrug it off as irrelevant when they went back to
their worldly concerns.

And the man who stood in the pulpit spoke in a way that
was in harmony with the style of the place of worship. The
wonderful acoustics of the auditorium relieved him of the need
to shout and thus to slip into the sing-song intonation and pulpit
pathos into which the ancient cathedrals so easily seduce a
preacher, especially when the attendance is meager. What may
begin as a need to fill up the space with sound ends up all too
readily in the tendency to step on the accelerator and thus produce an acoustical form of *coöperatio*. This auditorium permitted
Spurgeon to speak in a relaxed, almost conversational tone. The
complete absence of emotionalism in his delivery allowed his
message to sound forth in words and tones which were familiar
to people in everyday life, much as would be customary in a
conversation.

There are three points which seem to me to be important in
a theological evaluation of the worldliness of Spurgeon's preaching.

First, by plunging with his message into the world and emerging
in its climate, Spurgeon was fulfilling the original intention of
the gospel to meet man where he is. For, after all, the meaning
and intent of the incarnation of Jesus Christ is, as Paul Tillich
once expressed it, that God emerges "within the conditions of
historical reality" and subjects himself to its pressure in solidarity
with "his" people: that God is on man's side. These, his people,
no longer need to resort to a temple, a sacred place reserved for
God; they have no need for special ascetic disciplines, flights of
spiritual feeling, purgings and cleansings, and other methods of
spiritual training in order to come to him. Rather they meet their

Lord in *their* marketplaces, *their* highways and hedges; in short, God comes to meet them. To be sure, in all this, God also remains the "totally other," who cannot be imprisoned in any human formula. And if there is anything in the history of Christianity that bears witness to this inaccessibility of God, it is the failure of every form of the doctrine of the "two natures" which attempts to "think together" the divine and the human natures in one system of thought.

Now if the form of the service of worship is to help express this two-sided character of the reality of God—this nearness and this "total otherness"—then *both* must find expression in form. There must be both the liturgical presentation of the majesty of God, which reaches out beyond the ages and in the language of tradition transcends the present moment, *and* that nearness of God in our marketplaces and our highways and hedges.

It is true, of course, that when Spurgeon articulates in words, sounds, and sentences that side of the gospel which is oriented toward man, thus emphasizing only the "human nature" which is involved, he is being quite as one-sided as the pure liturgiologists who, at least in the "how" of their proclamation, are just definitely oriented toward the *theiotes,* the deity. I deliberately mention this one-sidedness of Spurgeon in order to avoid the impression that I wish to make him in too direct a sense an exemplary pattern of evangelical preaching. The paradoxy of the unity of deity and humanity in Christ must, in my opinion, have as its counterpart a corresponding tension involving the juxtaposition and coexistence of a liturgical adherence to tradition on the one hand and a historical immediacy in preaching on the other. Historically speaking, however, the balance between the two will never be something given and perfect, any more than the balance between the divine and the human has been in the doctrine of the two natures. Historically speaking, it will rather always be true that we shall be able to express in words this mystery of the divine and the human only by an interplay of statements which correct each other.

With this in mind, then, I would certainly think that we are in special need of the corrective which is provided for us in Spurgeon's "worldly" preaching. For the one-sidedness of *our* generation is the *liturgical* component, the possible withdrawal from the present of which we spoke above. Despite the immense concern with homiletical questions, we have forgotten the worldliness of preaching. And even where we have recognized that it is part of our task—how else could the universal respect for Dietrich Bonhoeffer's theological principles be explained?—we still have not succeeded.

The fact that this program for worldly preaching has repeatedly failed certainly has deeper causes than a mere mechanical failure to employ the proper kind of language. For even when this language is used—and here and there we have heard sermons and meditations in which the parlance of back-slapping brassiness and the tabloid press has been employed—we have hardly ever been stirred to say that here somebody has hit upon what could really be called worldly preaching. On the contrary, we have the somewhat painful feeling that what we are hearing is a calculated, tactical effort to be chummily familiar, that this is the very thing that is *not* appropriate to the subject, and that the substance of what is said is compromised by the very way in which it is said.

Here again it is evident that one cannot make up for theological deficiencies by means of artistic techniques, and that the techniques have to be "baptized" and made servants if they are to become trustworthy instruments. These theological deficiencies may consist in the fact that we have lost sight of the gospel as God's coming to meet man. We have forgotten the Christmas miracle and therefore foolishly devote ourselves to a useless attempt to recover what has been lost by means of popularizing the "Christian religion" and beating secularization with its own weapons. All efforts to arrive at a language for preaching that is close to life will remain illusory as long as we have not spelled out theologically the "what" of the Miracle of Bethlehem. And the worldly "how" of preaching will be "added to us" only when we have first learned about the worldliness of God and heard anew the words "God *so* loved the world."

Spurgeon can teach us something about this dogma of the worldliness of God, not only by what he says about it, but also by the way he deals with his congregation. For he not only spoke in a worldly way, he also went out into the world with his people. He actually went with his students from the Pastor's College into the highways and hedges and marketplaces. He turned up in the most dubious quarters and slums of London and gathered together the children from the streets. As far as I have been able to determine, when he did this he never preached a special sermon beamed at the particular situation of his hearers, but always preached in the same style, no matter whether he was speaking to the students in the Pastor's College, to a "mature" congregation in some church, or in the great forum of his Tabernacle where he had a mixed audience of proletarians and business men, aristocrats and middle-class people. Genuine worldliness can always remain the same, for the hedges and highways, the cellars and hovels, are the same in every life, and the powers of sin, suffering, and death pose the same questions everywhere. All of them who are gathered there we hear on Pentecost, praising the mighty works of God *"in their own tongues."*

Second, the worldly style of speaking has witnessing power in still another respect. Only he who is very familiar with and close to what he is saying can talk about it quite naturally and in a conversational tone. Only because the message here emerges as something that is almost tangibly a part of the person is its effect credible and trustworthy and, even for the skeptic, worth listening to. For here is a person, like ourselves, who lives with this message and has obviously tried it and found that one *can* live with it. The casual testimony of a man of the world, included in some incidental comment, often has more influence than the reasoned, carefully prepared speech of the "professional" witness.

Here I must go out of my way to correct a possible misunderstanding. Some may think that the worldliness of this speech with its natural flow represents an "accommodation" to the world and thus evades the necessary offense and scandal of the message. Just the opposite is true. One can shout from the pulpit in traditional academic language the most tremendous things—even that Christ rose from the dead!—without eliciting anything more than bored assent to the routine ecclesiastical vocabulary. Linguistic Docetism never offends anybody, because it never gets under a man's skin. Its effect is merely that of a report that "in far-off Turkey the nations are clashing," while I, withdrawn from all that, can bless my lucky stars for "peace and peaceful times" and "quaff my ale" in comfort.* This is no fateful encounter in which I hear *my* death sentence or *my* pardon. And even the refrain—added perhaps with some emotion—"This concerns *you!*" makes no impact at all, if the explosive is not already inherent in the message itself and brought to the kindling point.

The converse is true also: he who tells nothing more than a parable of Jesus, but tells it in the same way that one would speak of the weather or a hospital visit or the next election, evokes a shock because what he has said is now in the familiar realm of the ordinary; it gets at people where they are. So only he who accommodates and goes out to meet people in *this* way gets a confirmation of his faithful witness in a response of genuine resistance.

This, of course, is a different kind of accommodation from that which conforms to the *substantive* expectations of the hearers. The "German Christians" under Hitler performed this kind of substantive, and therefore disavowing, accommodation by fabricating a painless and innocuous synthesis of Christianity and contemporary ideologies. The genuine accommodation which is motivated by the purpose of reaching people where they are would have been quite different. It might be illustrated in this way:

---

*The quotations are from *Faust*, Part One, Scene II.—TRANS.

Imagine one of the great mass meetings in the Berlin Sport-palast at that time, in which a Nazi orator allows himself to be carried away in violent tirades against Christianity. If some-one had leaped to his feet and shouted out his counter-confession, "Christ is the Messiah!" the people sitting next to him would probably have looked up with some astonishment; but not much more would have happened. But if another had cried out, "Jesus Christ is the only Lord, and all who make themselves into gods by their own power will go to hell along with the pseudo-savior Adolf Hitler," he would probably have been torn to pieces by the crowd.

In reality both were saying the same thing. The one who de-clared that Christ is the Messiah was implicitly saying that all earthly entities are relative, and thus pronouncing judgment upon Hitler and his cohorts. But he was doing so in a veiled and cryptic way, for he was speaking in esoteric, churchly terminology. But the other said it in terms that were accommodated to the language and consciousness of those who were present. He spoke in clear terms. For this reason, and this reason *alone,* did it create dis-turbance and offense. Offense is not a sign that one has *not* understood, but a symptom of the fact that one *has* understood all too well, or at least is afraid he will *have* to understand. As a result of Jesus' parables, some people hardened their hearts and failed to understand (cf. Matt. 13:13; Mark 9:32; John 8:27; 10:6). Now, this effect was not the result of their ears being literally deaf and their hearts being literally closed. They pur-posely closed their ears and bolted their hearts. They understood very well what kind of aggression they were exposed to here, if they opened their ears and hearts. Perhaps, or rather probably, they had already taken precautions to alert the "wisdom of this world" in order to destroy the spiritual categories which might allow them to understand the foolishness of the cross and make it impossible for them to reject (cf. Rom. 1:22-23; I Cor. 1:20 ff.; and *katechein,* the term meaning "suppress," in Rom. 1:18).

This aim of meeting people where they are and of accommodating our speech to them can have a spiritual intent, and thus be in accord with the message itself, only if the primary consideration is not the technical and tactical question of how I can "get at" these people, how I can make myself understood and win my hearers; my chief concern must rather be faithfulness to the message: that I may portray the Word made flesh actually coming to meet men where they are, that I may speak of it in a manner that is appropriate to the fact itself, and hence that I may break through the facades of tradition and help men to see the granite walls of the foundations. The clerical mind which is sworn only to the traditional and speaks only in the code language of tradition is mortally sick. The mannered fustian, the grandiloquence, and the formalism which were once so potent in the religious world are gradually becoming obsolete. The truth and the life itself must win the victory, and their victory is nearest when they no longer need to drag about with them the ponderous clothes of the traditional and pretentious. It is a pleasure to break down the lath and plaster of old externals and formalities to make room for the granite walls of reality. This is one of my main aims. May God give success to my efforts!

Third, the worldly way of speaking is credible because it gives to the hearer what is the speaker's own. I hardly need to add that what is the speaker's own is not something he has gained himself, but rather the reservoir of talents bestowed upon him. But as such the *alienum* (the gift that comes from outside of him) has now become a *proprium* (his own). And this is what gives legitimacy to worldly preaching as the very opposite of that which often makes people today so skeptical of public speech, namely, propaganda.

The person who promotes propaganda is generally a professional advertising man who speaks his piece no matter which margarine or soft drink is being sold; and the deep tone of conviction in which he commends these products does not alter the skepticism of those who listen to his television utterances and read his ads. They know very well that he has to talk this way, because he is paid to do so; they know that the deep tone of conviction is no natural product, but a synthetic, very carefully and purposefully mixed cocktail designed to affect the nervous system.

But the professional advertising man is only the extreme example of a type that haunts us in many variations. One of these variations is the functionary who represents and advocates a group decision, even though his "private" views may be totally different. Another species is the manager, who does not act for himself but represents the stockholders.

All these people have one thing in common: basically they do not speak for themselves, but rather, acting on someone else's orders, they *must* speak the way they do. Hence in order really to know which soft drink is the best, we dare not listen to the advertiser's ballyhoo, but rather have to find out which one he himself drinks at home. And in order to learn what the functionary really thinks, we dare not trust what he says in a public statement, but rather have to get it out of what he says afterwards when he is speaking freely over beer and cigars in a familiar circle of trusted friends.

Because this type of speech, which is typical of professional advertising men, functionaries, and managers, is more than an isolated phenomenon of the moment, and because for many reasons it has now grown to immeasurable proportions compared with Spurgeon's time, our contemporaries have understandably come to distrust *all* forms of public speech, *every* kind of "speaking on someone else's orders"—and hence what the *church* says, too. "The minister has to talk that way": this is the dreadful phrase by which men seek to defend themselves and keep the demanding summons of the message at arm's length.

Why do people seek out the consulting room of the psychotherapist and hardly ever the pastor's study? Why do people not entrust themselves to the minister but write instead to the editor of the "worry column" in our newspapers and magazines?

Obviously because they think they know beforehand what the minister "has" to say; for, after all, he is an employee of that institution whose dogmatic stipulations stand, or at least *seem* to stand, like silent monuments in full view of everybody. Naturally, he has to be "against sin"; so it would hardly be worth his while, once he has diagnosed the problem as "sin," to consider impartially the matters confided to him. Naturally, he is against divorce, against love affairs on the part of married men, against disrespect for parents. Therefore he is incapable of evaluating exceptional cases; therefore he cannot recognize genuine crises, real conflict and borderline situations. As a "human being" he might perhaps understand, but he dare not let me know what he thinks about it personally. For his job is simply to carry out the collective will of his institution—and that is dogmatically fixed. "The minister has to talk that way."

We can hardly measure the extent to which this misguided prejudice—for, of course, that is what it is!—curbs people's willingness to listen and come to grips with Christianity. And if we examine this attitude more carefully it becomes clear that, strictly speaking, it is not a matter of their taking offense at the message itself, because they have not yet come even within earshot of it. Rather here again this offense springs from a reaction to the "how" of preaching. Distrust of the message increases to the extent to which it is presented in terms of formulas and expressed —even as regards the tone of voice—impersonally. For this only suggests the more strongly that here it is not the man himself who is speaking, but that he is a ventriloquist egurgitating voices other than his own.

And here again it is all too easy to put forward the parsonical self-justification and say that after all it is the task of the witness, not to present himself, but rather to retire behind the testimony and therefore to present it in a tone of aloof objectivity.

But this is quite wrong. The fact is that the witness does not withdraw; he comes forward. (If he puts himself in the foreground like a prima donna and misuses the message merely as a means to play up himself, then this is something quite different and has absolutely nothing to do with what is meant here.) The witness does not merely recite a confession; he confesses. He confesses that this is "his" confession, that he personally has made it his own and therefore that he himself is in it. Otherwise we should have to credit the remark of Alexander Schweizer (1808-88) that whereas the fathers once "confessed their beliefs," our modern Christian generation struggles largely just to "believe their confessions"—and hence to keep aloof from the matter itself. Only as the witness himself comes forward will men regard him as credible and worth listening to.

This coming forward of the witness, of course, need not by any means manifest itself in the use of the first person singular or an autobiographical tone of speech. Nevertheless the individuality of the preacher will undoubtedly make itself felt, or more cautiously stated, dare not fight shy of letting itself be known. The witness's own individual tone is itself a part of the witness. Only, his photograph need not be on the phonograph record— though on the higher levels there may be even here such a thing as an unmistakable handwriting—for the artist declares himself in the declaration he makes through his artistic statement.

When the instrument of the message knows that it has itself been chosen and prepared, it will—by allowing itself to be used in the hand of its Lord—at the same time say more about itself than the fact that it is only an instrument. For it is in truth also a *man,* called and appointed to act; it is a living being, whom God does not merely use as an "it," a thing, but rather addresses and confronts as a "thou." What happens is exactly what happened in the story of creation. There the stars, the animals, the plants, and the light are spoken about, in the third person: "*It* was so . . . *it* was good." Only man is spoken to in the second person: "I have given *you* . . ." Man, as one who has been addressed, will always have to "confess" or declare himself too whenever he confesses Him who has addressed him.

This indicates why it is that the term "instrument" *{Werkzeug}* is only an imperfect and halting metaphor of what witnessing *{Zeugenschaft}* means. If one takes this image in its literal, absolute sense—which is the very thing one dare not do—then there would be no difference at all between the witness and the functionary, since he too is an instrument. The witness, however, discloses himself in his own tone and individuality; for what characterizes him is not only that he testifies to *something,* but also that *he* is the one who is testifying and "standing up" for it. The mere instrument knows nothing of the one who is using it; nor does it know the purpose it is serving. But the witnessing person is so constituted that he consciously and purposely grasps and understands both who it is that is using him and the purpose he is serving. Therefore he must confess himself as one who accepts responsibility for his testimony (cf. I Pet. 3:15).

If I see aright, it was precisely this instinct for the personal character of witnessing that set Spurgeon so strongly against "formalism." It made him go out of his way to guard against the misunderstanding that it was not he but merely an institution that was speaking, and that his personal position might be something different from what he was saying.

But how does this "individual tone," which is itself witness, come into being? It comes into being through the worldliness of a man's speech and the immediate naturalness of his diction. For in order to be able to speak in this way I cannot simply declaim or recite a given statement, even if it is a passage from the Bible or a creed. Every statement requires translation, recasting, actualizing. Simply by going through these acts of assimilation and appropriation, preaching causes the medium of the message, namely, the preacher, to become a part of itself; it puts its stamp upon him, and also imparts to him his own individual stamp.

Hence it actually requires no first person singular, no forced subjective embellishments, and no exposition of "pious, Christian states of mind" (Schleiermacher) in order to bring out one's own individual tone, and thus differentiate oneself from the functionary—although none of these things need be feared either!

Anxious fear of subjectivism leads to the same kind of forced artificiality as does programmatic subjectivism. Here too the rule holds good: "All things are yours!" (I Cor. 3:22); or, to put it in Augustine's words: *Dilige et fac quod vis,* "Love, and do what you will!"

Just as in our prayers we do not need to use the carefully polished fair copy but are allowed to follow the "rough draft"—"as beloved children approach their dear father," often babbling foolishly and demanding stupid things of him—so in preaching we certainly do not need to weigh our words with the precision scales by which the legalists and formalists allow themselves to be tyrannized, but may rather assume the hazards and risks of speech to which we expose ourselves in natural, everyday conversation. Only he who runs the risk of heresy can gain the truth. Only he who risks good form and ventures to go even to the limits of good taste (so long as this is only a sign and remains an exceptional thing and does not itself become merely a routine!) can allow substance and content to break through. The man who will not utter anything that is not guarded and "safe" is not reckoning with him who is able from "stones to raise up children to Abraham." This passion to safeguard ourselves is not inspired by the Holy Spirit; it is based merely upon fleshly anxiety. The witness must venture something and dare not be afraid of the chips that fly as he hews. The discipline and the hard application must be taken care of *before* the witness begins to speak. But once he begins to speak, he must be free to venture and expose himself without defense. There is no real witness that is not utterly defenseless.

All this should be taken into account when one considers the homiletical risks that Spurgeon took. The dogmatician, the exegete, and also the professor of practical theology (the preceptor of the homiletical nursery) may often be impelled to wield their blue pencils; the aesthete may often see red and the liturgiologist turn purple when they read his sermons and hear what he did. For the priests and the Levites always have the hardest time listening with simplicity and without bias. Not only that; they also find it all too easy to pass by those who have fallen among thieves, those who can no longer hear because they have been corroded by distrust—and in this way too become as sheep without a shepherd.

Such critics ought to see in this man Spurgeon the shepherd who was content to allow his robe—including his clerical robe—to be torn to tatters by thorns and sharp stones as he clambered after the lost sheep, at times seeming to be engaged more in training for a cross-country race than in liturgical exercises. Worldly preaching is impossible without having the earth leave its traces on a man's wardrobe. Here there are no robes that look as if they had just come out of a bandbox. And sometimes the voice is rough and hoarse from much calling. The shepherds of the New Testament too were rough and ready fellows.

We have tried to think through the many aspects of the "how" of this worldly kind of preaching and we have tried to rescue it from the suspicion that it is merely a method, merely a kind of rhetorical pragmatism. We have tried to fix the theological locus of this how of preaching and have defined it, not merely as a *modus,* but as part of the content of the witness itself.

In doing so we have been constantly revolving about this content, the thing attested. And if in closing we desire to formulate this center of Spurgeon's message, we need only to quote his own words:

> The glory of God being our chief object we aim at it by seeking the edification of saints and the salvation of sinners . . . . To this end we must give clear statements of gospel doctrine, of vital experience, and of Christian duty, and never shrink from declaring the whole counsel of God.

Spurgeon's aim, therefore, is the saving of souls. He is concerned that we should be saved.

And there it is, so simple and so naïve—and suddenly all the worldliness, all the modernity of speech is wiped away. It sounds

quite old-fashioned, seems almost to belong under the classifica-
tion of Pietism and therefore among the relativities of the history
of theology. Perhaps it may be a little easier for us to take these
naïve and simple formulations seriously if we try to describe them
in negative terms and state what Spurgeon's purposes were *not*.

It was *not* the aim of his preaching to show people that their
life would be easier if they accepted the gospel; that it would
solve their problems; that civilization would perish without
Christianity; that the state and society need religion; that the
Christian social ethic is absolutely indispensable; that the world
order needs Christian foundations; that all the misery of modern
man comes from secularism; that if our world is to endure there
must be a renascence of the Christian West, and so on.*

All this is a kind of high-minded Christian pragmatism which
we are all too prone to promote these days, and which frequently
enough is smuggled into the holy city of Ilium under the guise of a
Trojan horse called "worldly Christianity." All this is completely
alien to Spurgeon. He is concerned only with salvation. He is so
unpragmatic that he is capable of arguing that the truths of the
Bible are not practical and not practicable. He warns against making practicality a criterion for the acceptability of the statements of
the Bible and the assertions of Christian preaching. Even if we do
not know what to make of them, he says, we must let the great
truths stand, for the Lord considered them important. "Woe unto
us, if we pretend to be wiser than he!"

The dictum "Whatever benefits is true" has no place in Spurg-

---

*"The question is . . . does our time want religion, that is to say, one form
of culture among or above others, in order to save its culture, in order to open
up a new source, perhaps a creative source, for its culture? Or does it want
God, simply and solely, regardless of anything else, no matter whether this
benefits culture or not? In the first case it is certain to fail, for a religion
which is sought for the sake of culture neither finds God nor does it create
culture. In the second case it is certain that God will be found; for it is utterly
impossible to seek him for his own sake without his being already present,
creating this will to seek him" (Paul Tillich). I deliberately quote this passage
from a theologian who employs a completely different terminology from that of
Spurgeon and who certainly would not speak of "being saved." And yet, behind
the facade of heterogeneous terms and styles, there is a similar intention.

eon's list of maxims. He would probably agree, though, if one were to say that in the long run that which is true also proves to be profitable. But at the outset one cannot have it, if one keeps his eye only on its practical utility. First it must simply be accepted disinterestedly, obediently, and trustingly. Then he who saves souls will *also* do something for the world; what he does will be done incidentally, over and above the chief thing, and the more so as he is exclusively concerned with souls and not with the world.

Perhaps we today are inclined to regard this as one of Spurgeon's limitations. Can the public claim and responsibility for the world which we take to be inherent in our message be reduced to the simple, childlike formula of "winning souls" and "saving souls"? Does not this narrow it down and make it individualistic?

The fact is that Spurgeon did have his eye primarily upon the individual; he gave little or no thought to the theology of social and political order and to Christ as the Lord of the cosmos. It is true, however, that at the beginning of the Civil War he vehemently and without regard for personal loss advocated the liberation of the slaves, and thus took a stand on a social problem. Where else in the nineteenth century was this done as emphatically? And he did it despite the fact that with one blow it cut off the tremendous circulation of his writings in the United States, and the financial loss had a considerable effect upon the support of his institutions and his work. But even this position taken toward a problem of the social order was determined by the center of his message of salvation. His concern was that man, who has been purchased and redeemed to be free, cannot be kept in slavery by a Christian society, and that therefore if slavery were tolerated without opposition this would rob the whole Christian message of its authority—and consequently it could no longer save souls!

Here too Spurgeon exercises for us the function of a corrective. For us and our kind of Christian social ethics the threatening danger is that we tend merely to enucleate the Christian "ideas" concerning the world order, the structuring of society, etc., and then to recommend them for their preservative and productive power. But since it is possible to have Christian ideas without actually believing, and to be taken up with the social teachings of Christianity(!) without becoming "engaged" personally, these ideas lose their connection with the *Lord* of Christendom and degenerate into ideologies, i.e., into instrumentalities of power and world mastery. They no longer appeal to the proof of the Spirit (in the sense of verification by the *testimonium spiritus sancti),* but only to the proof of power (in the sense of verification by what proves to be practicable and successful). Thus it is possible for Christianity to become merely a pervasive atmosphere, a climate of social order, while faith dwindles away and the matter of salvation is forgotten.

Therefore we stand in need of the simple way in which Spurgeon dares to say that what really and ultimately counts is to save sinners. Indeed, what really counts is "that we get to heaven." Anything else is watered-down social gospel *{kultur-protestantisches}* twaddle—including all the talk about the Christian West, and even Christian social ethics no matter how responsible it may be!—if, yes, *if* in our feeling of responsibility to the world we forget "heaven" and do not go out after those five brothers of Dives (cf. Luke 16:22) who are reeling and lurching toward the place of torment and losing sight of Abraham's bosom. Only if Moses and the prophets are mobilized at *this* point and to *this* end will the salt be prevented from losing its savor; and only *then*—really then *only!*—can it be the salt of the earth that stops the processes of decay.

True, we certainly have to say and do all this in a way that is different from Spurgeon's. We cannot merely repeat, but must translate what he said and did, even as he was no mere "repeater" but always a translator. We can, however, let him serve as a warning sign and a corrective. For our faithfulness to the fathers of the faith does not consist in our copying them but in our comprehending them. And the communion of saints does not consist in the fact that all of us say the same thing in the same words, but rather that we all drink from the same spring. Notable among those who have also stood watch by this spring is Spurgeon.

I am almost tempted to shout out to those who are serving the eternal Word as preachers, and to those who are preparing to do so, in what I hope will be a productive hyperbole: Sell all that you have (not least of all some of your stock of current sermonic literature) and buy Spurgeon (even if you have to grub through the second-hand bookstores). And even if you do not take all of the counsels for your ministry which he gives in the following pages, let him be a Socrates who helps you to find your own way. Use this seminar of his, to which you are here invited, not as a mere drill that will train you to homiletical perfection, but rather as an exercise in which you come to yourself and find your "own individual tone."

SELECTIONS FROM
"LECTURES TO MY STUDENTS"
AND TWO SERMONS

by Charles Haddon Spurgeon

1

On Conversion as Our Aim

THE grand object of the Christian ministry is the glory of God. Whether souls are converted or not, if Jesus Christ be faithfully preached, the minister has not laboured in vain, for he is a sweet savour unto God as well in them that perish as in them that are saved. Yet as a rule, God has sent us to preach in order that through the gospel of Jesus Christ the sons of men may be reconciled to him. Here and there a preacher of righteousness, like Noah, may labour on and bring none beyond his own family circle into the ark of salvation; and another, like Jeremiah, may weep in vain over an impenitent nation: but, for the most part, the work of preaching is intended to save the hearers. It is ours to sow even in the stony places, where no fruit rewards our toil; but still we are bound to look for a harvest, and mourn, if it does not appear in due time.

The glory of God being our chief object we aim at it by seeking the edification of saints and the salvation of sinners. It is a noble work to instruct the people of God, and to build them up in their most holy faith: we may by no means neglect this duty. To this end we must give clear statements of gospel doctrine, of vital experience, and of Christian duty, and never shrink from declaring the whole counsel of God. In too many cases sublime truths are held in abeyance under the pretence that they are not practical; whereas the very fact that they are revealed proves that the Lord thinks them to be of value, and woe unto us if we pretend to be wiser than he. We may say of any and every doctrine of Scripture—

"To give it then a tongue is wise in man."

If any one note is dropped from the divine harmony of truth the music may be sadly marred. Your people may fall into grave spiritual diseases through the lack of a certain form of spiritual nutriment, which can only be supplied by the doctrines which you withhold. In the food which we eat there are ingredients which do not at first appear to be necessary to life; but experience shows that they are requisite to health and strength. Phosphorus will not make flesh, but it is wanted for bone; many earths and salts come under the same description—they are necessary in due proportion to the human economy. Even thus certain truths which appear to be little adapted for spiritual nutriment are, nevertheless, very beneficial in furnishing believers with backbone and muscle, and in repairing the varied organs of Christian manhood. We must preach "the whole truth," that the man of God may be thoroughly furnished unto all good works. . . .

If we intensely desire to see our hearers believe on the Lord Jesus, how shall we act in order to be used of God for producing such a result? . . .

Since conversion is a divine work, we must take care that we *depend entirely upon the Spirit of God,* and look to him for power over men's minds. Often as this remark is repeated, I fear we too little feel its force; for if we were more truly sensible of our need of the Spirit of God, should we not study more in dependence upon his teaching? Should we not pray more importunately to be anointed with his sacred unction? Should we not in preaching give more scope for his operation? Do we not fail in many of our efforts, because we practically, though not doctrinally, ignore the Holy Ghost? His place as God is on the throne, and in all our enterprises he must be first, midst, and end: we are instruments in his hand, and nothing more.

This being fully admitted, what else should be done if we hope to see conversions? *Assuredly we should be careful to preach most prominently those truths which are likely to lead to this end.* What truths are those? I answer, we should first and foremost preach *Christ and him crucified.* Where Jesus is

exalted souls are attracted, "I, if I be lifted up, will draw all
men unto me." The preaching of the cross is to them that are
saved the wisdom of God and the power of God. The Christian
minister should preach all the truths which cluster around the
person and work of the Lord Jesus, and hence he must declare
very earnestly and pointedly *the evil of sin,* which created the
need of a Saviour. Let him show that sin is a breach of the law,
that it necessitates punishment, and that the wrath of God is
revealed against it. Let him never treat sin as though it were
a trifle, or a misfortune, but let him set it forth as exceeding
sinful. Let him go into particulars, not superficially glancing
at evil in the gross, but mentioning various sins in detail, especially those most current at the time: such as that all-
devouring hydra of drunkenness, which devastates our land; lying,
which in the form of slander abounds on all sides; and licentiousness, which must be mentioned with holy delicacy, and yet needs
to be denounced unsparingly. We must especially reprove those
evils into which our hearers have fallen, or are likely to fall.
Explain the ten commandments and obey the divine injunction:
"Show my people their transgressions, and the house of Jacob their
sins." Open up the spirituality of the law as our Lord did, and
show how it is broken by evil thoughts, intents, and imagina-
tions. By this means many sinners will be pricked in their hearts.

Old Robbie Flockhart used to say, "It is of no use trying to sew
with silken thread of the gospel unless we pierce a way for it with
the sharp needle of the law." The law goes first, like the needle,
and draws the gospel thread after it: therefore preach concerning
sin, righteousness, and judgment to come. Let such language as
that of the Fifty-First Psalm be often explained: show that God
requireth truth in the inward parts, and that purging with sacri-
ficial blood is absolutely needful. Aim at the heart. Probe the
wound and touch the very quick of the soul. Spare not the
sterner themes, for men must be wounded before they can be
healed, and slain before they can be made alive. No man will
ever put on the robe of Christ's righteousness till he is stripped

of his fig leaves, nor will he wash in the fount of mercy till he perceives his filthiness. Therefore, my brethren, we must not cease to declare the law, its demands, its threatenings, and the sinner's multiplied breaches of it.

Teach the depravity of human nature. Show men that sin is not an accident, but the genuine outcome of their corrupt hearts. Preach the doctrine of the natural depravity of man. It is an unfashionable truth; for nowadays ministers are to be found who are very fine upon "the dignity of human nature." The "lapsed state of man"—that is the phrase—is sometimes alluded to, but the corruption of our nature and kindred themes are carefully avoided: Ethiopians are informed that they may whiten their skins, and it is hoped that leopards will remove their spots. Brethren, you will not fall into this delusion, or, if you do, you may expect few conversions. To prophesy smooth things, and to extenuate the evil of our lost estate, is not the way to lead men to Jesus.

Brethren, *the necessity for the Holy Ghost's divine operations* will follow as a matter of course upon the former teaching, for dire necessity demands divine interposition. Men must be told that they are dead, and that only the Holy Spirit can quicken them; that the Spirit works according to his own good pleasure, and that no man can claim his visitations or deserve his aid. This is thought to be very discouraging teaching, and so it is, but men need to be discouraged when they are seeking salvation in a wrong manner. To put them out of conceit of their own abilities is a great help toward bringing them to look out of self to another, even the Lord Jesus. The doctrine of election and other great truths which declare salvation to be all of grace, and to be, not the right of the creature, but the gift of the Sovereign Lord, are all calculated to hide pride from man, and so to prepare him to receive the mercy of God.

We must also set before our hearers the justice of God and *the certainty that every transgression will be punished.* Often must we

> Before them place in dread array,
> The pomp of that tremendous day
> When Christ with clouds shall come.

Sound in their ears the doctrine of the second advent, not as a curiosity of prophecy, but as a solemn practical fact. It is idle to set forth our Lord in all the tinkling bravery of an earthly kingdom, after the manner of brethren who believe in a revived Judaism; we need to preach the Lord as coming to judge the world in righteousness, to summon the nations to his bar, and to separate them as a shepherd divideth the sheep from the goats. Paul preached of righteousness, temperance, and judgment to come, and made Felix tremble: these themes are equally powerful now. We rob the gospel of its power if we leave out its threatenings of punishment. It is to be feared that the novel opinions upon annihilation and restoration which have afflicted the church in these last days have caused many ministers to be slow to speak concerning the last judgment and its issues, and consequently the terrors of the Lord have had small influence upon either preachers or hearers. If this be so it cannot be too much re-gretted, for one great means of conversion is thus left unused.

Beloved brethren, we must be most of all clear upon the great soul-saving doctrine of *the atonement;* we must preach a real bona fide substitutionary sacrifice, and proclaim pardon as its result. Cloudy views as to atoning blood are mischievous to the last degree; souls are held in unnecessary bondage, and saints are robbed of the calm confidence of faith, because they are not definitely told that "God hath made him to be sin for us, who knew no sin; that we might be made the righteousness of God in him." We must preach substitution straightforwardly and unmistakably, for if any doctrine be plainly taught in Scripture it is this: "The chastisement of our peace was upon him, and with his stripes we are healed." "He, his own self, bare our sins in his own body on the tree." This truth gives rest to the con-science by showing how God can be just, and the justifier of him that believeth. This is the great net of gospel fishermen:

the fish are drawn or driven in the right direction by other truths but this is the net itself.

If men are to be saved, we must in the plainest terms preach *justification by faith* as the method by which the atonement becomes effectual in the soul's experience. If we are saved by the substitutionary work of Christ, no merit of ours is wanted, and all men have to do is by a simple faith to accept what Christ has already done. It is delightful to dwell on the grand truth that "This man, after he had offered one sacrifice for sins for ever, sat down on the right hand of God." . . .

Preach earnestly *the love of God in Christ Jesus,* and magnify the abounding mercy of the Lord; but always preach it in connection with his justice. Do not extol the single attribute of love in the method too generally followed, but regard love in the high theological sense, in which, like a golden circle, it holds within itself all the divine attributes: for God were not love if he were not just, and did not hate every unholy thing. Never exalt one attribute at the expense of another. Let boundless mercy be seen in calm consistency with stern justice and unlimited sovereignty. The true character of God is fitted to awe, impress, and humble the sinner: be careful not to misrepresent your Lord.

All these truths and others which complete the evangelical system are calculated to lead men to faith; therefore make them the staple of your teaching.

Secondly, if we are intensely anxious *to have souls saved* we must not only preach the truths which are likely to lead up to this end, but we must *use modes of handling those truths which are likely to conduce thereto.* Do you inquire, what are they? First, you must do a great deal by way of *instruction.* Sinners are not saved *in* darkness but *from* it: "That the soul be without knowledge, it is not good." Men must be taught concerning themselves, their sin, and their fall; their Saviour, redemption, regeneration, and so on. Many awakened souls would gladly accept God's way of salvation if they did but know it; they are akin to those of whom the apostle said, "And now, brethren, I wot

that through ignorance ye did it." If you will instruct them
God will save them: is it not written, "The entrance of thy
word giveth light"? If the Holy Spirit blesses your teaching,
they will see how wrong they have been, and they will be led to
repentance and faith. I do not believe in that preaching which
lies mainly in shouting, "Believe! Believe! Believe!" In common
justice you are bound to tell the poor people what they are to
believe. There must be instruction, otherwise the exhortation
to believe is manifestly ridiculous, and must in practice be
abortive. . . . The best way to preach sinners to Christ is to
preach Christ to sinners. Exhortations, entreaties, and beseechings, if not accompanied with sound instruction, are like firing
off powder without shot. You may shout and weep, and plead,
but you cannot lead men to believe what they have not heard,
nor to receive a truth which has never been set before them.
"Because the preacher was wise, he still taught the people
knowledge."

While giving instruction it is wise to *appeal to the understanding*. True religion is as logical as if it were not emotional. . . .
Should not persons of an argumentative cast of mind be provided for? We are to be all things to all men, and to these
men we must become argumentative and push them into a corner
with plain deductions and necessary inferences. Of carnal reasoning, we would have none, but of a fair, honest pondering,
considering, judging, and arguing, the more the better.

The class requiring logical argument is small compared with
the number of those who need to be pleaded with, by way of
emotional persuasion. They require not so much reasoning as
heart-argument—which is logic set on fire. You must argue with
them as a mother pleads with her boy that he will not grieve her,
or as a fond sister entreats a brother to return to their father's
home and seek reconciliation: argument must be quickened into
persuasion by the living warmth of love. Cold logic has its force,
but when made red hot with affection the power of tender argument is inconceivable. The power which one mind can gain

over others is enormous, but it is often best developed when the
leading mind has ceased to have power over itself. When passionate zeal has carried the man himself away his speech becomes
an irresistible torrent, sweeping all before it. A man known to
be godly and devout, and felt to be large-hearted and self-
sacrificing, has a power in his very person, and his advice and
recommendation carry weight because of his character; but when
he comes to plead and to persuade, even to tears, his influence
is wonderful, and God the Holy Spirit yokes it into his service.
Brethren, we must *plead.* Entreaties and beseechings must blend
with our instructions. Any and every appeal which will reach
the conscience and move men to fly to Jesus we must perpetually
employ, if by any means we may save some. I have sometimes
heard ministers blamed for speaking of themselves when they are
pleading, but the censure need not be much regarded while we
have such a precedent as the example of Paul. To a congregation
who love you it is quite allowable to mention your grief that
many of them are unsaved, and your vehement desire, and incessant prayer for their conversion. You are doing right when
you mention your own experience of the goodness of God in Christ
Jesus, and plead with men to come and taste the same. We must
not be abstractions or mere officials to our people, but we must
plead with them as real flesh and blood, if we would see them
converted. When you can quote yourself as a living instance of
what grace has done, the plea is too powerful to be withheld
through fear of being charged with egotism.

Sometimes, too, we must change our tone. Instead of in-
structing, reasoning, and persuading, we must come to *threatening,*
and declare the wrath of God upon impenitent souls. We must
lift the curtain and let them see the future. Show them their
danger, and warn them to escape from the wrath to come. This
done, we must return to *invitation,* and set before the awakened
mind the rich provisions of infinite grace which are freely presented to the sons of men. In our Master's name we must give
the invitation, crying, "Whosoever will, let him take the water of

life freely." Do not be deterred from this, my brethren, by those ultra-Calvinistic theologians who say, "You may instruct and warn the ungodly, but you must not invite or entreat them." . . . On what ground are we to address the ungodly at all? If we are only to bid them do such things as they are capable of doing without the Spirit of God, we are reduced to mere moralists. . . . Indeed, it would be idle altogether were it not that true preaching is an act of faith, and is owned by the Holy Spirit as the means of working spiritual miracles. If we were by ourselves, and did not expect divine interpositions, we should be wise to keep within the bounds of reason, and persuade men to do only what we see in them the ability to do. . . .

Again, brethren, if you wish to see souls saved, we must be wise as to *the times* when we address the unconverted. Very little common sense is spent over this matter. Under certain ministries there is a set time for speaking to sinners, and this comes as regularly as the hour of noon. . . . Why should the warning word be always at the hinder end of the discourse when hearers are most likely to be weary? . . . When their interest is excited, and they are least upon the defensive, then let fly a shaft at the careless, and it will frequently be more effectual than a whole flight of arrows shot against them at a time when they are thoroughly encased in armor of proof. Surprise is a great element in gaining attention and fixing a remark upon the memory, and times for addressing the careless should be chosen with an eye to that fact. . . .

Do not close a single sermon without addressing the ungodly, but at the same time set yourself seasons for a determined and continuous assault upon them, and proceed with all your soul to the conflict. On such occasions aim distinctly at immediate conversions; labor to remove prejudices, to resolve doubts, to conquer objections, and to drive the sinner out of his hiding-places at once. Summon the church-members to special prayer, beseech them to speak personally both with the concerned and the unconcerned, and be yourself doubly upon the watch to address individuals. . . . Winter is usually the preacher's harvest because the people can come together better in the long evenings, and are debarred from out-of-door exercises and amusements. Be well prepared for the appropriate season when "kings go forth to battle."

Among the important elements in the promotion of conversion are your own tone, temper, and spirit in preaching. If you preach the truth in a dull, monotonous style, God *may* bless it, but in all probability he will not; at any rate the tendency of such a style is not to promote attention, but to hinder it. It is not often that sinners are awakened by ministers who are themselves asleep. A hard, unfeeling mode of speech is also to be avoided; want of tenderness is a sad lack, and repels rather than attracts. The spirit of Elijah may startle, and where it is exceedingly intense it may go far to prepare for the reception of the gospel; but for actual conversion more of John is needed—love is the winning force. We must love men to Jesus. Great hearts are the main qualifications for great preachers, and we must cultivate our affections to that end. At the same time our manner must not degenerate into the soft and saccharine cant which some men affect who are forever "dearing" everybody, and fawning upon people as if they hoped to soft-sawder them into godliness. Manly persons are disgusted, and suspect hypocrisy when they hear a preacher talking molasses. Let us be bold and outspoken, and never address our hearers as if we were asking a favor of them, or as if they would oblige the Redeemer by allowing him to save them. We are bound to be lowly, but our office as ambassadors should prevent our being servile. . .

If we ourselves doubt the power of the gospel, how can we preach it with authority? Feel that you are a favored man in being allowed to proclaim the good news, and rejoice that your mission is fraught with eternal benefit to those before you. Let the people see how glad and confident the gospel has made you, and it will go far to make them long to partake in its blessed influences.

Preach very solemnly, for it is a weighty business, but let

your matter be lively and pleasing, for this will prevent solemnity from souring into dreariness. Be so thoroughly solemn that all your faculties are aroused and consecrated, and then a dash of humor will only add intenser gravity to the discourse, even as a flash of lightning makes midnight darkness all the more impressive. Preach to one point, concentrating all your energies upon the object aimed at. There must be no riding of hobbies, no introduction of elegancies of speech, no suspicion of personal display, or you will fail. Sinners are quick-witted people, and soon detect even the smallest effort to glorify self. Forego everything for the sake of those you long to save. Be a fool for Christ's sake if this will win them, or be a scholar, if that will be more likely to impress them. Spare neither labor in the study, prayer in the closet, nor zeal in the pulpit. If men do not judge their souls to be worth a thought, compel them to see that their minister is of a very different opinion.

Mean conversions, expect them, and prepare for them. Resolve that your hearers shall either yield to your Lord or be without excuse, and that this shall be the immediate result of the sermon now in hand. Do not let the Christians around you wonder when souls are saved, but urge them to believe in the undiminished power of the glad tidings, and teach them to marvel if no saving result follows the delivery of the testimony of Jesus. Do not permit sinners to hear sermons as a matter of course, or allow them to play with the edged tools of Scripture as if they were mere toys; but again and again remind them that every true gospel sermon leaves them worse if it does not make them better. Their unbelief is a daily, hourly sin; never let them infer from your teaching that they are to be pitied for continuing to make God a liar by rejecting his Son.

Impressed with a sense of their danger, give the ungodly no rest in their sins; knock again and again at the door of their hearts, and knock as for life and death. Your solicitude, your earnestness, your anxiety, your travailing in birth for them God will bless to their arousing. God works mightily by this instrumentality. But our agony for souls must be real and not feigned, and therefore our hearts must be wrought into true sympathy with God. Low piety means little spiritual power. Extremely pointed addresses may be delivered by men whose hearts are out of order with the Lord, but their result must be small. There is a something in the very tone of the man who has been with Jesus which has more power to touch the heart than the most perfect oratory: remember this and maintain an unbroken walk with God. You will need much night work in secret if you are to gather many of your Lord's lost sheep. Only by prayer and fasting can you gain power to cast out the worst of devils. Let men say what they will about sovereignty, God connects special success with special states of heart, and if these are lacking he will not do many mighty works.

In addition to earnest preaching it will be wise to use other means. If you wish to see results from your sermons you must be accessible to inquirers. A meeting after every service may not be desirable, but frequent opportunities for coming into direct contact with your people should be sought after, and by some means created. It is shocking to think that there are ministers who have no method whatever for meeting the anxious, and if they do see here and there one, it is because of the courage of the seeker, and not because of the earnestness of the pastor. From the very first you should appoint frequent and regular seasons for seeing all who are seeking after Christ, and you should continually invite such to come and speak with you.

In addition to this, hold numerous inquirers' meetings, at which the addresses shall be all intended to assist the troubled and guide the perplexed, and with these intermingle fervent prayers for the individuals present, and short testimonies from recent converts and others. As an open confession of Christ is continually mentioned in connection with saving faith, it is your wisdom to make it easy for believers who are as yet following Jesus by night to come forward and avow their allegiance to him. There must be no persuading to make a profession, but there should be every opportunity for so doing, and no stumbling block placed in the way of hopeful minds. . . . Doubts may be cleared away, errors rectified, and terrors dispelled by a few moments' conversation; I have known instances in which a lifelong misery has been ended by a simple explanation which might have been given years before. Seek out the wandering sheep one by one, and when you find all your thoughts needed for a single individual, do not grudge your labour, for your Lord in his parable represents the good shepherd as bringing home his lost sheep, not in a flock, but one at a time upon his shoulders, and rejoicing so to do.

With all that you can do, your desires will not be fulfilled, for soul-winning is a pursuit which grows upon a man; the more he is rewarded with conversions the more eager he becomes to see greater numbers born unto God. Hence you will soon discover that *you need help if many are to be brought in.* The net soon becomes too heavy for one pair of hands to drag to shore when it is filled with fishes, and your fellow-helpers must be beckoned to your assistance. Great things are done by the Holy Spirit when a whole church is aroused to sacred energy: then there are hundreds of testimonies instead of one, and these strengthen each other; then advocates for Christ succeed each other and work into each other's hands while supplication ascends to heaven with the force of united importunity; thus sinners are encompassed with a cordon of earnest entreaties, and heaven itself is called into the field. It would seem hard in some congregations for a sinner to be saved, for whatever good he may receive from the pulpit is frozen out of him by the arctic atmosphere with which he is surrounded; and on the other hand some churches make it hard for men to remain unconverted, for with holy zeal they persecute the careless into anxiety. It should be our ambition, in the power of the Holy Ghost, to work the entire church into a fine missionary condition, to make it like a Leyden jar charged to the full with divine electricity, so that whatever comes into contact with it shall feel its power. What can one man do alone?

What can he not do with an army of enthusiasts around him?

Contemplate at the outset the possibility of having a church of soul-winners. Do not succumb to the usual idea that we can only gather a few useful workers, and that the rest of the community must inevitably be a dead weight: it may possibly so happen, but do not set out with that notion or it will be verified. The usual need not be the universal; better things are possible than anything yet attained: set your aim high and spare no effort to reach it. Labour to gather a church alive for Jesus, every member energetic to the full, and the whole in incessant activity for the salvation of men. To this end there must be the best of preaching to feed the host into strength, continual prayer to bring down the power from on high, and the most heroic example on your own part to fire their zeal. . .

2

The Holy Spirit in Connection
with Our Ministry

I HAVE selected a topic upon which it would be difficult to say anything which has not been often said before; but as the theme is of the highest importance, it is good to dwell upon it frequently, and even if we bring forth only old things and nothing more, it may be wise to put you in remembrance of them. Our subject is the Holy Spirit in connection with our ministry, or—the work of the Holy Ghost in relation to ourselves as ministers of the gospel of Jesus Christ.

"*I believe in the Holy Ghost.*" Having pronounced that sentence as a matter of creed, I hope we can also repeat it as a devout soliloquy forced to our lips by personal experience. To us the presence and work of the Holy Spirit are the ground of our confidence as to the wisdom and hopefulness of our lifework. If we had not believed in the Holy Ghost we should have laid down our ministry long ere this, for "who is sufficient for these things?" Our hope of success, and our strength for continuing the service, lie in our belief that the Spirit of the Lord resteth upon us.

I will for the time being take it for granted that we are all of us conscious of the existence of the Holy Spirit. We have said we *believe* in him; but in very deed we have advanced beyond faith in this matter, and have come into the region of consciousness. Time was when most of us believed in the existence of our present friends, for we had heard of them by the hearing of the ear, but we have now seen each other, and returned the fraternal

grip, and felt the influence of happy companionships, and therefore we do not now so much believe as know. Even so we have
felt the Spirit of God operating upon our hearts, we have known
and perceived the power which he wields over human spirits,
and we know him by frequent, conscious, personal contact. By
the sensitiveness of our spirit we are as much made conscious of
the presence of the Spirit of God as we are made cognizant of the
existence of the souls of our fellow men by their action upon our
souls, or as we are certified of the existence of matter by its
action upon our senses. We have been raised from the dull sphere
of mere mind and matter into the heavenly radiance of the spirit-
world; and now, as spiritual men, we discern spiritual things, we
feel the forces which are paramount in the spirit-realm, and we
know that there is a Holy Ghost, for we feel him operating
upon our spirits. If it were not so, we should certainly have
no right to be in the ministry of Christ's church. Should we
even dare to remain in her membership? But, my brethren, we
have been spiritually quickened. We are distinctly conscious of a
new life, with all that comes out of it: we are new creatures in
Christ Jesus, and dwell in a new world. We have been illuminated,
and made to behold the things which eye hath not seen; we have
been guided into truth such as flesh and blood could never have
revealed. We have been comforted of the Spirit: full often
have we been lifted up from the deeps of sorrow to the heights of
joy by the sacred Paraclete. We have, also, in a measure, been
sanctified by him, and we are conscious that the operation of
sanctification is going on in us in different forms and ways.
Therefore, because of all these personal experiences, we know
that there is a Holy Ghost, as surely as we know that we ourselves exist. . . .

To us, as ministers, the Holy Spirit is absolutely essential.
Without him our office is a mere name. We claim no priesthood
over and above that which belongs to every child of God; but we
are the successors of those who, in olden times, were moved of
God to declare his work, to testify against transgression, and to

plead his cause. Unless we have the spirit of the prophets resting upon us, the mantle which we wear is nothing but a rough
garment to deceive. We ought to be driven forth with abhorrence
from the society of honest men for daring to speak in the name
of the Lord if the Spirit of God rests not upon us. We believe
ourselves to be spokesmen for Jesus Christ, appointed to continue
his witness upon earth; but upon him and his testimony the Spirit
of God always rested, and if it does not rest upon us, we are
evidently not sent forth into the world as he was. At Pentecost
the commencement of the great work of converting the world was
with flaming tongues and a rushing mighty wind, symbols of the
presence of the Spirit; if, therefore, we think to succeed without
the Spirit, we are not after the Pentecostal order. If we have
not the Spirit which Jesus promised, we cannot perform the com-
mission which Jesus gave. . . .

We are not the passive communicators of infallibility, but
the honest teachers of such things as we have learned, so far
as we have been able to grasp them. As our minds are active,
and have a personal existence while the mind of the Spirit is
acting upon them, *our* infirmities are apparent as well as *his*
wisdom; and while we reveal what he has made us to know, we are
greatly abased by the fear that our own ignorance and error are
in a measure manifested at the same time, because we have not
been more perfectly subject to the divine power. . . .

Wherein may we look for the aid of the Holy Spirit? I should
reply, in seven or eight ways.

1. First, *he is the Spirit of knowledge.* "He shall guide you
into all truth." In this character we need his teaching.

We have urgent need to study, for the teacher of others must
himself be instructed. Habitually to come into the pulpit unprepared is unpardonable presumption: nothing can more effectually lower ourselves and our office. After a visitation discourse by
the Bishop of Lichfield upon the necessity of earnestly studying
the Word, a certain vicar told his lordship that he could not
believe his doctrine, "For," said he, "often when I am in the vestry I

do not know what I am going to talk about; but I go into the
pulpit and preach, and think nothing of it." His lordship replied, "And you are quite right in thinking nothing of it, for
your church-wardens have told me that they share your opinion." . . .

It is in our study work, in that blessed labour when we are
alone with the Book before us, that we need the help of the Holy
Spirit. He holds the key of the heavenly treasury, and can enrich
us beyond conception; he has the clue of the most labyrinthine
doctrine, and can lead us in the way of truth. He can break in
pieces the gates of brass, and cut in sunder the bars of iron,
and give to us the treasures of darkness, and hidden riches of
secret places. You may study the original, consult the commentaries, and meditate deeply, yet if you neglect to cry mightily
unto the Spirit of God your study will not profit you; but even
if you are debarred the use of helps (which I trust you will not
be), if you wait upon the Holy Ghost in simple dependence
upon his teaching, you will lay hold of very much of the divine
meaning.

The Spirit of God is peculiarly precious to us, because he
especially instructs us as to the person and work of our Lord
Jesus Christ; and that is the main point of our preaching. He
takes of the things *of Christ,* and shows them unto us. If he had
taken of the things of doctrine or precept, we should have been
glad of such gracious assistance; but since he especially delights
in the things of Christ, and focusses his sacred light upon the
cross, we rejoice to see the centre of our testimony so divinely
illuminated, and we are sure that the light will be diffused over
all the rest of our ministry. Let us wait upon the Spirit of God
with this cry: "O Holy Spirit, reveal to us the Son of God, and
thus show us the Father."

As the Spirit of knowledge, he not only instructs us as to the
gospel, but he leads us to see the Lord in all other matters. We
are not to shut our eyes to God in nature, or to God in general
history, or to God in the daily occurrences of providence, or to
God in our own experience; and the blessed Spirit is the interpreter

to us of the mind of God in all these. If we cry, "Teach me what thou wouldst have me to do; or, show me wherefore thou contendest with me; or, tell me what is thy mind in this precious providence of mercy, or in that other dispensation of mingled judgment and grace," we shall in each case be well instructed; for the Spirit is the seven-branched candlestick of the sanctuary and by his light all things are rightly seen. As Goodwin well observes, "There must be light to accompany the truth if we are to know it. The experience of all gracious men proves this. What is the reason that you shall see some things in a chapter at one time, and not at another; some grace in your hearts at one time, and not at another; have a sight of spiritual things at one time, and not at another? The eye is the same, but it is the Holy Ghost that openeth and shutteth this dark lantern, as I may so call it; as he openeth it wider, or contracts it, or shutteth it narrower, so do we see more or less; and sometimes he shutteth it wholly, and then the soul is in darkness, though it have never so good an eye.". . .

2.   In the second place, the Spirit is called the *Spirit of wisdom*, and we greatly need him in that capacity; for knowledge may be dangerous if unaccompanied with wisdom, which is the art of rightly using what we know. Rightly to divide the Word of God is as important as fully to understand it, for some who have evidently understood a part of the gospel have given undue prominence to that one portion of it, and have therefore exhibited a distorted Christianity, to the injury of those who have received it. . . . We should not hide truth for a moment, but we should have wisdom so to preach it that there should be no needless jarring or offending, but a gradual enlightenment of those who cannot see it at all, and a leading of weaker brethren into the full circle of gospel doctrine.

We also need wisdom in the way of putting things to different people. You can cast a man down with the very truth which was intended to build him up. You can sicken a man with the honey with which you mean to sweeten his mouth. The great mercy of

God has been preached unguardedly, and has led hundreds into
licentiousness; and, on the other hand, the terrors of the Lord
have been occasionally fulminated with such violence that they
have driven men into despair, and so into a settled defiance
of the Most High. Wisdom is profitable to direct, and he who
hath it brings forth each truth in its season, dressed in its most
appropriate garments. Who can give us this wisdom but the blessed
Spirit? O, my brethren, see to it, that in lowliest reverence you
wait for his direction.

3. Thirdly, we need the spirit . . . as the live coal from
off the altar, touching our lips, so that when we have knowledge
and wisdom to select the fitting portion of truth, we may enjoy
freedom of utterance when we come to deliver it. "Lo, this hath
touched thy lips." . . .

We require the Holy Spirit also to incite us in our utterance.
I doubt not you are all conscious of different states of mind in
preaching. Some of those states arise from your body being in
different conditions. A bad cold will not only spoil the clearness
of the voice, but freeze the flow of the thoughts. For my own
part, if I cannot speak clearly I am unable to think clearly, and
the matter becomes hoarse as well as the voice....Are you not
conscious of changes altogether independent of the body? When
you are in robust health do you not find yourselves one day as
heavy as Pharaoh's chariot with the wheels taken off, and at
another time as much at liberty as "a hind let loose"? Today
your branch glitters with the dew, yesterday it was parched with
drought. Who knoweth not that the Spirit of God is in all this? . . .
Often and often, when I have had doubts suggested by the infidel,
I have been able to fling them to the winds with utter scorn, because I am distinctly conscious of a power working upon me
when I am speaking in the name of the Lord, infinitely trans-
cending any personal power of fluency, and far surpassing any
energy derived from excitement such as I have felt when delivering a secular lecture or making a speech—so utterly distinct
from such power that I am quite certain it is not of the same

order or class as the enthusiasm of the politician or the glow of
the orator. May we full often feel the divine energy, and speak
with power.

4. But then, fourthly, the Spirit of God acts also as *an
anointing oil,* and this relates to *the entire delivery*—not to the
utterance merely from the mouth, but to the whole delivery of
the discourse. He can make you feel your subject till it thrills
you, and you become depressed by it so as to be crushed into
the earth, or elevated by it so as to be borne upon its eagle wings;
making you feel, besides your subject, your object, till you yearn
for the conversion of men, and for the uplifting of Christians to
something nobler than they have known as yet. . . . The sacred
Spirit can multiply our mental states, and make us many times
the men we are by nature. How much he can make of us, and
how grandly he can elevate us, I will not dare to surmise: certainly, he can do exceeding abundantly above what we ask or
even think.

Especially is it the Holy Spirit's work to maintain in us a
devotional frame of mind whilst we are discoursing. This is a
condition to be greatly coveted—to continue praying while you
are occupied with preaching; to do the Lord's commandments,
hearkening unto the voice of his Word; to keep the eye on the
throne, and the wing in perpetual motion. I hope we know what
this means; I am sure we know, or may soon experience, its
opposite, namely, the evil of preaching in an undevotional spirit.
What can be worse than to speak under the influence of a proud
or angry spirit? What more weakening than to preach in an un-
believing spirit? But, oh, to burn in our secret heart while we
blaze before the eyes of others! This is the work of the Spirit
of God. . . .

In our pulpits we need the spirit of dependence to be mixed
with that of devotion, so that all along, from the first word to
the last syllable, we may be looking up to the strong for strength.
. . . Looking to the hills whence cometh your help all the sermon
through, with absolute dependence upon God, you will preach

in a brave, confident spirit all the while. Perhaps I was wrong
to say "brave," for it is not a brave thing to trust God: to
true believers it is a simple matter of sweet necessity—how can
they help trusting him? Wherefore should they doubt their
ever faithful Friend? I told my people the other morning, when
preaching from the text, "My grace is sufficient for thee," that
for the first time in my life I had experienced what Abraham felt
when he fell upon his face and laughed. I was riding home, very
weary with a long week's work, when there came to my mind this
text: "My grace is sufficient for thee"—but it came with the
emphasis laid upon two words: "*My* grace is sufficient for *thee.*"
My soul said, "Doubtless it is. Surely the grace of the infinite
God is more than sufficient for such a mere insect as I am,"
and I laughed, and laughed again, to think how far the supply
exceeded all my needs. It seemed to me as though I were a little
fish in the sea, and in my thirst I said, "Alas, I shall drink up
the ocean." Then the Father of the waters lifted up his head sublime, and smilingly replied, "Little fish, the boundless main is
sufficient for thee." The thought made unbelief appear supremely
ridiculous, as indeed it is.

Oh, brethren, we ought to preach feeling that God means to
bless the word, for we have his promise for it; and when we have
done preaching we should look out for the people who have
received a blessing. Do you ever say, "I am overwhelmed with
astonishment to find that the Lord has converted souls through
my poor ministry"? Mock humility! Your ministry is poor enough.
Everybody knows that, and you ought to know it most of all; but,
at the same time, is it any wonder that God, who said: "My word
shall not return unto me void," has kept his promise? . . .

We need the Spirit of God, then, all through the sermon to
keep our hearts and minds in a proper condition, for if we have
not the right spirit we shall lose the tone which persuades and
prevails. . . . To avoid errors of manners and tone, we must
be led of the Holy Spirit, who alone teacheth us to profit.

5. Fifthly, we depend entirely upon the Spirit of God *to*

produce actual effect from the gospel, and at this effect we must always aim. . . . Aim at the right sort of effect; the inspiring of saints to nobler things, the leading of Christians closer to their Master, the comforting of doubters till they rise out of their terrors, the repentance of sinners, and their exercise of immediate faith in Christ. . . . Miracles of grace must be the seals of our ministry; who can bestow them but the Spirit of God? Convert a soul without the Spirit of God! Why, you cannot even make a fly, much less create a new heart and a right spirit. . . . Our ends can never be gained if we miss the co-operation of the Spirit of the Lord. . . .

6. Next we need the Spirit of God as *the Spirit of supplications,* who maketh intercession for the saints according to the will of God. A very important part of our lives consists in praying in the Holy Ghost, and that minister who does not think so had better escape from his ministry. Abundant prayer must go with earnest preaching. . . . The habit of prayer is good, but the spirit of prayer is better. Regular retirement is to be maintained, but continued communion with God is to be our aim. As a rule, we ministers ought never to be many minutes without actually lifting up our hearts in prayer. Some of us could honestly say that we are seldom a quarter of an hour without speaking to God, and that not as a duty but as an instinct, a habit of the new nature for which we claim no more credit than a babe does for crying after its mother. How could we do otherwise? . . .

As to our prayers in public, let it never be truthfully said that they are official, formal, and cold; yet they will be so if the supply of the Spirit be scant. Those who use a liturgy I judge not; but to those who are accustomed to free prayer I say, you cannot pray acceptably in public year after year without the Spirit of God; dead praying will become offensive to the people long before that time. What then? Whence shall our help come? Certain weaklings have said, "Let us have a liturgy." Rather than seek divine aid they will go down to Egypt for help. Rather than be dependent upon the Spirit of God, they will pray by a book!

For my part, if I cannot pray, I would rather know it, and groan
over my soul's barrenness till the Lord shall again visit me with
fruitfulness of devotion. If you are filled with the Spirit, you will
be glad to throw off all formal fetters, that you may commit
yourself to the sacred current, to be borne along till you find waters
to swim in. Sometimes you will enjoy closer fellowship with God
in prayer in the pulpit than you have known anywhere else. To me
my greatest secrecy in prayer has often been in public; my truest
loneliness with God has occurred to me while pleading in the
midst of thousands. I have opened my eyes at the close of a
prayer and come back to the assembly with a sort of a shock at
finding myself upon earth and among men. Such seasons are not
at our command. Neither can we raise ourselves into such conditions by any preparations or efforts. How blessed they are both
to the minister and his people no tongue can tell! How full of
power and blessing habitual prayerfulness must also be I cannot
here pause to declare, but for it all we must look to the Holy
Spirit, and, blessed be God, we shall not look in vain, for it is
especially said of him that he helpeth our infirmities in prayer.

   7.   Furthermore, it is important that we be under the influence
of the Holy Ghost as he is the *Spirit of holiness;* for a very considerable and essential part of Christian ministry lies in example.
Our people take much note of what we say out of the pulpit,
and what we do in the social circle and elsewhere. Do you find
it easy, my brethren, to be saints?—such saints that others may
regard you as examples? We ought to be such husbands that
every husband in the parish may safely be such as we are. Is it
so? We ought to be the best of fathers. Alas! some ministers,
to my knowledge, are far from this, for as to their families, they
have kept the vineyards of others, but their own vineyards they
have not kept. Their children are neglected, and do not grow
up as a godly seed. Is it so with yours? In our converse with our
fellow men are we blameless and harmless, the sons of God
without rebuke? Such we ought to be. I admire Mr. Whitfield's
reasons for always having his linen scrupulously clean. "No, no,"

he would say, "these are not trifles; a minister must be without spot, even in his garments, if he can." Purity cannot be carried too far in a minister. . . . O to keep ourselves unspotted from the world! How can this be in such a scene of temptation, and with such besetting sins, unless we are preserved by superior power? If you are to walk in all holiness and purity, as becometh ministers of the gospel, you must be daily baptized into the Spirit of God.

8. Once again, we need the Spirit as *a Spirit of discernment*, for he knows the minds of men as he knows the mind of God, and we need this very much in dealing with difficult characters. There are in this world some persons who might possibly be allowed to preach, but they should never be suffered to become pastors. They have a mental or spiritual disqualification. In the church of San Zeno, at Verona, I saw the statue of that saint in a sitting posture, and the artist has given him knees so short that he has no lap whatever, so that he could not have been a nursing father. I fear there are many others who labor under a similar disability: they cannot bring their minds to enter heartily into the pastoral care. They can dogmatize upon a doctrine, and controvert upon an ordinance, but as to sympathizing with an experience, it is far from them. . . . In some such perplexity are those found who have never been taught of the Holy Spirit how to care for the souls of men. May his instructions save us from such wretched incompetence.

Moreover, brethren, whatever our tenderness of heart, or loving anxiety, we shall not know how to deal with the vast variety of cases unless the Spirit of God shall direct us, for no two individuals are alike; and even the same case will require different treatment at different times. At one period it may be best to console, at another to rebuke; and the person with whom you sympathized even to tears today may need that you confront him with a frown tomorrow, for trifling with the consolation which you presented. Those who bind up the brokenhearted and set free the captives must have the Spirit of the Lord upon them. . . .

I have given you a lengthened catalogue of matters wherein

the Holy Spirit is absolutely necessary to us, and yet the list is very far from complete. I have intentionally left it imperfect, because if I attempted its completion all our time would have expired before we were able to answer the question, *How may we lose this needful assistance?* Let none of us ever try the experiment, but it is certain that ministers may lose the aid of the Holy Ghost. Each man here may lose it. You shall not perish as believers, for everlasting life is in you; but you may perish as ministers, and be no more heard of as witnesses for the Lord. Should this happen it will not be without a cause. The Spirit claims a sovereignty like that of the wind which bloweth where it listeth; but let us never dream that sovereignty and capriciousness are the same thing. The blessed Spirit acts as he wills, but he always acts justly, wisely, and with motive and reason. At times he gives or withholds his blessing, for reasons connected with ourselves. Mark the course of a river like the Thames, how it winds and twists according to its own sweet will; yet there is a reason for every bend and curve—the geologist studying the soil and marking the conformation of the rock sees a reason why the river's bed diverges to the right or to the left—and so, though the Spirit of God blesses one preacher more than another, and the reason cannot be such that any man could congratulate himself upon his own goodness, yet there are certain things about Christian ministers which God blesses, and certain other things which hinder success. The Spirit of God falls like the dew, in mystery and power, but it is in the spiritual world as in the natural: certain substances are wet with the celestial moisture while others are always dry. Is there not a cause? The wind blows where it lists; but if we desire to feel a stiff breeze we must go out to sea, or climb the hills. The Spirit of God has his favored places for displaying his might. He is typified by a dove, and the dove has chosen haunts: to the rivers of water, to the peaceful and quiet places, the dove resorts; we meet it not upon the battlefield, neither does it alight on carrion. There are things congruous to the Spirit, and things contrary to his mind. The Spirit of God is compared to light, and light can shine where it wills, but some bodies are opaque, while others are transparent; and so there are men through whom God the Holy Ghost can shine, and there are others through whom his brightness never appears. Thus, then, it can be shown that the Holy Ghost, though he be the "free Spirit" of God, is by no means capricious in his operations.

But, dear brethren, the Spirit of God may be grieved and vexed, and even resisted: to deny this is to oppose the constant testimony of Scripture. Worst of all, we may do despite to him, and so insult him that he will speak no more by us, but leaves us as he left King Saul of old. Alas, that there should be men in the Christian ministry to whom this has happened; but I am afraid there are.

Brethren, what are those evils which will grieve the Spirit? I answer, anything that would have disqualified you as an ordinary Christian for communion with God also disqualifies you for feeling the extraordinary power of the Holy Spirit as a minister; but, apart from that, there are special hindrances.

Among the first we must mention a want of sensitiveness, or that unfeeling condition which arises from disobeying the Spirit's influences. We should be delicately sensitive to his faintest movement, and then we may expect his abiding presence, but if we are as the horse and as the mule, which have no understanding, we shall feel the whip, but we shall not enjoy the tender influences of the Comforter.

Another grieving fault is a want of truthfulness. . . . Some men's souls are not honest; they are sophistical and double-minded. Christ's Spirit will not be an accomplice with men in the wretched business of shuffling and deceiving. Does it really come to this—that you preach certain doctrines, not because you believe them, but because your congregation expects you to do so? Are you biding your time till you can, without risk, renounce your present creed and tell out what your dastardly mind really holds to be true? Then are you fallen indeed, and are baser than the meanest slaves. God deliver us from treacherous men! . . . If we feel an abhorrence of them, how much more must the Spirit of truth detest them!

You can greatly grieve the Holy Spirit by a general scantiness of grace. The phrase is awkward, but it describes certain persons better than any other which occurs to me. The Scanty-grace family usually have one of the brothers in the ministry. I know the man. He is not dishonest, nor immoral, he is not bad-tempered, nor self-indulgent, but there is a something wanting: it would not be easy to prove its absence by any overt offence, but it is wanting in the whole man, and its absence spoils everything. He wants the one thing needful. He is not spiritual, he has no savour of Christ, his heart never burns within him, his soul is not alive, he wants grace. We cannot expect the Spirit of God to bless a ministry which never ought to have been exercised, and certainly a graceless ministry is of that character.

Another evil which drives away the divine spirit is pride. The way to be very great is to be very little. To be very noteworthy in your own esteem is to be unnoticed of God. If you must needs dwell upon the high places of the earth, you shall find the mountain summits cold and barren: the Lord dwells with the lowly, but he knows the proud afar off.

The Holy Ghost is also vexed by laziness. I cannot imagine the Spirit waiting at the door of a sluggard, and supplying the deficiencies created by indolence. Sloth in the cause of the Redeemer is a vice for which no excuse can be invented. We ourselves feel our flesh creep when we see the dilatory movements of sluggards, and we may be sure that the active Spirit is equally vexed with those who trifle in the work of the Lord.

Neglect of private prayer and many other evils will produce the same unhappy result, but there is no need to enlarge, for your own consciences will tell you, brethren, what it is that grieves the Holy One of Israel.

And now, let me entreat you, listen to this word: *Do you know what may happen if the Spirit of God be greatly grieved and depart from us?* There are two suppositions. The first is that we never were God's true servants at all, but were only temporarily used by him, as Balaam was, and even the ass on which he rode. Suppose, brethren, that you and I go on comfortably preaching a while, and are neither suspected by ourselves nor others to be destitute of the Spirit of God: our ministry may all come to an end on a sudden, and we may come to an end with it; we may be smitten down in our prime, as were Nadab and Abihu, no more to be seen ministering before the Lord, or removed in riper years, like Hophni and Phinehas, no longer to serve in the tabernacle of the congregation. We have no inspired annalist to record for us the sudden cutting off of promising men, but if we had, it may be we should read with terror—of zeal sustained by strong drink, of public Phariseeism associated with secret defilement, of avowed orthodoxy concealing absolute infidelity, or of some other form of strange fire presented upon the altar till the Lord would endure it no more, and cut off the offenders with a sudden stroke. Shall this terrible doom happen to any one of us?

Alas, I have seen some deserted by the Holy Spirit, as Saul was. . . . See how the deserted preacher moodily plays the cynic, criticises all others, and hurls the javelin of detraction at a better man than himself. Saul was once among the prophets, but he was more at home among the persecutors. The disappointed preacher worries the true evangelist, resorts to the witchcraft of philosophy and seeks help from dead heresies; but his power is gone, and the Philistines will soon find him among the slain. . . .

Alas, some ministers become like Balaam. He was a prophet, was he not? Did he not speak in the name of the Lord? Is he not called the man whose eyes are opened, "which saw the vision of the Almighty"? Yet Balaam fought against Israel, and cunningly devised a scheme by which the chosen people might be overthrown. Ministers of the gospel have become Papists, infidels, and freethinkers, and plotted the destruction of what they once professed to prize. We may be apostles, and yet, like Judas, turn out to be sons of perdition. Woe unto us if this be the case! Brethren, I will assume that we really are the children of God, and what then?

Why, even then, if the Spirit of God depart from us, we may be taken away on a sudden, as the deceived prophet was who failed to obey the command of the Lord in the days of Jeroboam. He was no doubt a man of God, and the death of his body was no evidence of the loss of his soul, but he broke away from what he knew to be the command of God given specially to himself, and his ministry ended there and then, for a lion met him by the way and slew him. May the Holy Spirit preserve us from deceivers, and keep us true to the voice of God. . . .

Or—and this last has saddened me beyond all expression, because it is much more likely than any of the rest—we may be left by the Spirit of God, in a painful degree, to mar the close of our lifework as Moses did. Not to lose our souls, nay, not even to lose our crowns in heaven, or even our reputations on earth; but, still, to be under a cloud in our last days through once speaking unadvisedly with our lips. I have lately studied the later days of the great prophet of Horeb, and I have not yet recovered from the deep gloom of spirit which it cast over me. What was the sin of Moses? You need not inquire. It was not gross like the transgression of David, nor startling like the failure of Peter, nor weak and foolish like the grave fault of his brother Aaron; indeed, it seems an infinitesimal offence as weighed in the balances of ordinary judgment. But then, you see, it was the sin of Moses, of a man favored of God beyond all others, of a leader of the people, of a representative of the divine King. The Lord could have overlooked it in any one else, but not in Moses: Moses must be chastened by being forbidden to lead the people into the promised land. Truly, he had a glorious view from the top of Pisgah, and everything else which could mitigate the rigour of the sentence, but it was a great disappointment never to enter the land of Israel's inheritance, and that for once speaking unadvisedly. I would not shun my Master's service, but I tremble in his presence. Who can be faultless when even Moses erred? It is a dreadful thing to be beloved of God. "Who among us shall dwell with devouring fire? Who among us shall dwell

with everlasting burnings? He that walketh righteously and speaketh uprightly"—he alone can face that sin-consuming flame of
love. Brethren, I beseech you, crave Moses' place, but tremble
as you take it. Fear and tremble for all the good that God shall
make to pass before you. When you are fullest of the fruits of
the Spirit bow lowest before the throne, and serve the Lord
with fear. "The Lord our God is a jealous God." Remember that
God has come unto us, not to exalt *us,* but to exalt *himself,* and
we must see to it that his glory is the one sole object of all that
we do. "He must increase, and I must *decrease."* Oh, may God
bring us to this, and make us walk very carefully and humbly before him. God will search us and try us, for judgment begins
at his own house, and in that house it begins with his ministers.
Will any of us be found wanting? . . .

3

Earnestness: Its Marring and Maintenance

I F I were asked, "What in a Christian minister is the most essential quality for securing success in winning souls for Christ?" I should reply, "Earnestness"; and if I were asked a second or a third time, I should not vary the answer, for personal observation drives me to the conclusion that, as a rule, real success is proportionate to the preacher's earnestness. . . . In many instances ministerial success is traceable almost entirely to an intense zeal, a consuming passion for souls, and an eager enthusiasm in the cause of God, and we believe that in every case, other things being equal, men prosper in the divine service in proportion as their hearts are blazing with holy love. "The God that answereth by fire, let him be God"; and the man who has the tongue of fire, let him be God's minister.

Brethren, you and I must, as preachers, be always earnest in reference to our pulpit work. Here we must labour to attain the very highest degree of excellence. . . . The pulpit is the Thermopylae of Christendom: there the fight will be lost or won. To us ministers the maintenance of our power in the pulpit should be our great concern; we must occupy that spiritual watchtower with our hearts and minds awake and in full vigor. . . . When our hearers come to the house of God, and obtain "food convenient for them," they forget a great many grievances in the joy of the festival, but if we send them away hungry they will be in as irritable a mood as a bear robbed of her whelps.

Now, in order that we may be acceptable, *we must be earnest when actually engaged in preaching.* . . . To go into the pulpit with the listless air of those gentlemen who loll about, and lean upon the cushion as if they had at last reached a quiet resting place, is, I think, most censurable. To rise before the people to deal out commonplaces which have cost you nothing, as if anything would do for a sermon, is not merely derogatory to the dignity of our office, but is offensive in the sight of God. We must be earnest in the pulpit for our own sakes, for we shall not long be able to maintain our position as leaders in the church of God if we are dull. Moreover, for the sake of our church members, and converted people, we must be energetic, for if we are not zealous, neither will they be. It is not in the order of nature that rivers should run uphill, and it does not often happen that zeal rises from the pew to the pulpit. It is natural that it should flow down from us to our hearers; the pulpit must therefore stand at a high level of ardour if we are, under God, to make and to keep our people fervent. Those who attend our ministry have a great deal to do during the week. Many of them have family trials, and heavy personal burdens to carry, and they frequently come into the assembly cold and listless, with thoughts wandering hither and thither. . . . We ought each one to be like that reformer who is described as *"Vividus vultus, vividi oculi, vividae manus, denique omnia vivida,"* which I would rather freely render, "a countenance beaming with life, eyes and hands full of life, in fine, a vivid preacher, altogether alive." . . .

The world also will suffer as well as the church if we are not fervent. We cannot expect a gospel devoid of earnestness to have any mighty effect upon the unconverted around us. . . .

Earnestness in the pulpit must be real. It is not to be mimicked. We have seen it counterfeited, but every person with a grain of sense could detect the imposition. To stamp the foot, to smite the desk, to perspire, to shout, to bawl, to quote the pathetic portions of other people's sermons, or to pour out voluntary tears from a watery eye will never make up for true agony of soul and real tenderness of spirit. The best piece of acting is but acting; those who only look at appearances may be pleased by it, but lovers of reality will be disgusted. . . . We must be earnest in the pulpit because we are earnest everywhere; we must blaze in our discourses because we are continually on fire. . . . Be earnest, and you will *seem* to be earnest. A burning heart will soon find for itself a flaming tongue. To sham earnestness is one of the most contemptible of dodges for courting popularity; let us abhor the very thought. Go and be listless in the pulpit if you are so in your heart. Be slow in speech, drawling in tone, and monotonous in voice, if so you can best express your soul; even that would be infinitely better than to make your ministry a masquerade and yourself an actor.

But our zeal while in the act of preaching must be followed up by intense solicitude as to the after-results. . . . God will not send a harvest of souls to those who never watch or water the fields which they have sown. . . . Let the awful and important thought of souls being saved by our preaching, or left to perish and to be condemned to hell through our negligence—I say, let this awful and tremendous thought dwell ever upon our spirits. We are made watchmen to the house of Israel, as Ezekiel was; and, if we give no warnings of approaching danger, the souls of multitudes may perish through our neglect; then the blood of souls will be terribly required at our hands (Ezek. 3:17 ff.).

Such considerations should make us instant in season and out of season, and cause us at all times to be clad with zeal as with a cloak. We ought to be all alive, and always alive. A pillar of light and fire should be the preacher's fit emblem. Our ministry must be emphatic, or it will never affect these thoughtless times; and to this end our hearts must be habitually fervent, and our whole nature must be fired with an all-consuming passion for the glory of God and the good of men. . . .

We must by some means secure uninterrupted meditation, or we shall lose power. . . .

Earnestness may be, and too often is, diminished by neglect

of study. If we have not exercised ourselves in the word of God, we shall not preach with the fervour and grace of the man who has fed upon the truth he delivers, and is therefore strong and ardent. . . . Live on the substantial doctrines of grace, and you will outlive and outwork those who delight in the pastry and syllabubs of "modern thought."

Zeal may, on the other hand, be damped by our studies. There is, no doubt, such a thing as feeding the brain at the expense of the heart, and many a man in his aspirations to be literary has rather qualified himself to write reviews than to preach sermons. A quaint evangelist was wont to say that Christ hung crucified beneath Greek, Latin, and Hebrew. It ought not to be so, but it has often happened that the student in college has gathered fuel, but lost the fire which is to kindle it. It will be to our everlasting disgrace if we bury our flame beneath the faggots which are intended to sustain it. If we degenerate into book-worms it will be to the old serpent's delight, and to our own misery.

True earnestness may be greatly lessened by levity in con-versation, and especially by jesting with brother ministers, in whose company we often take greater liberties than we would like to do in society of other Christians. There are excellent reasons for our feeling at home with our brethren, but if this freedom be carried too far we shall soon feel that we have suffered dam-age through vanity of speech. Cheerfulness is one thing, and frivolity is another; he is a wise man who by a serious happiness of conversation steers between the dark rocks of moroseness, and the quicksands of levity.

We shall often find ourselves in danger of being deteriorated in zeal by the cold Christian people with whom we come in con-tact. What terrible wet blankets some professors are! . . . If these frost-bitten men should happen to be the officers of the church, from whom you naturally expect the warmest sympathy, the re-sult is chilling to the last degree, and all the more so if you are young and inexperienced: it is as though an angel were con-fined in an iceberg. . . .

Remembering then, dear brethren, that we must be in earnest, and that we cannot counterfeit earnestness, or find a substitute for it, and that it is very easy for us to lose it, let us consider for a while the ways and means for retaining all our fervour and gaining more. If it is to continue, *our earnestness must be kindled at an immortal flame,* and I know of but one—the flame of the love of Christ, which many waters cannot quench. A spark from that celestial sun will be as undying as the source from whence it came. If we can get it, yea, if we have it, we shall still be full of enthusiasm, however long we may live, however greatly we may be tried, and however much for many reasons we may be discouraged. To continue fervent for life we must possess the fervour of heavenly life to begin with. Have we this fire? . . . If not, why are we here? If a man *can* live without preaching, let him live without preaching. If a man can be content without being a soul-winner—I had almost said he had better not attempt the work, but I had rather say—let him seek to have the stone taken out of his heart, that he may feel for perishing men. Till then, as a minister, he may do positive mischief by occupying the place of one who might have succeeded in the blessed work in which *he* must be a failure.

The fire of our earnestness must burn upon the hearth of faith in the truths which we preach, and faith in their power to bless mankind when the Spirit applies them to the heart. He who declares what may or what may not be true, and what he considers upon the whole to be as good as any other form of teaching, will of necessity make a very feeble preacher. How can he be zealous about that which he is not sure of? If he knows nothing of the inward power of the truth within his own heart, if he has never tasted and handled the good word of life, how can he be enthusiastic? But if the Holy Ghost has taught us in secret places, and made our soul to understand within itself the doctrine which we are to proclaim, then shall we speak evermore with the tongue of fire. Brother, do not begin to teach others till the Lord has taught *you.* It must be dreary work to parrot forth dogmas which have no interest for your heart, and carry no conviction to your understanding. . . .

Fan the flame as well as feed it. Fan it with much supplication. . . . There is for our brethren and ourselves an absolute necessity for prayer. Necessity!—I hardly like to talk of that; let me rather speak of the deliciousness of prayer—the wondrous sweetness and divine felicity which come to the soul that lives in the atmosphere of prayer. John Fox said, "The time we spend with God in secret is the sweetest time, and the best improved. Therefore if thou lovest thy life, be in love with prayer." . . . There should be special seasons for devotion, and it is well to maintain them with regularity; but the spirit of prayer is even better than the habit of prayer: to pray without ceasing is better than praying at intervals. It will be a happy circumstance if we can frequently bow the knee with devout brethren, and I think it ought to be a rule with us ministers never to separate without a word of prayer. . . . It is a refreshing practice to have a minute or two of supplication in the vestry before preaching if you can call in three or four warmhearted deacons or other brethren. It always nerves me for the fight. But, for all that, to fan your earnestness to a vehement flame you should seek the spirit of continual prayer, so as to pray in the Holy Ghost, everywhere and always—in the study, in the vestry, and in the pulpit. It is well to be pleading evermore with God— when sitting down in the pulpit, when rising to give out the hymn, when reading the chapter, and while delivering the sermon—holding up one hand to God empty, in order to receive, and with the other hand dispensing to the people what the Lord bestows. Be in preaching like a conduit pipe between the everlasting and infinite supplies of heaven and the all but boundless needs of men; and to do this you must reach heaven, and keep up the communication without a break. Pray *for* the people while you preach *to* them; speak with God for them while you are speaking with them for God. Only so can you expect to be continually

in earnest. . . . Work and pray, as well as watch and pray; but
pray always. . . .

Far more weighty is the advice: *keep close to God, and keep
close to your fellow men whom you are seeking to bless.* Abide
under the shadow of the Almighty, dwell where Jesus manifests
himself, and live in the power of the Holy Ghost. Your very life
lies in this. . . .

Take care, also, to be on most familiar terms with those whose
souls are committed to your care. Stand in the stream and fish.
Many preachers are utterly ignorant as to how the bulk of the
people are living; they are at home among books, but quite at
sea among men. What would you think of a botanist who seldom
saw real flowers, or an astronomer who never spent a night with
the stars? Would they be worthy of the name of men of science?
Neither can a minister of the gospel be anything but a mere
empiric unless he mingles with men, and studies character for
himself. "Studies from the life"—gentlemen, we must have plenty
of these if we are to paint to the life in our sermons. Read men
as well as books, and love *men* rather than opinions, or you will
be inanimate preachers.

Get into close quarters with those who are in an anxious
state. . . . It will help to make you earnest when you see
their eagerness to find peace. . . .

If you have to labour in a large town I should recommend
you to familiarize yourself, wherever your place of worship may
be, with the poverty, ignorance, and drunkenness of the place.
Go if you can with a city missionary into the poorest quarter,
and you will see that which will astonish you, and the actual
sight of the disease will make you eager to reveal the remedy.
There is enough of evil to be seen even in the best streets of
our great cities, but there is an unutterable depth of horror in
the condition of the slums. As a doctor walks the hospitals, so
ought you to traverse the lanes and courts to behold the mischief
which sin has wrought. It is enough to make a man weep tears of
blood to gaze upon the desolation which sin has made in the

earth. . . . See the masses living in their sins, defiled with drinking and Sabbath-breaking, rioting and blaspheming; and see them dying sodden and hardened, or terrified and despairing: surely this will rekindle expiring zeal if anything can do it. The world is full of grinding poverty, and crushing sorrow; shame and death are the portion of thousands, and it needs a great gospel to meet the dire necessities of men's souls. . . . Go and see for yourselves. Thus will you learn to preach a great salvation, and magnify the great Saviour, not with your mouth only, but with your heart. . . .

Every unearnest minister is unfaithful. I would infinitely prefer to be consigned to Tophet as a murderer of men's bodies than as a destroyer of men's souls; neither do I know of any condition in which a man can perish so fatally, so infinitely, as in that of the man who preaches a gospel which he does not believe, and assumes the office of pastor over a people whose good he does not intensely desire. Let us pray to be found faithful always, and ever. God grant that the Holy Spirit may make and keep us so.

4

The Necessity of Ministerial Progress

D EAR fellow soldiers! We are few, and we have a desperate fight before us, therefore it is needful that every man should be made the most of, and nerved to his highest point of strength. It is desirable that the Lord's ministers should be the picked men of the church, yea, of the entire universe, for such the age demands; therefore, in reference to yourselves and your personal qualifications, I give you the motto, "Go forward." Go forward in personal attainments, forward in gifts and in grace, forward in fitness for the work, and forward in conformity to the image of Jesus. The points I shall speak upon begin at the base, and ascend.

1. First, dear brethren, I think it necessary to say to myself and to you that *we must go forward in our mental acquirements.* It will never do for us continually to present ourselves to God at our worst. We are not worth his having at our best; but at any rate let not the offering be maimed and blemished by our idleness. . . . We must cultivate ourselves to the highest possible point, and we should do this, first, by gathering in knowledge that we may fill the barn, then by acquiring discrimination that we may winnow the heap, and lastly by a firm retentiveness of mind, by which we may lay up the winnowed grain in the store-house. These three points may not be equally important, but they are all necessary to a complete man.

We must, I say, make great efforts to *acquire* information, especially of a biblical kind. We must not confine ourselves to one topic of study, or we shall not exercise our whole mental manhood. God made the world for man, and he made man with a mind intended to occupy and use all the world; he is the tenant, and nature is for a while his house; why should he shut himself out of any of its rooms? Why refuse to taste any of the cleansed meats the great Father has put upon the table? Still, our main business is to study the Scriptures. . . . Study the Bible, dear brethren, through and through, with all helps that you can possibly obtain; remember that the appliances now within the reach of ordinary Christians are much more extensive than they were in our fathers' days, and therefore you must be greater biblical scholars if you would keep in front of your hearers. Intermeddle with all knowledge, but above all things meditate day and night in the law of the Lord.

Be well instructed in theology, and do not regard the sneers of those who rail at it because they are ignorant of it. Many preachers are not theologians, and hence the mistakes which they make. It cannot do any hurt to the most lively evangelist to be also a sound theologian, and it may often be the means of saving him from gross blunders. Nowadays we hear men tear a single sentence of Scripture from its connection, and cry "Eureka! Eureka!" as if they had found a new truth; and yet they have not discovered a diamond, but a piece of broken glass. Had they been acquainted with the holy learning of the great Bible students of ages past, they would not have been quite so fast in vaunting their marvellous knowledge. Let us be thoroughly well acquainted with the great doctrines of the Word of God, and let us be mighty in expounding Scripture. I am sure that no preaching will last so long, or build up a church so well, as the expository. To renounce altogether the hortatory discourse for the expository would be running to a preposterous extreme; but I cannot too earnestly assure you that if your ministries are to be lastingly useful you must be expositors. For this you must understand the Word yourselves, and be able so to comment upon it that the people may be built up by the Word. Be master of your

Bibles, brethren: whatever other works you have not searched, be at home with the writings of the prophets and apostles. "Let the word of God dwell in you richly."

Having given precedence to the inspired writings, neglect no field of knowledge. The presence of Jesus on earth has sanctified the realms of nature, and what he has cleansed call not you common. All that your Father has made is yours, and you should learn from it. . . . Follow the trails of knowledge, according as you have the time, the opportunity, and the peculiar faculty, and do not hesitate to do so because of any apprehension that you will educate yourselves up to too high a point. When grace abounds, learning will not puff you up, or injure your simplicity in the gospel. Serve God with such education as you have. . . .

I have said that we must also learn to discriminate. . . . Be ready for fresh truth, *if it be truth,* but be very chary how you subscribe to the belief that a better light has been found than that of the sun. Those who hawk new truths about the street, as the boys do a second edition of the evening paper, are usually no better than they should be. The fair maid of truth does not paint her cheeks and tire her head like Jezebel, following every new philosophic fashion; she is content with her own native beauty, and her aspect is in the main the same yesterday, today, and forever. . . . He who has no assured truth to tell must not wonder if his hearers set small store by him. . . . Brethren, I charge you, seek to know and to discriminate; and then, having discriminated, labour to be rooted and grounded in the truth. Keep in full operation the processes of filling the barn, winnowing the grain, and storing it in granaries—so shall you mentally "Go forward."

2. *We need to go forward in oratorical qualifications.* I am beginning at the bottom, but even this is important, for it is a pity that even the feet of this image should be of clay. Nothing is trifling which can be of any service to our grand design. . . . . A man may be irretrievably ruined for spiritual usefulness, not because he fails either in character or spirit, but because he breaks

down mentally or oratorically, and, therefore, I have begun with these points, and again remark that we must improve in utterance. It is not every one of us who can speak as some can do, and even these men cannot speak up to their own ideal. If there be any brother here who thinks he can preach as well as he should, I would advise him to leave off altogether. If he did so he would be acting as wisely as the great painter who broke his palette, and, turning to his wife, said, "My painting days are over, for I have satisfied myself, and therefore I am sure my power is gone." Whatever other perfection may be reachable, I am certain that he who thinks he has gained perfection in oratory mistakes volubility for eloquence, and verbiage for argument. . . .

Brethren, we should cultivate a clear style. When a man does not make me understand what he means, it is because he does not himself know what he means. An average hearer who is unable to follow the course of thought of the preacher ought not to worry himself, but to blame the preacher, whose business it is to make the matter plain. If you look down into a well, if it be empty it will appear to be very deep, but if there be water in it you will see its brightness. I believe that many "deep" preachers are simply so because they are like dry wells with nothing whatever in them, except decaying leaves, a few stones, and perhaps a dead cat or two. If there be living water in your preaching it may be very deep, but the light of truth will give clearness to it. It is not enough to be so plain that you can be understood; you must speak so that you cannot be misunderstood.

We must cultivate a cogent as well as a clear style; our speech must be forceful. Some imagine that this consists in speaking loudly, but I can assure them they are in error. Nonsense does not improve by being bellowed. . . . Let us be forcible by reason of the excellence of our matter, and the energy of spirit which we throw into the delivery of it. In a word, let our speaking be natural and living. . . . May a living, natural, simple way of talking out the gospel be learned by us all; for I am persuaded that such a style is one which God is likely to bless. . . .

Learn the art of pleading with men. You will do this well if you often see the Lord. If I remember rightly, the old classic story tells us that, when a soldier was about to kill Darius, his son, who had been dumb from his childhood, suddenly cried out in surprise, "Know you not that he is the king?" His silent tongue was unloosed by love to his father, and well may ours find earnest speech when the Lord is seen by us crucified for sin. . . .

Let your oratory, therefore, constantly improve in clearness, cogency, naturalness, and persuasiveness. Try, dear brethren, to get such a style of speaking that you *suit yourselves to your audiences*. Much lies in that. The preacher who should address an educated congregation in the language which he would use in speaking to a company of costermongers would prove himself a fool; and on the other hand, he who goes down amongst miners and colliers with technical theological terms and drawing-room phrases acts like an idiot. . . . In our modes of speech we should aim at being "all things to all men." He is the greatest master of oratory who is able to address any class of people in a manner suitable to their condition, and likely to touch their hearts. . . .

3.   Brethren, we must be even more earnest to go forward in *moral qualities*. Let the points I shall mention here come home to those who shall require them, but I assure you I have no special persons among you in my mind's eye. We desire to rise to the highest style of ministry, and if so, even if we obtain the mental and oratorical qualifications, we shall fail, unless we also possess high moral qualities. There are evils which we must shake off, as Paul shook the viper from his hand, and there are virtues which we must gain at any cost.

Self-indulgence has slain its thousands; let us tremble lest we perish by the hands of that Delilah. Let us have every passion and habit under due restraint: if we are not masters of ourselves we are not fit to be leaders in the church.

We must put away all notion of self-importance. God will not bless the man who thinks himself great. To glory even in the work of God the Holy Spirit in yourself is to tread dangerously near to self-adulation. "Let another praise thee, and not thine own lips," and be very glad when that other has sense enough to hold his tongue.

We must also have our tempers well under restraint. A vigorous temper is not altogether an evil. Men who are as easy as an old shoe are generally of as little worth. I would not say to you, "Dear brethren, have a temper," but I do say, "If you have it, control it carefully." I thank God when I see a minister have temper enough to be indignant at wrong, and to be firm for the right; still temper is an edged tool, and often cuts the man who handles it, "Gentle, easy to be entreated," preferring to bear evil rather than inflict it, this is to be our spirit. . . .

We must acquire certain moral faculties and habits, as well as put aside their opposites. He will never do much for God who has not integrity of spirit. . . . Resolve, dear brethren, that you can be poor, that you can be despised, that you can lose life itself, but that you cannot do a crooked thing. . . .

May you also possess the grand moral characteristic of courage. By this we do not mean impertinence, impudence, or self-conceit, but real courage to do and say calmly the right thing, and to go straight on at all hazards, though there should be none to give you a good word. I am astonished at the number of Christians who are afraid to speak the truth to their brethren. I thank God I can say this, there is no member of my church, no officer of the church, and no man in the world to whom I am afraid to say before his face what I would say behind his back. Under God I owe my position in my own church to the absence of all policy, and the habit of saying what I mean. The plan of making things pleasant all round is a perilous as well as a wicked one. If you say one thing to one man, and another to another, they will one day compare notes and find you out, and then you will be despised. The man of two faces will sooner or later be the object of contempt, and justly so. Above all things, avoid cowardice, for it makes men liars. If you have anything that you feel you ought to say about a man, let the measure of what you say be this: "How much dare I say to his face?" You must not allow yourselves a word more in censure of any man living. If that be your rule, your courage will save you from a thousand difficulties, and win you lasting respect.

Having the integrity and the courage, dear brethren, may you be gifted with an indomitable zeal. Zeal—what is it? How shall I describe it? Possess it, and you will know what it is. Be consumed with love for Christ, and let the flame burn continuously, not flaming up at public meetings and dying out in the routine work of every day. We need indomitable perseverance, dogged resolution, and a combination of sacred obstinacy, self-denial, holy gentleness, and invincible courage.

Excel also in one power, which is both mental and moral, namely, the power of concentrating all your forces upon the work to which you are called. Collect your thoughts, rally all your faculties, mass your energies, focus your capacities. . . . Some men lack this quality. They scatter themselves and fail. . . . Do not try to be great at this and great at that—to be "everything by turns, and nothing long"—but suffer your entire nature to be led in captivity by Jesus Christ, and lay everything at his dear feet who bled and died for you.

4. Above all these, we need *spiritual qualifications*, graces which must be wrought in us by the Lord himself. This is the main matter, I am sure. Other things are precious, but this is priceless; we must be rich towards God.

We need to know ourselves. The preacher should be great in the science of the heart, the philosophy of inward experience. There are two schools of experience, and neither is content to learn from the other; let us be content, however, to learn from both. The one school speaks of the child of God as one who knows the deep depravity of his heart, who understands the loathsomeness of his nature, and daily feels that in his flesh there dwelleth no good thing. "That man has not the life of God in his soul," say they, "who does not know and feel this, and feel it by bitter and painful experience from day to day." It is in vain to talk to them about liberty, and joy in the Holy Ghost; they will not have it. Let us learn from these one-sided brethren. They know much that should be known, and woe to that minister who ignores their set of truths. Martin Luther used to say that temptation is the best teacher for a minister. There is truth on that side of the question. Another school of believers dwell much upon the glorious work of the Spirit of God, and rightly and blessedly so. They believe in the Spirit of God as a cleansing power, sweeping the Augean stable of the soul, and making it into a temple for God. But frequently they talk as if they had ceased to sin, or to be annoyed by temptation; they glory as if the battle were already fought, and the victory won. Let us learn from these brethren. All the truth they can teach us let us know. . . . Do not be afraid of being too full of the Holy Spirit. I would have you wise on all sides, and able to deal with man both in his conflicts and in his joys, as one familiar with both. . . .

Brethren, know man in Christ, and out of Christ. Study him at his best, and study him at his worst; know his anatomy, his secrets, and his passions. You cannot do this by books; you must have personal spiritual experience; God alone can give you that.

Among spiritual acquirements, it is beyond all other things needful to know him who is the sure remedy for all human diseases. Know Jesus. Sit at his feet. Consider his nature, his work, his sufferings, his glory. Rejoice in his presence: commune with him from day to day. To know Christ is to understand the most excellent of sciences. You cannot fail to be wise if you commune with wisdom; you cannot miss of strength if you have fellowship with the mighty Son of God. I saw the other day in an Italian grotto a little fern which grew where its leaves continually glistened and danced in the spray of a fountain. It was always green, and neither summer's drought nor winter's cold affected it. So let us for ever abide under the sweet influence of Jesus' love. Dwell in God, brethren; do not occasionally visit him, but abide in him. . . .

Brethren, as the outcome of this, if we are to be strong men, we must be conformed to our Lord. Oh, to be like him! Blessed be that cross on which we shall suffer, if we suffer for being made like unto the Lord Jesus. If we obtain conformity to Christ, we shall have a wondrous unction upon our ministry, and without that, what is a ministry worth?

In a word, we must labour for holiness of character. What is holiness? Is it not wholeness of character, a balanced condition in which there is neither lack nor redundance? It is not morality—that is a cold, lifeless statue; holiness is life. You must have holiness; and, dear brethren, if you should fail in mental qualifications (as I hope you will not), and if you should have a slender measure of the oratorical faculty (as I trust you will not), yet, depend upon it, a holy life is in itself a wonderful power, and will make up for many deficiencies; it is, in fact, the best sermon the best man can deliver. Let us resolve that all the purity which can be had we will have, that all the sanctity which can be reached we will obtain, and that all the likeness to Christ that is possible in this world of sin shall certainly be in us through the work of the Spirit of God. . . .

5. Still I have not done, dear brethren. I have to say to you, go forward in *actual work,* for, after all, we shall be known by what we have done. We ought to be mighty in deed as well as word. There are good brethren in the world who are impractical. . . . Be not so taken up with speculations as to prefer a Bible reading of a dark passage in the Revelation to teaching in a ragged-school or discoursing to the poor concerning Jesus. We must have done with daydreams, and get to work. . . . It is all very well to write essays, but what souls have you saved from going down to hell? Your excellent management of your school interests me, but how many children have been brought into the church by it? . . . Brethren, do something; do something; do something. While committees waste their time over resolutions, do something. While Societies and Unions are making constitutions, let us win souls. Too often we discuss, and dis-

cuss, and discuss, and Satan laughs in his sleeve. It is time we had done planning and sought something to plan. I pray you, be men of action all of you. Get to work and quit yourselves like men. Old Suwarrow's idea of war is mine: "Forward and strike! No theory! Attack! Form column! Charge bayonets! Plunge into the centre of the enemy." Our one aim is to save sinners, and this we are not to talk about, but to do in the power of God.

6. Lastly, . . . go forward in the matter of *the choice of your sphere of action*. I plead this day for those who cannot plead for themselves, namely, the great outlying masses of the heathen world. Our existing pulpits are tolerably well supplied, but we need men who will build on new foundations. Who will do this? Are we, as a company of faithful men, clear in our consciences about the heathen? Millions have never heard the name of Jesus. Hundreds of millions have seen a missionary only once in their lives, and know nothing of our King. Shall we let them perish? Can we go to our beds and sleep while China, India, Japan, and other nations are being damned? Are we clear of their blood? Have they no claim upon us? We ought to put it on this footing—not "Can I prove that I *ought* to go?" but "Can I prove that I *ought not* to go?" When a man can prove honestly that he ought not to go, then he is clear, but not else. . . . We must have the heathen converted; God has myriads of his elect among them, we must go and search for them till we find them. Many difficulties are now removed, all lands are open to us, and distance is annihilated. True we have not the Pentecostal gift of tongues, but languages are now readily acquired, while the art of printing is a full equivalent for the lost gift. The dangers incident to missions ought not to keep any true man back, even if they were very great, but they are now reduced to a minimum. There are hundreds of places where the cross of Christ is unknown, to which we can go without risk. Who will go? . . .

I wish that our churches would imitate that of Pastor Harms, in Germany, where every member was consecrated to God indeed

and of a truth. The farmers gave the produce of their lands, the
workingmen their labour; one gave a large house to be used as a
missionary college, and Pastor Harms obtained money for a ship
which he fitted out, to make voyages to Africa, and then he sent
missionaries, and little companies of his people with them, to
form Christian communities among the Bushmen. When will our
churches be equally self-denying and energetic? Look at the
Moravians! how every man and woman becomes a missionary, and
how much they do in consequence. Let us catch their spirit. Is it
a right spirit? Then it is right for us to have it. It is not enough
for us to say, "Those Moravians are very wonderful people!"
We ought to be wonderful people too. Christ did not purchase
the Moravians any more than he purchased us; they are under no
more obligation to make sacrifices than we are. Why then this
backwardness! When we read of heroic men who gave up all for
Jesus, we are not merely to admire, but to imitate them. Who
will imitate them now? . . .

Forward! In God's name, *forward!!*

5

The Need of Decision for the Truth

SOME things are true and some things are false—I regard that as an axiom; but there are many persons who evidently do not believe it. The current principle of the present age seems to be, "Some things are either true or false, according to the point of view from which you look at them. Black is white, and white is black, according to circumstances, and it does not particularly matter which you call it. Truth of course is true, but it would be rude to say that the opposite is a lie; we must not be bigoted, but remember the motto, 'So many men, so many minds,'" . . . Still, for all that, my firm old-fashioned belief is that some doctrines are true, and that statements which are diametrically opposite to them are not true—that when "No" is the fact, "Yes" is out of court, and when "Yes" can be justified, "No" must be abandoned. . . .

We have a fixed faith to preach, my brethren, and we are sent forth with a definite message from God. We are not left to fabricate the message as we go along. . . . There is something told me in the Bible—told me for certain—not put before me with a "but" and a "perhaps" and an "if" and a "maybe," and fifty thousand suspicions behind it, so that really the long and the short of it is that it may not be so at all; but revealed to me as infallible fact, which must be believed, the opposite of which is deadly error and comes from the father of lies.

Believing, therefore, that there is such a thing as truth, and such a thing as falsehood, that there are truths in the Bible, and that the gospel consists in something definite which is to be believed by men, it becomes us to be decided as to what we teach, and to teach it in a decided manner. We have to deal with men who will be either lost or saved, and they certainly will not be saved by erroneous doctrine. We have to deal with God, whose servants we are, and he will not be honoured by our delivering falsehoods; neither will he give us a reward, and say, "Well done, good and faithful servant, thou has mangled the gospel as judiciously as any man that ever lived before thee." We stand in a very solemn position, and ours should be the spirit of old Micaiah, who said, "As the Lord my God liveth, before whom I stand, whatsoever the Lord saith unto me that will I speak." Neither less nor more than God's word are we called to state, but that word we are bound to declare in a spirit which convinces the sons of men that, whatever they may think of it, we believe God, and are not to be shaken in our confidence in him.

Brethren, in what ought we to be positive? Well, there are gentlemen alive who imagine that there are no fixed principles to go upon. "Perhaps a few doctrines," said one to me, "perhaps a few doctrines may be considered as established. It is, perhaps, ascertained that there is a God; but one ought not to dogmatize upon his personality: a great deal may be said for pantheism." Such men creep into the ministry, but they are generally cunning enough to conceal the breadth of their minds beneath Christian phraseology thus acting in consistency with their principles, for their fundamental rule is that truth is of no consequence.

As for us—as for me, at any rate—I am certain that there is a God, and I mean to preach it as a man does who is absolutely sure. He is the Maker of heaven and earth, the Master of providence, and the Lord of Grace: let his name be blessed for ever and ever! We will have no questions and debates as to him.

We are equally certain that the book which is called "the Bible" is his word, and is inspired. . . . We believe that everything stated in the book that comes to us from God is to be accepted by us as his sure testimony, and nothing less than that.

God forbid we should be ensnared by those various interpretations of the *modus* of inspiration, which amount to little more than frittering it away. The book is a divine production; it is perfect, and is the last court of appeal—"the judge which ends the strife." I would as soon dream of blaspheming my Maker as of questioning the infallibility of his word.

We are also sure concerning the doctrine of the blessed Trinity. We cannot explain how it is that the Father, Son, and Spirit can be each one distinct and perfect in himself, and yet that these three are one, so that there is but one God; yet we do verily believe it, and mean to preach it, nothwithstanding Unitarian, Socinian, Sabellian, or any other error. We shall hold fast evermore the doctrine of the Trinity in Unity.

And, brethren, there will be no uncertain sound from us as to the atonement of our Lord Jesus Christ. We cannot leave the blood out of our ministry, or the life of it will be gone; for we may say of the gospel, "The blood is the life thereof." The proper substitution of Christ, the vicarious sacrifice of Christ, on the behalf of his people, that they might live through him— this we must publish till we die.

Neither can we waver in our minds for a moment concerning the great and glorious Spirit of God—the fact of his existence, his personality, the power of his working, the necessity of his influences, the certainty that no man is regenerated except by him; that we are born again by the Spirit of God, and that the Spirit dwells in believers, and is the author of all good in them, their sanctifier and preserver, without whom they can do no good thing whatsoever—we shall not at all hesitate as to preaching these truths.

The absolute necessity of the new birth is also a certainty. . . . We shall never poison our people with the notion that a moral reformation will suffice, but we will over and over again say to them, "Ye must be born again." . . .

The tremendous evil of sin—we shall not hesitate about that. We shall speak on that matter both sorrowfully and positively. . . .

Neither will we ever give an uncertain sound as to the glorious truth that salvation is all of grace. If ever we ourselves are saved, we know that sovereign grace alone has done it, and we feel it must be the same with others. . . .

We shall be very decided, also, as to justification by faith; for salvation is "Not of works, lest any man should boast." "Life in a look at the Crucified One" will be our message. Trust in the Redeemer will be that saving grace which we will pray the Lord to implant in all our hearers' hearts. And everything else which we believe to be true in the Scriptures we shall preach with decision. If there be questions which may be regarded as moot, or comparatively unimportant, we shall speak with such a measure of decision about them as may be comely. But points which cannot be moot, which are essential and fundamental, will be declared by us without any stammering, without any inquiring of the people, "What would you wish us to say?" Yes, and without the apology, "Those are my views, but other people's views may be correct."

We ought to preach the gospel, not as our views at all, but as the mind of God—the testimony of Jehovah concerning his own Son, and in reference to salvation for lost men. . . . This, then, is the matter concerning which we are decided.

How are we to show this decision? We need not be careful to answer this question; our decision will show itself in its own way. If we really believe a truth, we shall be decided about it. . . . Don't go about the world with your fist doubled up for fighting, carrying a theological revolver in the leg of your trousers. There is no sense in being a sort of doctrinal game-cock, to be carried about to show your spirit, or a terrier of orthodoxy, ready to tackle heterodox rats by the score. Practice the *suaviter in modo* as well as the *fortiter in re*. Be prepared to fight, and always have your sword buckled on your thigh, but wear a scabbard; there can be no sense in waving your weapon about before everybody's eyes to provoke conflict. . . .

If you really believe the gospel, you will be decided for

it in more sensible ways. Your very tone will betray your sincerity; you will speak like a man who has something to say
which he knows to be true. Have you ever watched a rogue when
he is about to tell a falsehood? Have you noticed the way in
which he has to mouth it? It takes a long time to be able to
tell a lie well, for the facial organs were not originally constituted and adapted for the complacent delivery of a falsehood. When a man knows he is telling you the truth, everything
about him corroborates his sincerity. . . . There ought to be
always that same air of truth about the Christian minister; only
as he is not only bearing witness to the truth, but wants other
people to feel that truth and own the power of it, he ought to
have more decision in his tone than a mere witness who is stating
facts which may be believed or not without any serious conse-
quences following either way. Luther was the man for decision.
Nobody doubted that he believed what he spoke. He spoke with
thunder, for there was lightning in his faith. The man preached
all over, for his entire nature believed. You felt, "Well, he may
be mad, or he may be altogether mistaken, but he assuredly
believes what he says. He is the incarnation of faith; his heart is
running over at his lips."

If we would show decision for the truth, we must not only
do so by our tone and manner, but by our daily actions. A man's
life is always more forcible than his speech; when men take stock
of him they reckon his deeds as pounds and his words as pence.
If his life and his doctrines disagree, the mass of lookers-on
accept his practice and reject his preaching. A man may know
a great deal about truth, and yet be a very damaging witness
on its behalf, because he is no credit to it. The quack who in
the classic story cried up an infallible cure for colds, coughing
and sneezing between every sentence of his panegyric, may serve
as the image and symbol of an unholy minister. . . . It is very
ridiculous to hear good truth from a bad man; it is like flour
in a coal-sack. . . .

Brother, if the truth be in thee it will flow out of thine

entire being as the perfume streams from every bough of the
sandalwood tree; it will drive thee onward as the trade wind
speeds the ships, filling all their sails; it will consume thy whole
nature with its energy as the forest fire burns up all the trees of
the wood. Truth has not fully given thee her friendship till all
thy doings are marked with her seal.

We must show our decision for the truth by the sacrifices we
are ready to make. This is, indeed, the most efficient as well
as the most trying method. We must be ready to give up anything
and everything for the sake of the principles which we have
espoused, and must be ready to offend our best supporters, to
alienate our warmest friends, sooner than belie our consciences.
We must be ready to be beggars in purse, and offscourings in
reputation, rather than act treacherously. We can die, but we
cannot deny the truth. The cost is already counted, and we are
determined to buy the truth at any price, and sell it at no price.
Too little of this spirit is abroad nowadays. Men have a saving
faith, and save their own persons from trouble; they have great
discernment, and know on which side their bread is buttered;
they are largehearted, and all things to all men, if by any means
they may save a sum. There are plenty of curs about, who would
follow at the heel of any man who would keep them in meat.
They are among the first to bark at decision, and call it obstinate
dogmatism and ignorant bigotry. Their condemnatory verdict
causes us no distress; it is what we expected.

Above all we must show our zeal for the truth by continually,
in season and out of season, endeavoring to maintain it in the
tenderest and most loving manner, but still very earnestly and
firmly. . . .

My brethren, you will *strengthen your decision* by the recollection of the importance of these truths to your own souls. Are
your sins forgiven? Have you a hope of heaven? How do the
solemnities of eternity affect you? Certainly you are not saved
apart from these things, and therefore you must hold them, for
you feel you are a lost man if they be not true. You have to

die, and, being conscious that these things alone can sustain you in the last article, you hold them with all your might. You cannot give them up. How can a man resign a truth which he feels to be vitally important to his own soul? He daily feels, "I have to live on it, I have to die on it, I am wretched now, and lost forever apart from it, and therefore by the help of God I cannot relinquish it."

Your own experience from day to day will sustain you, beloved brethren. I hope you have realized already and will experience much more the power of the truth which you preach. I believe the doctrine of election, because I am quite sure that if God had not chosen me I should never have chosen him; and I am sure he chose me before I was born, or else he never would have chosen me afterwards; and he must have elected me for reasons unknown to me, for I never could find any reason in myself why he should have looked upon me with special love. So I am forced to accept that doctrine. I am bound to the doctrine of the depravity of the human heart, because I find myself depraved in heart, and have daily proofs that there dwelleth in my flesh no good thing. I cannot help holding that there must be an atonement before there can be pardon, because my conscience demands it, and my peace depends upon it. The little court within my own heart is not satisfied unless some retribution be exacted for dishonour done to God. They tell us sometimes that such and such statements are not true; but when we are able to reply that we have tried them and proved them, what answer is there to such reasoning? A man propounds the wonderful discovery that honey is not sweet. "But I had some for breakfast, and I found it very sweet," say you, and your reply is conclusive. . . . If you are daily and habitually experienced in the truth of God's Word, I am not afraid of your being shaken in mind in reference to it. Those young fellows who have never felt conviction of sin, but obtain their religion as they get their bath in the morning, by jumping into it—these will as readily leap out of it as they leaped in. Those who feel neither the joys nor yet the depressions of spirit which indicate spiritual life are torpid, and their palsied hand has no firm grip of truth. Mere skimmers of the word, who, like swallows, touch the water with their wings, are the first to fly from one land to another as personal considerations guide them. They believe this, and then believe that, for, in truth, they believe nothing intensely. If you have ever been dragged through the mire and clay of soul-despair, if you have been turned upside down, and wiped out like a dish as to all your own strength and pride, and have then been filled with the joy and peace of God, through Jesus Christ, I will trust you among fifty thousand infidels. Whenever I hear the sceptic's stale attacks upon the word of God, I smile within myself, and think, "Why, you simpleton! How can you urge such trifling objections? I have felt, in the contentions of my own unbelief, ten times greater difficulties." . . .

If, my brethren, we have fellowship with the Lord Jesus Christ, we cannot be made to doubt the fundamentals of the gospel; neither can we be undecided. A glimpse at the thorn-crowned head and pierced hands and feet is the sure cure for "modern doubt" and all its vagaries. Get into the "Rock of Ages, cleft for you," and you will abhor the quicksand. . . .

We have tasted and handled the good word of life. What we have seen and heard, that we do testify; and whether men receive our testimony or not, we cannot but speak it, for we speak what we do know, and testify what we have seen. That, my brethren, is the sure way to be decided. . . .

6

On Spiritualizing

. . . Within limits, my brethren, be not afraid to spiritualize, or to take singular texts. Continue to look out passages of Scripture, and not only give their plain meaning, as you are bound to do, but also draw from them meanings which may not lie upon their surface. . . . I counsel you to employ spiritualizing within certain limits and boundaries, but I pray you do not, under cover of this advice, rush headlong into incessant and injudicious "imaginings," as George Fox would call them. Do not drown yourselves because you are recommended to bathe, or hang yourselves on an oak because tannin is described as a valuable astringent. An allowable thing carried to excess is a vice, even as fire is a good servant in the grate, but a bad master when raging in a burning house. Too much even of a good thing surfeits and disgusts, and in no case is this fact more sure than in the one before us.

The first canon to be observed is this: *do not violently strain a text by illegitimate spiritualizing.* This is a sin against common sense. How dreadfully the word of God has been mauled and mangled by a certain band of preachers who have laid texts on the rack to make them reveal what they never would have otherwise spoken. . . .

We have heard of a performer who delivered his mind upon Proverbs 20:17, "He that loveth pleasure shall be a poor man; he that loveth wine and oil shall not be rich." The Proverbs are a favorite field for spiritualizers to disport themselves withal. Our worthy disposed of the proverb in this fashion: " 'He that loveth pleasure,' that is, the Christian who enjoys the means of grace, 'shall be a poor man,' that is, he shall be poor in spirit; and 'he that loveth wine and oil,' that is to say, rejoices in covenant provisions, and enjoys the oil and wine of the gospel, 'shall not be rich,' that is, he shall not be rich in his own esteem": showing the excellence of those who are poor in spirit, and how they shall enjoy the pleasures of the gospel—a very proper sentiment, but my carnal eyes fail to see it in the text. . . .

Ludicrous results sometimes arise from sheer stupidity inflated with conceit. One instance may suffice. A worthy minister told me the other day that he had been preaching lately to his people upon the nine-and-twenty knives of Ezra. I am sure he would handle these edged tools discreetly, but I could not refrain from saying that I hoped he had not imitated the very sage interpreter who saw in that odd number of knives a reference to the four-and-twenty elders of the Apocalypse. . . .

These are a few specimens of ecclesiastical curiosities which are as numerous and valuable as the relics which are every day gathered so plentifully on the battlefield of Waterloo, and accepted by the more verdant as priceless treasures. . . . Such maunderings dishonor the Bible; they are an insult to the common sense of the hearers, and a deplorable lowering of the minister. This, however, is no more the spiritualizing which we recommend to you than the thistle in Lebanon is the cedar of Lebanon. . . .

Our second [canon] is *never spiritualize upon indelicate subjects.* It is needful to say this, for the Slopdash family are never more at home than when they speak in a way to crimson the cheek of modesty. . . . What abominable things have been said upon some of the sterner and more horrifying similes of Jeremiah and Ezekiel! Where the Holy Spirit is veiled and chaste, these men have torn away the veil, and spoken as none but naughty tongues would venture to do. . . . I know it is said, *"Honi soit qui mal y pense,"* but I aver that no pure mind ought to be subjected to the slightest breath of indelicacy from the pulpit. Caesar's wife must be without suspicion, and Christ's ministers must be without speck in their lives or stain in their speech. Gentlemen, the kissing and hugging which some preachers delight in is disgusting: Solomon's Song had better be let alone than dragged in the mire as it often is. . . .

Next, and thirdly, *never spiritualize for the sake of showing what an uncommonly clever fellow you are.* Such an intention will be wicked, and the method used will be foolish. Only an egregious simpleton will seek to be noted for doing what nine men out of ten could do quite as well. A certain probationer once preached a sermon upon the word "but," thus hoping to ingratiate himself with the congregation, who would, he thought, be enraptured with the powers of a brother who could enlarge so marvellously upon a mere conjunction. His subject appears to have been, the fact that whatever there may be of good in a man's character, or admirable in a man's position, there is sure to be some difficulty, some trial in connection with us all: "Naaman was a great man with his master, but—." When the orator descended from the pulpit the deacons said, "Well, sir, you have given us a singular sermon, *but*—you are not the man for the place; that we can see very clearly." Alas! for wit when it becomes so common, and withal puts a weapon into the hand of its own adversaries! Remember that spiritualizing is not such a wonderful display of ingenuity, even if you are able to do it well, and that without discretion it is the most ready method of revealing your egregious folly. Gentlemen, if you aspire to emulate Origen in wild, daring interpretations, it may be as well to read his life and note attentively the follies into which even his marvellous mind was drawn by allowing a wild fancy to usurp absolute authority over his judgment. . . .

Our fourth caution is *never pervert Scripture* to give it a novel and so-called spiritual meaning, lest you be found guilty of that solemn curse with which the roll of inspiration is guarded and closed. . . .

Once more, *in no case allow your audience to forget that the narratives which you spiritualize are facts,* and not mere myths or parables. The first sense of the passage must never be drowned in the overflow of your imagination; it must be distinctly declared and allowed to hold the first rank; your accommodation of it must never thrust out the original and native meaning, or even push it into the background. The Bible is not a compilation of clever allegories or instructive poetical traditions; it teaches literal facts and reveals tremendous realities: let your full persuasion of this truth be manifest to all who attend your ministry....

However, there is a legitimate range for spiritualizing, or rather for the particular gift which leads men to spiritualize. For instance, you have frequently been shown that *the types* yield ample scope for the exercise of a sanctified ingenuity. Why need you go about to find "odious women" to preach upon, when you have before you the tabernacle in the wilderness, with all its sacred furniture, the burnt-offering, the peace offering, and all the various sacrifices which were offered before God? Why struggle for novelties when the temple and all its glories are before you? The largest capacity for typical interpretation will find abundant employment in the undoubted symbols of the Word of God, and it will be safe to enter upon such an exercise, because the symbols are of divine appointment. When you have exhausted all the Old Testament types, you have left to you an heirloom of a thousand *metaphors. . . .*

But supposing you have expounded all the usually accepted types, and have cast light upon the emblems and figurative expressions, must your fancy and delight in similitudes go to sleep? By no means. When the apostle Paul finds a mystery in Melchizedek, and speaking of Hagar and Sarah says, "Which things are an allegory," he gives us a precedent for discovering scriptural *allegories* in other places besides the two mentioned. Indeed, the historical books not only yield us here and there an allegory, but seem as a whole to be arranged with a view to symbolical teaching.

A passage from Mr. Andrew Jukes' preface to his work on the types of Genesis will show how, without violence, a most elaborate theory may be constructed by a devout mind:

As a base or ground for what is to follow, we first are shown what springs from man, and all the different forms of life, which either by nature or grace can grow out of the root of old Adam. This is the book of Genesis. Then we see, that be it bad or good which has come out of Adam, there must be redemption; so an elect people by the blood of the Lamb are saved from Egypt. This is Exodus. After redemption is known, we come to the experience of the elect as needing access, and learning the way of it, to God the Redeemer in the sanctuary. This we get in Leviticus. Then in the wilderness of this world, as pilgrims from Egypt, the house of bondage, to the promised land beyond Jordan, the trials of the journey are learned, from that land of wonders and man's wisdom to the land flowing with milk and honey. This is the book of Numbers. Then comes the desire to exchange the wilderness for the better land, from entering which for a season after redemption is known the elect yet shrink; answering to the desire of the elect at a certain stage to know the power of the resurrection, to live even now as in heavenly places. The rules and precepts which must be obeyed, if this is to be done, come next. Deuteronomy, a second giving of the law, a second cleansing, tells the way of progress. After which Canaan is indeed reached. We go over Jordan: we know practically the death of the flesh, and what it is to be circumcised, and to roll away the reproach of Egypt. We know now what it is to be risen with Christ, and to wrestle, not with flesh and blood, but with principalities and powers in heavenly places. This is Joshua. Then comes the failure of the elect in heavenly places, failure arising from making leagues with Canaanites instead of overcoming them. This is Judges. After which the different forms of rule, which the church may know, pass in review in the books of Kings, from the first setting up of rule in Israel down to its extinction, when for their sin the rule of Babylon supersedes that of the elect. When this is known with all its shame, we see the remnants of the elect, each according to its measure, doing what may be done, if possible, to restore Israel; some, like Ezra, returning to build the temple, that is, to restore the forms of true worship; and some coming up, like Nehemiah, to build the wall, that is, to re-establish, by Gentile permission, a feeble imitation of the ancient polity; while a third remnant in Esther is seen in bonds, but faithful, providentially saved, though God's name (and this is characteristic of their state) never appears throughout the whole record.

I should be far from recommending you to become as fanciful as the ingenious author I have just quoted sometimes becomes, through the large indulgence of his tendency to mysticism, but nevertheless, you will read the Word with greatly increased interest if you are a sufficiently careful reader to have noticed the general run of the books of the Bible, and their consecutiveness as a system of types.

Then, too, the faculty which turns to spiritualizing will be well employed in *generalizing the great universal principles evolved by minute and separate facts.* This is an ingenious, instructive, and legitimate pursuit. . . . In hundreds of scriptural incidents you may find great general principles which may nowhere be expressed in so many words. . . .

The *parables* of our Lord in their expounding and enforcement afford the amplest scope for a matured and disciplined fancy, and if these have all passed before you, the *miracles* still remain, rich in symbolical teaching. There can be no doubt that the miracles are the acted sermons of our Lord Jesus Christ. You have his "word sermons" in his matchless teaching, and his "deed sermons" in his peerless acts. . . . All our Lord's mighty works are full of teaching. Take the story of the healing of the deaf-and-dumb man. The poor creature's maladies are eminently suggestive of man's lost estate, and our Lord's mode of procedure most instructively illustrates the plan of salvation. "Jesus took him aside from the multitude"—the soul must be made to feel its own personality and individuality, and must be led into loneliness. He "put his finger into his ears"—the source of the mischief is indicated; sinners are convinced of their state. "And spat"— the gospel is a simple and a despised means, and the sinner, in order to obtain salvation, must humble himself to receive it. He "touched his tongue"—further pointing out where the mischief lay; our sense of need grows on us. He "looked up to heaven"— Jesus reminded his patient that all strength must come from above, a lesson which every seeker must learn. "He sighed," showing that the sorrows of the Healer are the means of our healing. And when he said, *"Ephphatha,* Be opened"—here was the effectual word of grace which wrought an immediate, perfect, and lasting cure. From this one exposition learn all, and ever believe that the miracles of Christ are a great picture gallery, illustrating his work among the sons of men. Let it be an instruction, however, to all who handle either the parables or the metaphors, to be discreet. . . .

I am tempted before I close this address to give a sketch or two of spiritualizings which were familiar to me in my earliest days. I shall never forget a sermon preached by an uneducated but remarkable man, who was my near neighbor in the county. I had the notes of the discourse from his own lips, and I trust they will remain as notes, and never be preached from again in this world. The text was, "The nighthawk, the owl, and the cuckoo." That might not strike you as being exceedingly rich in matter; it did not so strike me, and therefore I innocently inquired, "And what were the heads?" He replied most archly, "Heads? Why, wring the birds' necks, and there are three directly: the nighthawk, the owl, and the cuckoo." He showed that these birds were all unclean under the law, and were plain types of unclean sinners. Nighthawks were persons who pilfered on the sly, also people who adulterated their goods, and cheated their neighbors in an underhand way without being suspected to be rogues. As for the owls, they typified drunkards, who are always liveliest at night, while by day they will almost knock their heads against a post because they are so sleepy. There were owls also among professors. The owl is a very small bird when he is plucked; he only looks big because he wears so many feathers; so, many professors are all feathers, and if you could take away their boastful professions there would be very little left of them. The cuckoos were the church clergy, who always utter the same note whenever they open their mouths in the church, and live on other birds' eggs with their church-rates and tithes. The cuckoos were also, I think, the free-willers, who were always saying, "Do-do-do-do."

Was not this rather too much of a good thing? Yet from the man who delivered it the sermon would not seem at all remarkable or odd. The same venerable brother delivered a sermon equally singular but far more original and useful; those who heard it will remember it to their dying day. It was from this text: "The slothful man roasteth not that which he took in hunting." The good old man leaned upon the top of the pulpit, and said, "Then, my brethren, he *was* a lazy fellow!" That was the exordium; and then he went on to say, "He went out a-hunting, and after much trouble he caught his hare, and then was too idle to roast it. He was a lazy fellow indeed!" The good man made us all feel how ridiculous such idleness was, and then he said, "But then you are very likely quite as much to blame as this man, for you do just the same. You hear of a popular minister coming down from London, and you put the horse to the cart, and drive ten or twenty miles to hear him; and then when you have heard the sermon you forget to profit by it. You catch the hare and do not roast it; you go hunting after the truth, and then you do not receive it." Then he went on to show that just as meat needs cooking to prepare it for assimilation in the bodily system—I do not think he used that word though—so the truth needs to go through a process before it can be received into the mind so that we may feed thereon and grow. He said he should show how to cook a sermon, and he did so most instructively. He began as the cookery books do—"First catch your hare." "So," he said, "first get a gospel sermon." Then he declared that a great many sermons were not worth hunting for, and that good sermons were mournfully scarce, and it was worthwhile to go any distance to hear a solid, old-fashioned, Calvinistic discourse. Then after the sermon had been caught, there was much about it which might be necessary because of the preacher's infirmity, which was not profitable, and must be put away. Here he enlarged upon discerning and judging what we heard, and not believing every word of any man. Then followed directions as to roasting a sermon; run the spit of memory through it from end to end, turn it round upon the roasting-jack of meditation, before the fire of a really warm and earnest heart, and in that way the sermon would be cooked and ready to yield real spiritual nourishment.

I do but give you the outline, and though it may look somewhat laughable, it was not so esteemed by the hearers. It was full of allegory, and kept up the attention of the people from the beginning to the end. . . .

With this I close, reasserting the opinion, that guided by discretion and judgment, we may occasionally employ spiritualizing with good effect to our people; certainly we shall interest them and keep them awake.

7

The Preacher's Private Prayer

OF course the preacher is above all others distinguished as a man of prayer. He prays as an ordinary Christian, else he were a hypocrite. He prays more than ordinary Christians, else he were disqualified for the office which he has undertaken. "It would be wholly monstrous," says Bernard, "for a man to be highest in office and lowest in soul; first in station and last in life." Over all his other relationships the pre-eminence of the pastor's responsibility casts a halo, and if true to his Master, he becomes distinguished for his prayerfulness in them all. As a citizen, his country has the advantage of his intercession; as a neighbor those under his shadow are remembered in supplication. He prays as a husband and as a father; he strives to make his family devotions a model for his flock; and if the fire on the altar of God should burn low anywhere else, it is well tended in the house of the Lord's chosen servant—for he takes care that the morning and evening sacrifice shall sanctify his dwelling. But there are some of his prayers which concern his office, and of those our plan in these lectures leads us to speak most. He offers peculiar supplications *as a minister,* and he draws near to God in this respect, over and above all his approaches in his other relationships.

I take it that as a minister *he is always praying.* Whenever his mind turns to his work, whether he is in it or out of it, he ejaculates a petition, sending up his holy desires as well-directed arrows to the skies. He is not always in the act of prayer, but he lives in the spirit of it. If his heart be in his work, he cannot eat or drink, or take recreation, or go to his

bed, or rise in the morning, without evermore feeling a fervency
of desire, a weight of anxiety, and a simplicity of dependence
upon God; thus, in one form or other he continues in prayer.
If there be any man under heaven who is compelled to carry
out the precept "Pray without ceasing," surely it is the Christian
minister. . . . If you as ministers are not very prayerful, you
are much to be pitied. If, in the future, you shall be called to
sustain pastorates, large or small, if you become lax in secret
devotion, not only will you need to be pitied, but your people
also; and, in addition to that, you shall be blamed, and the day
cometh in which you shall be ashamed and confounded.

It may scarcely be needful to commend to you the sweet uses
of private devotion, and yet I cannot forbear. . . . All our
libraries and studies are mere emptiness compared with our
closets. We grow, we wax mighty, we prevail in private prayer.

*Your prayers will be your ablest assistants while your dis-
courses are yet upon the anvil.* While other men, like Esau, are
hunting for their portion, you, by the aid of prayer, will find
the savoury meat near at home, and may say in truth what Jacob
said so falsely, "The Lord brought it to me." . . . Prayer, as a
mental exercise, will bring many subjects before the mind, and
so help in the selection of a topic, while as a high spiritual
engagement it will cleanse your inner eye that you may see
truth in the light of God. Texts will often refuse to reveal their
treasures till you open them with the key of prayer. How wonder-
fully were the books opened to Daniel when he was in supplication! How much Peter learned upon the housetop! The closet
is the best study. The commentators are good instructors, but
the Author himself is far better, and prayer makes a direct appeal
to him and enlists him in our cause. It is a great thing to pray
one's self into the spirit and marrow of a text, working into it
by sacred feeding thereon, even as the worm bores its way into
the kernel of the nut. Prayer supplies a leverage for the uplifting
of ponderous truths. One marvels how the stones of Stonehenge
could have been set in their places; it is even more to be inquired

after whence some men obtained such admirable knowledge of mysterious doctrines: was not prayer the potent machinery which wrought the wonder? Waiting upon God often turns darkness into light. Persevering inquiry at the sacred oracle uplifts the veil and gives grace to look into the deep things of God. . . .

You will frequently find fresh streams of thought leaping up from the passage before you, as if the rock had been struck by Moses' rod; new veins of precious ore will be revealed to your astonished gaze as you quarry God's Word and use diligently the hammer of prayer. You will sometimes feel as if you were entirely shut up, and then suddenly a new road will open before you. He who hath the key of David openeth, and no man shutteth. If you have ever sailed down the Rhine, the water scenery of that majestic river will have struck you as being very like in effect to a series of lakes. Before and behind, the vessel appears to be enclosed in massive walls of rock, or circles of vine-clad terraces, till on a sudden you turn a corner, and before you the rejoicing and abounding river flows onward in its strength. So the laborious student often finds it with a text; it appears to be fast closed against you, but prayer propels your vessel, and turns its prow into fresh waters, and you behold the broad and deep stream of sacred truth flowing in its fulness, and bearing you with it. Is not this a convincing reason for abiding in supplication? . . .

The best and holiest men have ever made prayer the most important part of pulpit preparation. It is said of M'Cheyne, "Anxious to give his people on the Sabbath what had cost him somewhat, he never, without an urgent reason, went before them without much previous meditation and prayer." . . .

Prayer will singularly assist you in the delivery of your sermon; in fact, nothing can so gloriously fit you to preach as descending fresh from the mount of communion with God to speak with men. None are so able to plead with men as those who have been wrestling with God on their behalf. . . . A truly pathetic delivery, in which there is no affectation, but much affection, can only be the offspring of prayer. There is no rhetoric like that of the heart, and no school for learning it but the foot of the cross. . . .

As fresh springs of thought will frequently break up during preparation, in answer to prayer, so will it be in *the delivery of the sermon.* Most preachers who depend upon God's Spirit will tell you that their freshest and best thoughts are not those which have been premeditated, but ideas which come to them flying as on the wings of angels, unexpected treasures brought on a sudden by celestial hands, seeds of the flowers of paradise, wafted from the mountains of myrrh. Often and often when I have felt hampered, both in thought and expression, my secret groaning of heart has brought me relief, and I have enjoyed more than usual liberty. But how dare we pray in the battle if we have never cried to the Lord while buckling on the harness! The remembrance of his wrestlings at home comforts the fettered preacher when in the pulpit: God will not desert us unless we have deserted him. You, brethren, will find that prayer will insure you strength equal to your day. . . .

After the sermon, how would a conscientious preacher give vent to his feelings and find solace for his soul if access to the mercy seat were denied him? Elevated to the highest pitch of excitement, how can we relieve our souls but in importunate pleadings? Or depressed by a fear of failure, how shall we be comforted but in moaning out our complaint before our God? How often have some of us tossed to and fro upon our couch half the night because of conscious shortcomings in our testimony! How frequently have we longed to rush back to the pulpit again to say over again more vehemently what we have uttered in so cold a manner! Where could we find rest for our spirits but in confession of sin and passionate entreaty that our infirmity or folly might in no way hinder the Spirit of God! . . . If we cannot prevail with men for God, we will, at least, endeavour to prevail with God for men. We cannot save them, or even persuade them to be saved, but we can at least bewail their madness and entreat the interference of the Lord. Like Jeremiah we can make it our resolve: "If ye will not hear it, my soul shall weep in secret places for your pride, and mine eye shall weep sore and run down with tears." To such pathetic appeals the Lord's heart can never be indifferent; in due time the weeping intercessor will become the rejoicing winner of souls. There is a distinct connection between importunate agonizing and true success, even as between the travail and the birth, the sowing in tears and the reaping in joy. . . . The secret of Luther's power lay in the same direction. Theodorus said of him: "I overheard him in prayer, but, good God, with what life and spirit did he pray! It was with so much reverence, as if he were speaking to God, yet with so much confidence as if he were speaking to his friend." My brethren, let me beseech you to be men of prayer. Great talents you may never have, but you will do well enough without them if you abound in intercession. . . .

When we have done with preaching, we shall not, if we are true ministers of God, have done with praying, because the whole church with many tongues will be crying, in the language of the Macedonian, "Come over and help us" in prayer. If you are enabled to prevail in prayer you will have many requests to offer for others who will flock to you, and beg a share in your intercessions, and so you will find yourself commissioned with errands to the mercy seat for friends and hearers. Such is always my lot, and I feel it a pleasure to have such requests to present before my Lord. Never can you be short of themes for prayer, even if no one should suggest them to you. Look at your congregation. There are always sick folk among them, and many more who are soul-sick. Some are unsaved, others are seeking and cannot find. Many are desponding, and not a few believers are backsliding or mourning. There are widows' tears and orphans' sighs to be put into our bottle, and poured out before the Lord. If you are a genuine minister of God you will stand as a priest before the Lord, spiritually wearing the ephod and the breast-plate whereon you bear the names of the children of Israel, pleading for them within the veil. I have known brethren who have kept a list of persons for whom they felt bound especially to pray, and I doubt not such a record often reminded them of what might otherwise have slipped their memory. Nor will your people wholly engross you; the nation and the world will claim their share. The man who is mighty in prayer may be a wall of fire around his country, her guardian angel and her shield. We have all heard how the enemies of the Protestant cause dreaded the prayers of Knox more than they feared armies of ten thousand men. . . . oh, that we were thus wrestling at midnight, crying, "Lord, wilt thou not grant us our hearers' souls?"

The minister who does not earnestly pray over his work must surely be a vain and conceited man. He acts as if he thought himself sufficient of himself, and therefore needed not to appeal to God. Yet what a baseless pride to conceive that our preaching can ever be in itself so powerful that it can turn men from their sins, and bring them to God without the working of the Holy Ghost. If we are truly humble-minded we shall not venture down to the fight until the Lord of Hosts has clothed us with all power, and said to us, "Go in this thy might." The preacher who neglects to pray much must be very careless about his ministry. He cannot have comprehended his calling. He cannot have computed the value of a soul, or estimated the meaning of eternity. He must be a mere official, tempted into a pulpit because the piece of bread which belongs to the priest's office is very necessary to him, or a detestable hypocrite who loves the praise of men, and cares not for the praise of God. He will surely become a mere superficial talker, best approved where grace is least valued and a vain show most admired. He cannot be one of those who plough deep and reap abundant harvests. He is a mere loiterer, not a labourer. As a preacher he has a name to live and is dead. . . .

How much of a blessing we may have missed through remissness in supplication we can scarcely guess, and none of us can know how poor we are in comparison with what we might have been if we had lived habitually nearer to God in prayer.

Vain regrets and surmises are useless, but an earnest determination to amend will be far more useful. We not only ought to pray more, but we *must*. The fact is, the secret of all ministerial success lies in prevalence at the mercy seat.

One bright benison which private prayer brings down upon the ministry is an indescribable and inimitable something, better understood than named; it is a dew from the Lord, a divine presence which you will recognize at once when I say it is "an unction from the Holy One." What is it? I wonder how long we might beat our brains before we could plainly put into words what is meant by *preaching with unction*. . . . Such is the mystery of spiritual anointing; we know, but we cannot tell to others what it is. It is as easy as it is foolish to counterfeit it, as some do who use expressions which are meant to betoken fervent love, but oftener indicate sickly sentimentalism or mere cant. "Dear Lord!" "Sweet Jesus!" "Precious Christ!" are by them poured out wholesale, till one is nauseated. These familiarities may have been not only tolerable, but even beautiful when they first fell from a saint of God, speaking, as it were, out of the excellent glory, but when repeated flippantly they are not only intolerable, but indecent, if not profane. Some have tried to imitate unction by unnatural tones and whines; by turning up the whites of their eyes, and lifting their hands in a most ridiculous manner. . . . All mere mannerism without power is as foul carrion of all life bereft, obnoxious, mischievous. Certain brethren aim at inspiration through exertion and loud shouting, but it does not come; some we have known to stop the discourse, and exclaim, "God bless you," and others gesticulate wildly, and drive their fingernails into the palms of their hands as if they were in convulsions of celestial ardor. Bah! The whole thing smells of the greenroom and the stage. The getting up of fervour in hearers by the simulation of it in the preacher is a loathsome deceit to be scorned by honest men. . . . To the secret pleader with God this secret is committed; upon him rests the dew of the Lord, about him is the perfume which makes glad the heart. If the anointing which we bear come not from the Lord of hosts we are deceivers, and since only in prayer can we obtain it, let us continue instant, constant, fervent in supplication. Let your fleece lie on the threshing floor of supplication till it is wet with the dew of heaven. Go not to minister in the temple till you have washed in the laver. Think not to be a messenger of grace to others till you have seen the God of grace for yourselves, and had the word from his mouth.

Time spent in quiet prostration of soul before the Lord is most envigourating. David "sat before the Lord." It is a great thing to hold these sacred sittings; the mind being receptive, like an open flower drinking in the sunbeams, or the sensitive photographic plate accepting the image before it. Quietude, which some men cannot abide because it reveals their inward poverty, is as a palace of cedar to the wise, for along its hallowed courts the king in his beauty deigns to walk. . . . I am persuaded that we most of us think too much of speech, which after all is but the shell of thought. Quiet contemplation, still worship, unuttered rapture—these are mine when my best jewels are before me. Brethren, rob not your heart of the deep-sea joys; miss not the far-down life by for ever babbling among the broken shells and foaming surges of the shore.

I would seriously recommend to you, when settled in the ministry, the celebration of extraordinary seasons of devotion. If your ordinary prayers do not keep up the freshness and vigour of your souls, and you feel that you are flagging, get alone for a week, or even a month if possible. We have occasional holidays, why not frequent holy days? We hear of our richer brethren finding time for a journey to Jerusalem; could we not spare time for the less difficult and far more profitable journey to the heavenly city? . . . It would be a great thing every now and then for a band of truly spiritual brethren to spend a day or two with each other in real burning agony of prayer. Pastors alone could use much more freedom than in a mixed company. Times of humiliation and supplication for the whole church will also benefit us if we enter into them heartily. Our seasons of fasting and prayer at the [Metropolitan] Tabernacle have been high days indeed; never has heaven-gate stood wider; never have our hearts been nearer the central glory. I look forward to our month of special devotion, as mariners reckon upon reaching land. Even if our public work were laid aside to give us space for special prayer, it might be a great gain to our churches. A voyage to the golden rivers of fellowship and meditation would be well repaid by a freight of sanctified feeling and elevated thought. Our silence might be better than our voices if our solitude were spent with God. That was a grand action of old Jerome, when he laid all his pressing engagements aside to achieve a purpose to which he felt a call from heaven. He had a large congregation, as large a one as any of us need want, but he said to his people, "Now it is of necessity that the New Testament should be translated, you must find another preacher: the translation must be made; I am bound for the wilderness, and shall not return till my task is finished." Away he went with his manuscripts, and prayed and laboured, and produced a work—the Latin Vulgate—which will last as long as the world stands; on the whole a most wonderful translation of Holy Scripture. As learning and prayerful retirement together could thus produce an immortal work, if we were sometimes to say to our people when we felt moved to do so, "Dear friends, we really must be gone for a little while to refresh our souls in solitude," our profiting would soon be apparent, and if we did not write Latin Vulgates, yet we should do immortal work, such as would abide the fire.

8

Our Public Prayer

. . . Be assured that free prayer is the most scriptural, and should be the most excellent form of public supplication. If you lose faith in what you are doing you will never do it well; settle it in your minds, therefore, that before the Lord you are worshipping in a manner which is warranted by the Word of God, and accepted of the Lord. The expression "reading prayers," to which we are now so accustomed, is not to be found in Holy Scripture, rich as it is in words for conveying religious thought; and the phrase is not there because the thing itself had no existence. Where in the writings of the apostles meet we with the bare idea of a liturgy? Prayer in the assemblies of the early Christians was unrestricted to any form of words. . . .

Be it ours to prove the superiority of extempore prayer by making it more spiritual and earnest than liturgical devotion. It is a great pity when the observation is forced from the hearer, our minister preaches far better than he prays: this is not after the model of our Lord; he spake as never man spake—and as for his prayers, they so impressed his disciples that they said, "Lord *teach* us to pray." All our faculties should concentrate their energy, and the whole man should be elevated to his highest point of vigour while in public prayer, the Holy Ghost meanwhile baptizing soul and spirit with his sacred influence; but slovenly, careless, lifeless talk in the guise of prayer, made to fill up a certain space in the service, is a weariness to man, and an abomination to God. Had free prayer been universally of a higher order a liturgy would never have been thought of, and today forms of prayer have no better apology than the feebleness of extempora-

125

neous devotions. The secret is that we are not so really devout at heart as we should be. (Habitual communion with God must be maintained, or our public prayers will be vapid or formal.) If there be no melting of the glacier high up in the ravines of the mountain, there will be no descending rivulets to cheer the plain. Private prayer is the drill ground for our more public exercises, neither can we long neglect it without being out of order when before the people. . . .

Let the Lord alone be the object of your prayers. Beware of having an eye to the auditors; beware of becoming rhetorical to please the listeners. Prayer must not be transformed into "an oblique sermon." It is little short of blasphemy to make devotion an occasion for display. Fine prayers are generally very wicked prayers. In the presence of the Lord of hosts it ill becomes a sinner to parade the feathers and finery of tawdry speech with the view of winning applause from his fellow mortals. . . . We may aim at exciting the yearnings and aspirations of those who hear us in prayer; but every word and thought must be Godward, and only so far touching upon the people as may be needful to bring them and their wants before the Lord. Remember the people in your prayers, but do not mould your supplications to win their esteem; look up, look up with both eyes. . . .

Avoid that kind of prayer which may be called—though the subject is one on which language has not given us many terms—*a sort of peremptory demanding of God.* It is delightful to hear a man wrestle with God, and say "I will not let thee go except thou bless me," but that must be said softly, and not in a hectoring spirit, as though we could command and exact blessings from the Lord of all. Remember, it is still a man wrestling, even though permitted to wrestle, with the eternal I Am. . . . We are taught to say, "Our Father," but still it is, "Our Father *who art in heaven.*" Familiarity there may be, but holy familiarity; boldness, but the boldness which springs from grace and is the work of the Spirit; not the boldness of the rebel who carries a brazen front in the presence of his offended king, but the boldness of the child who fears because he loves, and loves because he fears. Never fall into a vainglorious style of impertinent address to God; he is not to be assailed as an antagonist, but entreated with as our Lord and God. Humble and lowly let us be in spirit, and so let us pray.

Pray when you profess to pray, and don't talk about it. Business men say, "A place for everything and everything in its place"; preach in the sermon and pray in the prayer. Disquisitions upon our need of help in prayer are not prayer. Why do not men go at once to prayer—why stand beating about the bush; instead of saying what they ought to do and want to do, why not set to work in God's name and do it? In downright earnestness address yourself to intercession, and set your face towards the Lord. Plead for the supply of the great and constant needs of the church, and do not fail to urge, with devout fervor, the special requirements of the present time and audience. Let the sick, the poor, the dying, the heathen, the Jew, and all forgotten classes of people be mentioned as they press upon your heart. Pray for your people as saints and sinners—not as if they were all saints. Mention the young and the aged; the impressed and the careless; the devout and the backsliding. (Never turn to the right hand or to the left, but plough on in the furrow of real prayer.) Let your confessions of sin and your thanksgivings be truthful and to the point; and let your petitions be presented as if you believed in God and had no doubt as to the efficacy of prayer: I say this, because so many pray in such a formal manner as to lead observers to conclude that they thought it a very decent thing to pray, but, after all, a very poor and doubtful business as to any practical result. Pray as one who has tried and proved his God, and therefore comes with undoubting confidence to renew his pleadings: and do remember to pray to God right through the prayer, and never fall to talking or preaching—much less, as some do, to scolding and grumbling.

As a rule, if called upon to preach, conduct the prayer yourself; and if you should be highly esteemed in the ministry, as I trust you may be, make a point, with great courtesy, but equal firmness, to resist the practice of choosing men to pray with the idea of honouring them by giving them something to do. Our public devotions ought never to be degraded into opportunities for compliment. I have heard prayer and singing now and then called "the preliminary services," as if they were but a preface to the sermon; this is rare, I hope, among us—if it were common it would be to our deep disgrace. I endeavour invariably to take all the service myself for my own sake, and I think also for the people's. I do not believe that "anybody will do for the praying." No, sirs, it is my solemn conviction that the prayer is one of the most weighty, useful, and honorable parts of the service, and that it ought to be even more considered than the sermon. There must be no putting up of anybodies and nobodies to pray, and then the selection of the abler man to preach. It may happen through weakness, or upon a special occasion, that it may be a relief to the minister to have someone to offer prayer for him; but if the Lord has made you love your work you will not often or readily fulfil this part of it by proxy. If you delegate the service at all, let it be to one in whose spirituality and present preparedness you have the fullest confidence; but to pitch on a giftless brother unawares, and put him forward to get through the devotions, is shameful:

> Shall we serve *heaven* with less respect
> Than we do minister to our gross selves?

Appoint the ablest man to pray, and let the sermon be slurred sooner than the approach to heaven. Let the Infinite Jehovah be served with our best; let prayer addressed to the Divine Majesty be carefully weighed, and presented with all the powers of an awakened heart and a spiritual understanding. He who has been by communion with God prepared to minister to the people is usually of all men present the most fit to engage in prayer; to lay out a programme which puts up another brother in his place is to mar the harmony of the service, to rob the preacher of an exercise which would brace him for his sermon, and in many instances to suggest comparisons between one part of the service and the other which ought never to be tolerated. If unprepared brethren are to be sent into the pulpit to do my praying for me when I am engaged to preach, I do not see why I might not be allowed to pray, and then retire to let these brethren do the sermonizing. I am not able to see any reason for depriving me of the holiest, sweetest, and most profitable exercise which my Lord has allotted me; if I may have my choice, I will sooner yield up the sermon than the prayer. Thus much I have said in order to impress upon you that you must highly esteem public prayer, and seek of the Lord for the gifts and graces necessary to its right discharge. . . .

I have been at funerals when the burial service of the Church of England has been galloped through so indecorously that it has taken all the grace I had to prevent my throwing a hassock at the creature's head. I have felt so indignant that I have not known what to do, to hear, in the presence of mourners whose hearts were bleeding, a man rattling through the service as if he were paid by the piece, and had more work to follow, and therefore desired to get it through as quickly as possible. What effect he could think he was producing, or what good result could come from words jerked forth and hurled out with vengeance and vehemence, I cannot imagine. It is really shocking to think of how that very wonderful burial service is murdered, and made into an abomination, by the mode in which it is frequently read. I merely mention this because, if they criticise our prayers too severely, we can bring a formidable countercharge to silence them. Better far, however, for us to amend our own blunders than find fault with others.

In order to make our *public prayer* what it should be, the first necessary is that it *must be a matter of the heart*. . . . It must be true prayer, and if it be such, it will, like love, cover a multitude of sins. You can pardon a man's familiarities and his vulgarities too, when you clearly see that his inmost heart is speaking to his Maker, and that it is only the man's defects of education which create his faults, and not any moral or spiritual vices of his heart. The pleader in public must be in earnest; for a sleepy prayer—what can be worse preparation for a sermon? A sleepy prayer—what can make people more dislike going up to the house of God at all? Cast your whole soul into the exercise. If ever your whole manhood was engaged in anything, let it be in drawing near unto God in public. So pray that, by a divine attraction, you draw the whole congregation with you up to the throne of God. So pray, that by the power of the Holy Spirit resting on you, you express the desires and thoughts of everyone present, and stand as the one voice for the hundreds of beating hearts which are glowing with fervour before the throne of God.

Next to this, *our prayers must be appropriate.* I do not say go into every minute detail of the circumstances of the congregation. As I have said before, there is no need to make the public prayer a gazette of the week's events, or a register of the births, deaths, and marriages of your people, but the general movements that have taken place in the congregation should be noted by the minister's careful heart. He should bring the joys and sorrows of his people alike before the throne of grace, and ask that the divine benediction may rest upon his flock in all their movements, their exercises, engagements, and holy enterprises, and that the forgiveness of God may be extended to their shortcomings and innumerable sins.

Then, by way of negative canon, I should say, *do not let your prayer be long.* . . . You cannot pray too long in private. . . . The more you are on your knees alone the better. We are now speaking of those public prayers which come before or after the sermon, and for these, ten minutes is a better limit than fifteen. Only one in a thousand would complain of you for being too short, while scores will murmur at your being wearisome in length. "He prayed me into a good frame of mind,"

George Whitfield once said of a certain preacher, "and if he had stopped there, it would have been very well; but he prayed me out of it again by keeping on." The abundant long-suffering of God has been exemplified in his sparing some preachers, who have been great sinners in this direction; they have done much injury to the piety of God's people by their long-winded orations, and yet God, in his mercy, has permitted them still to officiate in the sanctuary. Alas! for those who have to listen to pastors who pray in public for five-and-twenty minutes, and then ask God to forgive their "shortcomings"! Do not be too long, for several reasons. First, because you weary yourselves and the people; and secondly, because being too long in prayer puts your people out of heart for hearing the sermon. All those dry, dull, prolix talkifications in prayer do but blunt the attention, and the ear gets, as it were, choked up. Nobody would think of blocking up ear-gate with mud or stones when he meant to storm the gate. No, let the portal be cleared that the battering-ram of the gospel may tell upon it when the time comes to use it. Long prayers consist of repetitions, or else of unnecessary explanations which God does not require; or else they degenerate into downright preachings, so that there is no difference between the praying and the preaching, except that in the one the minister has his eyes shut, and in the other he keeps them open. It is not necessary in prayer to rehearse the Westminster Assembly's catechism. It is not necessary in prayer to relate the experience of all the people who are present, or even your own. It is not necessary in prayer to string a selection of texts of Scripture together, and quote David, and Daniel, and Job, and Paul, and Peter, and every other body, under the title of "thy servant of old." It *is* necessary in prayer to draw near unto God, but it is not required of you to prolong your speech till everyone is longing to hear the word "Amen."

One little hint I cannot withhold—never appear to be closing, and then start off again for another five minutes. When friends make up their minds that you are about to conclude, they cannot with a jerk proceed again in a devout spirit. I have known men tantalize us with the hope that they were drawing to a close, and then take a fresh lease two or three times; this is most unwise and unpleasant.

Another canon is *do not use cant phrases.* My brethren, have done with those vile things altogether; they have had their day, and let them die. These pieces of spiritual fustian cannot be too much reprobated. Some of them are pure inventions; others are passages taken from the Apocrypha; others are texts fathered upon Scripture. . . . "Thy poor unworthy dust" [for example], an epithet generally applied to themselves by the proudest men in the congregation, and not seldom by the most moneyed and grovelling, in which case the last two words are not so very inappropriate. We have heard of a good man who, in pleading for his children and grandchildren, was so completely beclouded in the blinding influence of this expression that he exclaimed, "O Lord, save thy dust, and thy dust's dust, and thy dust's dust's dust." . . .

It ought to be a point of honour among ministers always to quote Scripture correctly. . . . You who so unwaveringly believe in the verbal-inspiration theory (to my intense satisfaction) ought never to quote at all until you can give the precise words, because, according to your own showing, by the alteration of a single word you may miss altogether God's sense of the passage. If you cannot make extracts from Scripture correctly, why quote at all in your petitions? Make use of an expression fresh from your own mind, and it will be quite as acceptable to God as a scriptural phrase defaced or clipped. Vehemently strive against garblings and perversions of Scripture, and renounce for ever all cant phrases, for they are the disfigurement of free prayer.

I have noticed a habit among some—I hope you have not fallen into it—of praying with their eyes open. It is unnatural, unbecoming, and disgusting. Occasionally the opened eye uplifted to heaven may be suitable and impressive, but to be gazing about while professing to address the unseen God is detestable. In the earliest ages of the church the fathers denounced this unseemly practice. Action in prayer should be very little used, if at all. It is scarcely comely to lift and move the arm, as if in preaching; the outstretched arms however, or the clasped hands, are natural and suggestive when under strong holy excitement. The voice should accord with the matter, and should never be boisterous or self-asserting: humble and reverent let those tones be in which man talketh with his God. Doth not even nature itself teach you this? If grace does not, I despair. . . .

Vary the current of your prayers in intercession. There are many topics which require your attention: the church in its weakness, it backslidings, its sorrows, and its comforts; the outside world; the neighborhood; unconverted hearers; the young people; the nation. Do not pray for all these every time, or otherwise your prayers will be long and uninteresting. Whatever topic shall come uppermost to your heart, let that be uppermost in your supplications. There is a way of taking a line of prayer, if the Holy Spirit shall guide you therein, which will make the service all of a piece, and harmonize with the hymns and discourse. It is very useful to maintain unity in the service where you can—not slavishly, but wisely, so that the effect is one. . . . Hardly commendable is the practice, common with some preachers, of rehearsing the sermon in the last prayer. It may be instructive to the audience, but that is an object altogether foreign to prayer. . . .

As you would avoid a viper, *keep from all attempts to work up spurious fervour in public devotion.* Do not labour to seem earnest. Pray as your heart dictates, under the leading of the Spirit of God, and if you are dull and heavy tell the Lord so. It will be no ill thing to confess your deadness, and bewail it, and cry for quickening; it will be real and acceptable prayer; but simulated ardour is a shameful form of lying. Never imitate those who are earnest. You know a good man who groans, and another whose voice grows shrill when he is carried away with zeal, but do not therefore moan or squeak in order to appear as zealous as they are. Just be natural the whole way through, and ask of God to be guided in it all.

Lastly . . . *prepare your prayer.* You say with astonishment, "Whatever can you mean by that?" Well, I mean what some do not mean. The question was once discussed in a society of ministers, "Was it right for the minister to prepare his prayer beforehand?" It was earnestly asserted by some that it was wrong; and very properly so. It was with equal earnestness maintained by others that it was right; and they were not to be gainsayed. I believe both parties to have been right. The first brethren understood by preparing the prayer, the studying of expressions, and the putting together of a train of thought, which they all said was altogether opposed to spiritual worship, in which we ought to leave ourselves in the hand of God's Spirit to be taught of him both as to matter and words. In these remarks we altogether agree; for if a man writes his prayers and studies his petitions, let him use a liturgy at once. But the brethren in opposition meant by preparation quite another thing, not the preparation of the head, but of the heart, which consists in the solemn considera-tion beforehand of the importance of prayer, meditation upon the needs of men's souls, and a remembrance of the promises which we are to plead; and thus coming before the Lord with a petition written upon the fleshy tables of the heart. This is surely better than coming to God at random, rushing before the throne at haphazard, without a definite errand or desire. "I never am tired of praying," said one man, "because I always have a definite errand when I pray." Brethren, are your prayers of this sort? Do you strive to be in a fit frame to lead the supplications of your people? Do you order your cause in coming before the Lord? . . . We counsel, therefore, the committing to memory of the inspired devotional exercises of the word of truth, and then your continued reading of the Scriptures will keep you always furnished with fresh supplications. . . .

Let your petitions be plain and heartfelt; and while your people may sometimes feel that the sermon was below the mark, may they also feel that the prayer compensated for all. . . .

9

On the Voice

OUR first rule with regard to the voice would be: *do not think too much about it,* for recollect the sweetest voice is nothing without something to say. . . .

Whitfield's voice, without his heart-power, would have left no more lasting effects upon his hearers than Paganini's fiddle. You are not singers but preachers: your voice is but a secondary matter. . . .

On the other hand, *do not think too little of your voice,* for its excellence may greatly conduce to the result which you hope to produce. . . . Exceedingly precious truths may be greatly marred by being delivered in monotonous tones. I once heard a most esteemed minister, who mumbled sadly, compared to "a humble bee in a pitcher," a vulgar metaphor no doubt, but so exactly descriptive, that it brings to my mind the droning sound at this instant most distinctly, and reminds me of the parody upon Gray's Elegy:

> Now fades the glimmering subject from the sight,
> And all the air a sleepy stillness holds,
> Save where the parson hums his droning flight,
> And drowsy tinklings lull the slumb'ring folds.

What a pity that a man who from his heart delivered doctrines of undoubted value, in language the most appropriate, should commit ministerial suicide by harping on one string, when the Lord had given him an instrument of many strings to play upon! . . .

When you do pay attention to the voice, *take care not to fall into the habitual and common affectations of the present day.* Scarcely one man in a dozen in the pulpit talks like a man.

This affectation is not confined to Protestants, for the Abbe Mullois remarks:

> Everywhere else, men speak: they speak at the bar and the tribune; but they no longer speak in the pulpit, for there we only meet with a factitious and artificial language, and a false tone. This style of speaking is only tolerated in the church, because, unfortunately, it is so general there; elsewhere it would not be endured. What would be thought of a man who should converse in a similar way in a drawing room? He would certainly provoke many a smile. Some time ago there was a warder at the Pantheon —a good sort of fellow in his way—who, in enumerating the beauties of the monument, adopted precisely the tone of many of our preachers, and never failed thereby to excite the hilarity of the visitors, who were as much amused with his style of address as with the objects of interest which he pointed out to them. A man who has not a natural and true delivery, should not be allowed to occupy the pulpit from whence, at least, everything that is false should be summarily banished . . . . In these days of mistrust everything that is false should be set aside . . . . The instant you abandon the natural and the true, you forego the right to be believed, as well as the right of being listened to.

. . . The moment some men shut the pulpit door, they leave their own personal manhood behind them, and become as official as the parish beadle. There they might almost boast with the Pharisee that they are not as other men are, although it would be blasphemy to thank God for it. No longer are they carnal and speaking as men; but a whine, a broken hum-haw, an *ore rotundo,* or some other graceless mode of noise-making is adopted, to prevent all suspicion of being natural and speaking out of the abundance of the heart. When that gown is once on, how often does it prove to be the shroud of the man's true self, and the effeminate emblem of officialism! . . . All mimicry is in the pulpit near akin to an unpardonable sin. . . . I have heard many different varieties, from the fulness of the Johnsonian to the thinness of the little genteel whisper; from the roaring of the bulls of Bashan up to the chip, chip, chip of a chaffinch. . . . I do not condemn them—let every creature speak in its own tongue; but the fact is, that in nine cases out of ten, these sacred brogues, which I hope will soon be dead languages, are unnatural and strained. I am persuaded that these tones and semitones and monotones are Babylonian, that they are not at all the Jerusalem dialect; for the Jerusalem dialect has this one distinguishing mark, that it is a man's own mode of speech, and is the same out of the pulpit as it is in it. . . . I maintain that the best notes a man's voice is capable of should be given to the proclamation of the gospel, and these are such as nature teaches him to use in earnest conversation. . . .

In the next place, *if you have any idiosyncrasies of speech which are disagreeable to the ear correct them if possible.* It is admitted that this is much more easy for the teacher to inculcate than for you to practice. . . .

One of the surest ways to kill yourself is to speak from the throat instead of the mouth. This misuse of nature will be terribly avenged by her; escape the penalty by avoiding the offence. It may be well in this place to urge you as soon as you detect yourself interposing hum-haw pretty plentifully in your discourse, to purge yourself of the insinuating but ruinous habit at once. There is no need whatever for it, and although those who are now its victims may never be able to break the chain, you, who are beginners in oratory, must scorn to wear the galling yoke. It is even needful to say, open your mouths when you speak, for much of inarticulate mumbling is the result of keeping the mouth half closed. It is not in vain that the evangelists have written of our Lord, *"He opened his mouth and taught them."* Open wide the doors from which such goodly truth is to march forth. . . . Abhor the practice of some men, who will not bring out the letter *r;* such a habit is "vewy wuinous, and wediculous, vewy wetched and wepwehensible." Now and then a brother has the felicity to possess a most winning and delicious lisp. This is perhaps among the least of evils, *where the brother*

---

*"Take care of anything awkward or affected either in your gesture, phrase, or pronunciation."—JOHN WESLEY

himself is little and winning, but it would ruin any being who
aimed at manliness and force. I can scarcely conceive of Elijah
lisping to Ahab, or Paul prettily chipping his words on Mars'
Hill. There may be a peculiar pathos about a weak and watery
eye, and a faltering style; we will go further, and admit that
where these are the result of intense passion, they are sublime;
but some possess them by birth, and use them rather too freely:
it is, to say the least, unnecessary for you to imitate them. Speak
as educated nature suggests to you, and you will do well; but
let it be educated, and not raw, rude, uncultivated nature. Demosthenes took, as you know, unbounded pains with his voice, and
Cicero, who was naturally weak, made a long journey into Greece
to correct his manner of speaking. With far nobler themes, let us
not be less ambitious to excel. . . .

Always speak so as to be heard. . . . What is the use of a
preacher whom men cannot hear? Modesty should lead a voiceless
man to give place to others who are more fitted for the work of
proclaiming the messages of the King. Some men are loud enough,
but they are not distinct; their words overlap each other, play
at leap-frog, or trip each other up. Distinct utterance is far
more important than wind-power. Do give a word a fair chance; do
not break its back in your vehemence, or run it off its legs in
your haste. It is hateful to hear a big fellow mutter and whisper
when his lungs are quite strong enough for the loudest speech;
but at the same time, let a man shout ever so lustily, he will
not be well heard unless he learns to push his words forward
with due space between. To speak too slowly is miserable work, and
subjects active-minded hearers to the disease called "the horrors."
It is impossible to hear a man who crawls along at a mile an
hour. One word today and one tomorrow is a kind of slow-fire
which martyrs only could enjoy. Excessively rapid speaking, tear-
ing and raving into utter rant, is quite as inexcusable; it is not,
and never can be powerful, except with idiots, for it turns what
should be an army of words into a mob, and most effectually
drowns the sense in floods of sound. . . .

Pause soon enough to prevent that "hough, hough," which rather creates pity for the breathless orator than sympathy with the subject in hand. Your audience ought not to know that you breathe at all—the process of respiration should be as unobserved as the circulation of the blood. It is indecent to let the mere animal function of breathing cause any hiatus in your discourse.

Do not as a rule exert your voice to the utmost in ordinary preaching. . . . Men do not hear in proportion to the noise created; in fact, too much noise stuns the ear, creates reverberations and echoes, and effectually injures the power of your sermons.

Adapt your voice to your audience; when twenty thousand are before you, draw out the stops and give the full peal, but not in a room which will only hold a score or two. . . . Why speak so as to be heard in the street when there is nobody there who is listening to you? Whether indoors or out, see that the most remote hearers can follow you, and that will be sufficient. By the way, I may observe that brethren should out of mercy to the weak always attend carefully to the force of their voices in sick rooms, and in congregations where some are known to be very infirm. It is a cruel thing to sit down by a sick man's bedside, and shout out "THE LORD IS MY SHEPHERD." If you act so thoughtlessly, the poor man will say as soon as you are downstairs, "Dear me! How my head aches. I am glad the good man is gone, Mary; that is a very precious Psalm and so quietlike, but he read it out like thunder and lightning, and almost stunned me!". . .

Observe carefully the rule to *vary the force of your voice.* The old rule was to begin very softly, gradually rise higher, and bring out your loudest notes at the end. Let all such regulations be blown to pieces at the cannon's mouth; they are impertinent and misleading. Speak softly or loudly, as the emotion of the moment may suggest, and observe no artificial or fanciful rules. Artificial rules are an utter abomination. . . . In imitation of a popular preacher, to whom it was unavoidable, a certain minister was accustomed in the commencement of his sermon to speak in so low a key that no one could possibly hear him. Everybody leaned forward, fearing something good was being lost in the air, but their straining was in vain, a holy mutter was all they could discern. If the brother *could not* have spoken out none should have blamed him, but it was a most absurd thing to do this when in a short time he proved the power of his lungs by filling the whole structure by sonorous sentences. If the first half of his discourse was of no importance, why not omit it? and if of any value at all, why not deliver it distinctly? *Effect,* gentlemen, that was the point aimed at; he knew that one who spake in that fashion had produced great effects, and he hoped to rival him. . . . Never do anything for effect, but scorn the stratagems of little minds, hunting after the approval of connoisseurs in preaching, who are a race as obnoxious to a true minister as locusts to the Eastern husbandman. . . .

Your exordia are too good to be whispered to space. Speak them out boldly, and command attention at the very outset by your manly tones. Do not start at the highest pitch as a rule, for then you will not be able to rise when you warm with the work; but still be outspoken from the first. Lower the voice when suitable, even to a whisper; for soft, deliberate, solemn utterances are not only a relief to the ear, but have a great aptitude to reach the heart. Do not be afraid of the low keys, for if you throw force into them they are as well heard as the shouts. You need not speak in a loud voice in order to be heard well. . . . It is not the loudness of your voice, it is the force which you put into it that is effective. . . . If you wish to be understood, and so to be of service, shun the reproach of being "impotent and loud.". . . A bell will be heard much farther off than a drum; and very singularly, the more musical a sound is the farther it travels. It is not the thumping of the piano which is needed, but the judicious sounding of the best keys. You will therefore feel at liberty to ease the strain very frequently in the direction of loudness, and you will be greatly relieving both the ears of the audience and your own lungs. . . . Be, indeed, just what every common-sense person is in his speech when he talks naturally, pleads vehemently, whispers confidentially, appeals plaintively, or publishes distinctly.

Next to the moderation of lung-force, I should place the rule *modulate your tones.* Alter the key frequently and vary the strain constantly. Let the bass, the treble, and the tenor take their turn. I beseech you to do this out of pity to yourself and to those who hear you. God has mercy upon us and arranges all things to meet our cravings for variety; let us have mercy upon our fellow creatures, and not persecute them with the tedium of sameness. . . .

However musical your voice may be in itself, if you continue to sound the same chord perpetually, your hearers will perceive that its notes are by distance made more sweet. Do in the name of humanity cease intoning and take to rational speaking. . . . If you wish to ruin your throats, you can speedily do so, but if you wish to preserve them, note what is now laid before you. I have often in this room compared the voice to a drum. If the drummer should always strike in one place on the head of his drum, the skin would soon wear into a hole; but how much longer it would have lasted him if he had varied his thumping and had used the entire surface of the drumhead! So it is with a man's voice. If he uses always the same tone, he will wear a hole in that part of the throat which is most exercised in producing that monotony, and very soon he will suffer from bronchitis. . . . Actors and barristers have much occasion to strain their vocal powers, and yet there is no such thing as a counsel's sore throat, or a tragedian's bronchitis, simply because these men dare not serve the public in so slovenly a manner as some preachers serve their God. . . .

I was pleased to find my opinion that infrequent preaching is the root of many diseases thus plainly declared by Dr. Fenwick. . . :

The example of the most celebrated orators the world has seen proves the advantages of regular and constant practice of speaking:

and I would on this account, most strongly recommend all persons subject to this complaint to read aloud once or twice a day, using the same pitch of voice as in the pulpit, and paying especial attention to the position of the chest and throat, and to clear and proper articulation of the words.

. . . Gentlemen, a needful rule—*always suit your voice to your matter.* Do not be jubilant over a doleful subject, and on the other hand, do not drag heavily where the tones ought to trip along merrily, as though they were dancing to the tune of the angels in heaven. This rule I shall not enlarge upon, but rest assured it is of the utmost importance, and if obediently followed, will always secure attention, provided your matter is worth it. Suit your voice to your matter always, and above all, *in everything be natural.* Away forever with slavish attention to rules and models. Do not imitate other people's voices, or, if from an unconquerable propensity you must follow them, emulate every orator's excellences, and the evil will be lessened. . . . The mimic is for the playhouse, the cultured man in his sanctified personality is for the sanctuary. I would repeat this rule till I wearied you if I thought you would forget it; be natural, be natural, be natural evermore. . . .

We are bound to add—*endeavour to educate your voice.* Grudge no pains or labour in achieving this, for as it has been well observed, "However prodigious may be the gifts of nature to her elect, they can only be developed and brought to their extreme perfection by labour and study." Think of Michelangelo working for a week without taking off his clothes, and Handel hollowing out every key of his harpsichord, like a spoon, by incessant practice. Gentlemen, after this, never talk of difficulty or weariness. It is almost impossible to see the utility of Demosthenes' method of speaking with stones in his mouth, but anyone can perceive the usefulness of his pleading with the boisterous billows, that he might know how to command a hearing amidst the uproarious assemblies of his countrymen; and in his speaking as he ran up hill that his lungs might gather force from laborious use the

reason is as obvious as the self-denial is commendable. We are
bound to use every possible means to perfect the voice by which
we are to tell forth the glorious gospel of the blessed God. Take
great care of the consonants, enunciate every one of them clearly;
they are the features and expressions of the words.   Practise
indefatigably till you give every one of the consonants its due;
the vowels have a voice of their own, and therefore they can
speak for themselves. . . . Get a friend to tell you your faults,
or better still, welcome an enemy who will watch you keenly
and sting you savagely. What a blessing such an irritating critic
will be to a wise man, what an intolerable nuisance to a fool!
Correct yourself diligently and frequently, or you will fall into
errors unawares; false tones will grow, and slovenly habits
will form insensibly: therefore criticise yourself with unceasing
care. Think nothing little by which you may be even a little
more useful. But, gentlemen, never degenerate in this business
into pulpit fops, who think gesture and voice to be everything.
I am sick at heart when I hear of men taking a whole week
to get up a sermon, much of the getting up consisting in repeating their precious productions before a glass! Alas for this
age, if graceless hearts are to be forgiven for the sake of graceful manners! Give us all the vulgarities of the wildest backwoods itinerant rather than the perfumed prettinesses of effeminate gentility. . . .

When you have done preaching, take care of your throat by
never wrapping it up tightly. From personal experience I venture
with some diffidence to give this piece of advice. If any of you
possess delightfully warm woollen comforters, with which there
may be associated the most tender remembrances of mother or
sister, treasure them—treasure them in the bottom of your trunk,
but do not expose them to any vulgar use by wrapping them round
your necks. If any brother wants to die of influenza let him wear
a warm scarf round his neck, and then one of these nights he
will forget it, and catch such a cold as will last him the rest of his
natural life. You seldom see a sailor wrap his neck up. No, he

always keeps it bare and exposed, and has a turndown collar, and if he has a tie at all, it is but a small one loosely tied, so that the wind can blow all round his neck. In this philosophy I am a firm believer, having never deviated from it for these fourteen years, and having before that time been frequently troubled with colds, but very seldom since. If you feel that you want something else, why, then grow your beards! A habit most natural, scriptural, manly, and beneficial. . . . If your throats become affected, consult a good physician, or if you cannot do this, give what attention you please to the following hint. Never purchase "Marsh-mallow Rock," "Cough-no-more Lozenges," "Pulmonic Wafers," horehound, ipecacuanha, or any of the ten thousand emollient compounds. They may serve your turn for a time by removing present uneasiness, but they ruin the throat by their laxative [relaxant] qualities. If you wish to improve your throat take a good share of pepper—good Cayenne pepper, and other astringent substances, as much as your stomach can bear. Do not go beyond that, because you must recollect that you have to take care of your stomach as well as your throat, and if the digesting apparatus be out of order, nothing can be right. Common sense teaches you that astringents must be useful. Did you ever hear of a tanner making a piece of hide into leather by laying it to soak in sugar? Neither would tolu, ipecacuanha, or treacle serve his purpose, but the very reverse; if he wants to harden and strengthen the skin, he places it in a solution of oak-bark, or some astringent substance which draws the material together and strengthens it. When I began to preach at Exeter Hall my voice was weak for such a place—as weak as the usual run of voices—and it had frequently failed me altogether in street preaching, but in Exeter Hall (which is an unusually difficult place to preach in, from its excessive width in proportion to its length), I always had a little glass of Chili vinegar and water just in front of me, a draught of which appeared to give a fresh force to the throat whenever it grew weary and the voice appeared likely to break down. When my throat becomes a little relaxed I

usually ask the cook to prepare me a basin of beef-tea, as strong
with pepper as can be borne, and hitherto this has been a sovereign
remedy. However, as I am not qualified to practise in medicine, you
will probably pay no more attention to me in medical matters
than to any other quack. . . .

I shall not detain you longer, but express the hope that your
chest, lungs, windpipe, larynx, and all your vocal organs may
last you till you have nothing more to say.

10

Posture, Action, Gesture, Etc.

THE subjects of this lecture are to be posture, gesture, and action in the delivery of a sermon. I shall not attempt to draw any hard and fast line of division between the one and the other; for it would need a very highly discriminating mind to keep them separate; indeed, it could not be done at all, for they naturally merge into each other. . . .

The sermon itself is the main thing: its matter, its aim, and the spirit in which it is brought before the people, the sacred anointing upon the preacher, and the divine power applying the truth to the hearer—these are infinitely more important than any details of manner. Posture and action are comparatively small and inconsiderable matters; but still even the sandal in the statue of Minerva should be correctly carved, and in the service of God even the smallest things should be regarded with holy care. . . .

Doubtless, faults in even so secondary a matter as posture have prejudiced men's minds, and so injured the success of what would otherwise have been most acceptable ministries. A man of more than average abilities may, by ridiculous action, be thrown into the rear rank and kept there. This is a great pity, even if there were only one such case, but it is to be feared that many are injured by the same cause. Little oddities and absurdities of mode and gesture which wise men would endeavour not to notice are not overlooked by the general public; in fact, the majority of hearers fix their eyes mainly upon those very things, while those who come to scoff observe nothing else. Persons are either disgusted or diverted by the oddities of certain preachers, or else they want an excuse for inattention, and jump at this convenient one. There can be no reason why we should help men to resist our own endeavours for their good. No minister would willingly cultivate a habit which would blunt his arrows, or drift them aside from the mark; and therefore, since these minor matters of movement, posture, and gesture may have that effect, you will give them your immediate attention. . . . It is not so much incumbent upon you to acquire right pulpit action as it is to get rid of that which is wrong. If you could be reduced to motionless dummies, it would be better than being active and even vigorous incarnations of the grotesque, as some of our brethren have been. Some men by degrees fall into a suicidal style of preaching, and it is a very rare thing indeed to see a man escape when once he has entangled himself in the meshes of an evil mannerism. No one likes to tell them of their queer antics, and so they are unaware of them; but it is surprising that their wives do not mimic them in private and laugh them out of their awkwardness. . . .

If you do not care to cultivate proper action, at least be wise enough to steer clear of that which is grotesque or affected. There is a wide range between playing the fop, curling and perfuming his locks, and permitting one's hair to hang in matted masses like the mane of a wild beast. We should never advise you to practice posture before a glass, nor to imitate great divines, nor to ape the fine gentleman; but there is no need, on the other hand, to be vulgar or absurd. Postures and attitudes are merely a small part of the dress of a discourse, and it is not in dress that the substance of the matter lies: a man in fustian is "a man for a' that," and so a sermon which is oddly delivered may be a good sermon for all that; but still, as none of you would care to wear a pauper's suit if you could procure better raiment, so you should not be so slovenly as to clothe truth like a mendicant when you might array her as a prince's daughter.

Some men are naturally very awkward in their persons and movements. I suppose we must blame what the countryman called

their "broughtens up." The rustic's gait is heavy, and his walk
is slouching. You can see that his natural habitat is a ploughed
field. . . . There is a shape and handiness, a general propriety
of form, which the human body acquires under proper drill
which seldom comes in any other manner. Drill brings a man's
shoulders down, keeps his arms from excessive swinging, expands
the chest, shows him what to do with his hands, and, in a
word, teaches a man how to walk uprightly, and to bring himself
into something like shipshape without any conscious effort to
do so, which effort would be a sure betrayal of his awkwardness.
Very spiritual people will think me trifling, but indeed I am
not. I hope the day will come when it will be looked upon as an
essential part of education to teach a young man how to carry
himself, and move without clumsiness.

*It may happen that awkward gestures arise from feeble utter-
ance, and a nervous consciousness of lack of power in that direction.*
. . . Let us wherever we see awkwardness, which is evidently
unavoidable, take little or no notice of it, and take care to
commend the brother that he does so well under the circumstances; counting it no small achievement for a divine to cover
by richness of thought and fitness of language the ungainliness
of his outer man, thus making the soul triumph over the body.
Yet should we ourselves be afflicted with any fault of manner,
let us resolve to overcome it, for it is not an impossible task. . . .

Many men are made awkward through fear. It is not the man's
nature, nor his pulpit, but his nervousness which makes a guy
of him. To some it is a display of great courage even to stand
before an audience, and to speak is an ordeal indeed: no wonder
that their attitude is constrained, for they are twitching and
trembling all over. Every nerve is in a state of excitement,
and their whole body is tremulous with fear. Especially are they
perplexed what to do with their hands, and they move them about
in a restless, irregular, meaningless manner; if they could have
them strapped down to their sides they might rejoice in the
deliverance. . . . Practice is a great remedy, and faith in God

is a still more potent cure. When the minister becomes accustomed to the people, he stands at ease because he is at ease, he feels at home, and as to his hands or legs, or any other part of his person, he has no thought: he goes to work with all his heart, and soon drops into the positions most natural to an earnest man, and these are the most appropriate. Unstudied gestures, to which you never turned your thoughts for a moment, are the very best, and the highest result of art is to banish art, and leave the man as free to be graceful as the gazelle among the mountains.

Occasional oddities of posture and gesture may arise from the difficulty of finding the next word. . . .

The posture of the minister should be natural, but his nature must not be of a coarse type; it should be graceful, educated nature. He should avoid especially those positions which are unnatural to a speaker, because they hamper the organs of utterance, or cramp his lungs. He should use his common sense, and not make it difficult for himself to speak by leaning forward over the Bible or book-board. Bending over as if you were speaking confidentially to the persons immediately below may be tolerated occasionally, but as a customary position it is as injurious as it is ungraceful. Who thinks of stooping when he speaks in the parlor? What killing work it would be to conduct a long conversation while pressing the breathing apparatus against the edge of a table! Stand upright, get a firm position, and then speak like a man. A few orators even err in the other direction, and throw their heads far back, as though they were addressing the angels, or saw a handwriting upon the ceiling. This also cometh of evil, and unless the occasional sublime apostrophe requires it, is by no means to be practised. . . .

Too many men assume a slouching attitude, lolling and sprawling as if they were lounging on the parapet of a bridge and chatting with somebody down in a boat on the river. We do not go into the pulpit to slouch about, and to look free and easy, but we go there upon very solemn business, and our posture should be such as becomes our mission. A reverent and earnest spirit will not be indicated by a sluggish lounge or a careless slouch. It is said that among the Greeks even the ploughmen and herdsmen take up graceful attitudes without any idea that they are doing so. I think it is also true of the Italians, for wherever I have seen a Roman man or woman—no matter whether they are sleeping upon the Spagna steps, or sitting upon a fragment of the baths of Caracalla, or carrying a bundle on their heads, or riding a mule—they always look like studies for an artist; yet this is the last thing which ever crosses their minds. . . . We should be foolish to imitate Greeks or Italians, except in their freedom from all imitation, but it were well if we could copy their unconstrained and natural action. There is no reason why a Christian should be a clown, and there are a great many reasons why a minister should not be a boor. . . .

Now leaving posture, let us more distinctly notice *action* in preaching; this also is a secondary and yet an important item. Our first observation shall be, *it should never be excessive.* In this matter bodily exercise profiteth little. We cannot readily judge when action is excessive, for what would be excessive in one man may be most fitting and proper in another. Different races employ different action in speaking. Two Englishmen will talk very quietly and soberly to one another compared with a couple of Frenchmen. Notice our Gallic neighbors: they talk all over, and shrug their shoulders, and move their fingers, and gesticulate most vehemently. Very well, then, we may allow a French preacher to be more demonstrative in preaching than an Englishman, because he is so in ordinary speech. I am not sure that a French divine is so as a matter of fact, but if he were so it could be accounted for by the national habit. . . . As it is with races so is it with men: some naturally gesticulate more than others, and if it be really natural, we have little fault to find. . . . Martin Luther was wont to smite with his fist at such a rate that they show, at Eisenach, a board—I think a three-inch board—which he broke while hammering at a text. The truth of the legend has been doubted, for it has been asserted that those delicate hands, which could play so charmingly upon the guitar, could hardly have been treated so roughly; but if the hand be an index of its owner's character, we can well believe it, for strength and tenderness were marvellously combined in Luther. There was much delicacy and sensitiveness about Luther's mind, yet these never diminished, but rather increased, its tremendous energy. It is by no means difficult to believe that he could smash up a plank, from the style in which he struck out at the Pope; and yet we can well imagine that he would touch the strings of his guitar with a maiden's hand; even as David could play skilfully upon the harp, and yet a bow of steel was broken by his arms. . . . Come upon consciences with a crash, and aim at breaking hard hearts by the power of the Spirit, but these require spiritual power; physical energy is not the power of God unto salvation.

It is very easy to overdo the thing so much as to make yourself appear ridiculous. . . . He who beats the air, and bawls, and raves, and stamps, means nothing: and the more a man really means what he says the less of vulgar vehemence will there be. . . . Perhaps a man is nearest to the golden mean in action when his manner excites no remark either of praise or censure, because it is so completely of a piece with the discourse that it is not regarded as a separate item at all. That action which gains conspicuous notice is probably out of proportion, and excessive. . . .

Action should be expressive and appropriate. We cannot express so much by action as by language, but one may express a few things with even greater force. Indignantly to open a door and point to it is quite as emphatic as the words, "Leave the room!" To refuse the hand when another offers his own is a very marked declaration of ill-will, and will probably create a more enduring bitterness than the severest words. A request to remain silent upon a certain subject could be well conveyed by laying the finger across the lips. A shake of the head indicates disapprobation in a very marked manner. The lifted eyebrows express surprise in a forcible style; and every part of the face has its own eloquence of pleasure and of grief. What volumes can be condensed into a shrug of the shoulders, and what mournful mischief that same shrug has wrought! Since, then, gesture and posture can speak powerfully, we must take care to let them speak correctly. It will never do to imitate the famous Grecian who cried, "O heaven!" with his finger pointing to the earth; nor to describe dying weakness by thumping upon the book-board. . . . No brother among you would, I hope, be so stupid as to clasp his hands while saying: "The gospel is not meant to be confined to a few. Its spirit is generous and expansive. It opens its arms to men of all ranks and nations." It would be an equal solecism if you were to spread forth your arms and cry, "Brethren, concentrate your energies! Gather them up, as a commander gathers his troops to the royal standard in the day of battle." Now, put the gestures into their proper places and see how diffusion may be expressed by the opened arms, and concentration by the united hands.

Action and tone together may absolutely contradict the meaning of the words. . . . What force may the language of Scripture lose through the preacher's ill delivery! . . . Too many speakers appear to have taken lessons from Bendigo, or some other professor of the noble art of self-defence, for they hold their fists as if they were ready for a round. It is not pleasant to watch brethren preaching the gospel of peace in that pugnacious style; yet it is by no means rare to hear of an evangelist preaching a free Christ with a clinched fist. It is amusing to see them putting themselves into an attitude and saying, "Come unto me," and then, with a revolution of both fists, "and I will give you—rest." Better not suggest such ridiculous ideas, but they have been suggested more than once by men who earnestly desired above all things to make their hearers think of better things. . . .

Those awkward hands, if once brought into subjection, become our best allies. We can talk with them almost as well as with our tongues, and make a sort of silent music with them which will add to the charm of our words. If you have never read Sir Charles Bell on "The Hand," be sure to do so, and note well the following passage:

> We must not omit to speak of the hand as an instrument of expression. Formal dissertations have been written on this. But were we constrained to seek authorities, we might take the great painters in evidence, since by the position of the hands, in conformity with the figure, they have expressed every sentiment. Who, for example, can deny the eloquence of the hands in the Magdalens of Guidio; their expression in the cartoons of Raphael, or in "The Last Supper," by Leonardo da Vinci? We see there expressed all that Quinctilian says the hand is capable of expressing. "For other parts of the body," says he, "assist the speaker, but these, I may say, speak themselves. By them we ask, we promise, we invoke, we dismiss, we threaten, we entreat, we deprecate, we express fear, joy, grief, our doubts, our assent, our penitence: we show moderation, or profusion; we mark number and time."

The face, and especially the eyes, will play a very important part in all appropriate action. It is very unfortunate when ministers cannot look at their people. It is singular to hear them pleading with persons whom they do not see. They are entreating them to look to Jesus upon the cross! You wonder where the sinners are. The preacher's eyes are turned upon his book, or up to the ceiling, or into empty space. It seems to me that you *must* fix your eyes upon the people when you come to exhortation. There are parts of a sermon in which the sublimity of the doctrine may call for the uplifted gaze, and there are other portions which may allow the eyes to wander as you will; but when pleading time has come, it will be inappropriate to look anywhere but to the persons addressed. . . .

The man who would be perfect in posture and gesture must regulate his whole frame, for in one case a man's most suitable action will be that of his head, and in another that of his hands, and in a third that of his trunk alone. . . .

Let the gesture tally with the words, and be a sort of running commentary and practical exegesis upon what you are saying. . . .

We have said that gesture should not be excessive, and secondly that it should be appropriate: now comes the third canon, *action and gesture should never be grotesque.* This is plain enough, and I shall not enforce it except by giving specimens of the grotesque, that you may not only avoid the identical instances, but all of a similar character. . . .

The first species of grotesque action may be named *the stiff;* and this is very common. Men who exhibit this horror appear to have no bend in their bodies and to be rigid about the joints. The arms and legs are moved as if they were upon iron hinges, and were made of exceedingly hard metal. A wooden anatomical doll, such as artists use, might well represent their limbs so straight and stiff, but it would fail to show the jerks with which those limbs are thrown up and down. There is nothing round in the action of these brethren; everything is angular, sharp, mechanical. . . . Surely any sort of physical exercise might help to cure this mischief, which in some living preachers almost amounts to a deformity. . . . It is certain that much good speech is bereft of power through the awkward deportment of the speaker. . . .

The second form of the grotesque is not unlike the first, and may be best distinguished as *the regular and mechanical.* Men in this case move as if they were not living beings possessed of will and intellect, but as if they were automatons formed to go through prescribed movements at precise intervals. At the back of the [Metropolitan] Tabernacle a cottager has placed over his house a kind of vane, in the form of a little soldier, which lifts first one arm and then the other with rather an important air. It has made me smile many a time by irresistibly reminding me of——, who alternately jerks each arm, or if he allows one arm to lie still, chops the other up and down as persistently as if he were moved by wind or by clockwork. Up and down, up and down the hand goes, turning neither to the right nor to the left, every other movement being utterly abjured, except this one

monotonous ascent and descent. It matters little how unobjection-
able a movement may be in itself, it will become intolerable if
it be continued without variation. . . .

Now, the jerking, sawing, pumping, and pounding might all
be endurable and even appropriate if they were blended; but the
perpetual iteration of any one becomes wearisome and unmeaning.
The figures of mandarins in a teashop, continually nodding their
heads, and the ladies in wax which revolve with uniform motions
in the hairdresser's window, are not fit models for men who have
before them the earnest work of winning men to grace and virtue.
You ought to be so true, so real, so deeply in earnest, that mere
mechanical movements will be impossible to you, and everything
about you will betoken life, energy, concentrated faculty, and
intense zeal.

Another method of the grotesque may be correctly called *the
laborious*. Certain brethren will never fail in their ministry from
want of physical exertion: when they mount the rostrum they
mean hard work, and before long they puff and blow at it as
if they were labourers working by the piece. They enter upon a
sermon with the resolve to storm their way through it, and carry
all before them: the kingdom of heaven suffereth violence
with them in another sense besides that which is intended in
Scripture. . . .

Laborious action is frequently a relic of the preacher's trade
in former days: as an old hunter cannot quite forget the hounds,
so the good man cannot shake off the habits of the shop. One
brother who has been a wheelwright always preaches as if he
were making wheels. If you understand the art of wheelwrighting,
you can see most of the processes illustrated during one of his
liveliest discourses. You can detect the engineer in another friend,
the cooper in a third, and the grocer with his scales in a fourth.
A brother who has been a butcher is pretty sure to show us
how to knock down a bullock when he gets at all argumentative.
As I have watched the discourse proceed from strength to strength,
and the preacher has warmed to his work, I have thought to

myself, "Here comes the pole-axe, there goes the fat ox, down falls the prize bullock."

Now, these reminiscences of former occupations are never very blameworthy, and are at all times less obnoxious than the altogether inexcusable awkwardnesses of gentlemen who from their youth up have dwelt in the halls of learning. These will sometimes labour quite as much, but with far less likeness to useful occupations; they beat the air and work hard at doing nothing. Gentlemen from the universities are frequently more hideous in their action than commonplace people; perhaps their education may have deprived them of confidence, and made them all the more fidgety and awkward. . . .

But here we must not overlook another laborious orator who is in our mind's eye. We will name him the perpetual-motion preacher, who is all action, and lifts his finger, or waves his hand, or strikes his palm at every word. He is never at rest for a moment. So eager is he to be emphatic that he effectually defeats his object, for where every word is emphasized by a gesture nothing whatever is emphatic. This brother takes off men's minds from his words to his movement: the eye actually carries the thoughts away from the ear, and so a second time the preacher's end is missed. This continual motion greatly agitates some hearers, and gives them the fidgets, and no wonder, for who can endure to see such incessant patting, and pointing, and waving? In action, as well as everything else, "Let your moderation be known unto all men."

Thus I have mentioned three species of the grotesque—the stiff, the mechanical, and the laborious—and I have also glanced at the laxly dignified. I will close the list by mentioning two others. There is *the martial,* which also sufficiently borders on the grotesque to be placed in this category. Some preachers appear to be fighting the good fight of faith every time they stand before a congregation. They put themselves into a fencing attitude, and either stand on guard against an imaginary foe, or else assault the unseen adversary with stern determination. . . .

The last singularity of action which I shall place under this head is *the ill-timed*. In this case the hands do not keep time with the lips. The good brother is a little behindhand with his action, and therefore the whole operation is out of order. You cannot at first make the man out at all: he appears to chop and thump without rhyme or reason, but at last you perceive that his present action is quite appropriate to what he said a few seconds before. The effect is strange to the last degree. It puzzles those who do not possess the key to it, and when fully understood it loses none of its oddness. . . .

I must confess, however, that I do not think so badly of any of these singularities, or all of them put together, as I do of *the superfine* style, which is utterly despicable and abominable. It is worse than the commonly vulgar, for it is the very essence of vulgarity, flavoured with affectations and airs of gentility. . . .

"Rustic coarseness" is quite refreshing after one has been wearied with inane primness. Well did Cicero exhort orators to adopt their gestures rather from the camp or the wrestling ring than from the dancers with their effeminate niceties. Manliness must never be sacrificed to elegance. Our working classes will never be brought even to consider the truth of Christianity by teachers who are starched and fine. The British artisan admires manliness, and prefers to lend his ear to one who speaks in a hearty and natural style: indeed, working men of all nations are more likely to be struck by a brave negligence than by a foppish attention to personal appearances. . . .

All foreign matters of attitude, tone, or dress are barricades between us and the people; we must talk like men if we would win men. . . .

God save us from fine deportment and genteel propriety, if these are to keep the masses in alienation from the public worship of God. In our own day this sickening affectation is, we hope, far more rare, but it still survives. . . . Slovenliness of any sort is to be avoided in a minister, but manliness more often falls into this fault than into the other effeminate vice; therefore shun most heartily this worst error. Cowper says, "In my soul I loathe all affectation," and so does every sensible man. All tricks and stage effects are unbearable when the message of the Lord is to be delivered. Better a ragged dress and rugged speech, with artless, honest manner, than clerical foppery. Better far to violate every canon of gracefulness than to be a mere performer, a consummate actor, a player upon a religious stage. . . .

Our last rule is one which sums up all the others: *be natural in your action.* Shun the very appearance of studied gesture. Art is cold, only nature is warm; let grace keep you clear of all seeming, and in every action, and in every place, be truthful, even if you should be considered rough and uncultivated. Your mannerism must always be your own, it must never be a polished lie—and what is the aping of gentility, the simulation of passion, the feigning of emotion, or the mimicry of another man's mode of delivery but a practical lie.

> Therefore, avaunt all attitude and stare,
> And start theatric, practised at the glass!

Our object is to remove the excrescences of uncouth nature, not to produce artificiality and affectation; we would prune the tree and by no means clip it into a set form. . . .

You are not sent of God to court smiles but to win souls; your teacher is not the dancing master, but the Holy Spirit, and your pulpit manner is only worth a moment's thought because it may hinder your success by causing people to make remarks about the preacher when you want all their thoughts for the subject. If the best action had this effect I would urge you to forswear it, and if the worst gestures would prevent such a result I would advise you to practise them. All that I aim at is to advocate quiet, graceful, natural movements, because they are the least likely to be observed. The whole business of delivery should be *one;* everything should harmonize; the thought, the spirit, the language, the tone, and the action should be all of a piece, and the whole should be, not for the winning of honor to ourselves, but for the glory of God and the good of men; if it be so there is no fear of your violating the rule as to being natural, for it will not occur to you to be otherwise. Yet have I one fear, and it is this: you may fall into a foolish imitation of some admired minister, and this will to some extent put you off from the right track. Each man's action should suit himself and grow out of his own personality. . . . A rumor is current that there are one or two young Spurgeons about, but if so I hope that the reference is to my own sons, who have a right to the name by birth. If any of you become mere copyists of me I shall regard you as thorns in the flesh, and rank you among those whom Paul says "we suffer gladly." Yet it has been wisely said that every beginner must of necessity be for a time a copyist; the artist follows his master while as yet he has barely acquired the elements of the art, and perhaps for life he remains a painter of the school to which he at first attached himself; but as he becomes proficient he develops his own individuality, grows into a painter with a style of his own, and is all the better and none the worse for having been in his earliest days content to sit at a master's feet. It is of necessity the same in oratory, and therefore it may be too much to say never copy anyone, but it may be better to exhort you to imitate the best action you can find, in order that your own style during its formation may be rightly moulded. Correct the influence of any one man by what you see of excellence in others; but still create a manner of your own. Slavish imitation is the practice of an ape, but to follow another where he leads aright, *and there only,* is the wisdom of a prudent man. Still never let a natural originality be missed by your imitating the best models of antiquity, or the most esteemed among the moderns.

In conclusion, do not allow my criticisms upon various grotesque postures and movements to haunt you in the pulpit; better perpetrate them all than be in fear, for this would make you cramped and awkward. Dash at it whether you blunder or no. A few mistakes in this matter will not be half so bad as being nervous. It may be that what would be eccentric in another may be most proper in *you;* therefore take no man's dictum as applicable to every case, or to your own. . . .

Be yourself; even if you should be ungainly and awkward, be yourself. Your own clothes, though they be homespun, will fit you better than another man's, though made of the best broadcloth; you may follow your tutor's style of dress if you like, but do not borrow his coat; be content to wear one of your own. Above all, be so full of matter, so fervent, and so gracious that the people will little care how you hand out the word; for if they perceive that it is fresh from heaven, and find it sweet and abundant, they will pay little regard to the basket in which you bring it to them. Let them, if they please, say that your bodily presence is weak, but pray that they may confess that your testimony is weighty and powerful. Commend yourself to every man's conscience in the sight of God, and then the mere mint and anise of posture will seldom be taken into account.

11

Open-Air Preaching

... It can be argued, with small fear of refutation, that open-air preaching is as old as preaching itself. We are at full liberty to believe that Enoch, the seventh from Adam, when he prophesied, asked for no better pulpit than the hillside, and that Noah, as a preacher of righteousness, was willing to reason with his contemporaries in the shipyard wherein his marvellous ark was builded. Certainly, Moses and Joshua found their most convenient place for addressing vast assemblies beneath the un-pillared arch of heaven. Samuel closed a sermon in the field at Gilgal amid thunder and rain, by which the Lord rebuked the people and drove them to their knees. Elijah stood on Carmel, and challenged the vacillating nation with "How long halt ye between two opinions?" Jonah, whose spirit was somewhat similar, lifted up his cry of warning in the streets of Nineveh, and in all her places of concourse gave forth the warning utterance, "Yet forty days and Nineveh shall be overthrown!" To hear Ezra and Nehemiah "all the people gathered themselves together as one man into the street that was before the water gate." Indeed, we find examples of open-air preaching everywhere around us in the records of the Old Testament.

It may suffice us, however, to go back as far as the origin of our own holy faith, and there we hear the forerunner of the Saviour crying in the wilderness and lifting up his voice from the river's bank. Our Lord himself, who is yet more our pattern, delivered the larger proportion of his sermons on the mountain's side, or by the seashore or in the streets. Our Lord was to all intents and purposes an open-air preacher. He did not remain

162

silent in the synagogue, but he was equally at home in the field. We have no discourse of his on record delivered in the chapel royal, but we have the sermon on the mount, and the sermon in the plain; so that the very earliest and most divine kind of preaching was practised out-of-doors by him who spake as never man spake.

There were gatherings of his disciples after his decease, within walls, especially that in the upper room; but the preaching was even then most frequently in the court of the temple, or in such other open spaces as were available. The notion of holy places and consecrated meetinghouses had not occurred to them as Christians; they preached in the temple because it was the chief place of concourse, but with equal earnestness "in every house they ceased not to teach and preach Jesus Christ.". . .

As the Dark Ages lowered, the best preachers of the gradually declining church were also preachers in the open air; as were also those itinerant friars and great founders of religious orders who kept alive such piety as remained. We hear of Berthold, of Ratisbon, with audiences of sixty or a hundred thousand, in a field near Glatz in Bohemia. There were also Bernards, and Bernardines, and Anthonys, and Thomases of great fame as travelling preachers, of whom we cannot find time to speak particularly. . . .

When Antichrist had commenced its more universal sway, the reformers before the Reformation were full often open-air preachers, as, for instance, Arnold of Brescia, who denounced papal usurpations at the very gates of the Vatican.

It would be very easy to prove that revivals of religion have usually been accompanied, if not caused, by a considerable amount of preaching out-of-doors, or in unusual places. The first avowed preaching of Protestant doctrine was almost necessarily in the open air, or in buildings which were not dedicated to worship, for these were in the hands of the papacy. True, Wycliffe for a while preached the gospel in the church at Lutterworth; Huss, and Jerome, and Savonarola for a time delivered semi-gospel addresses in connection with the ecclesiastical arrangements around them; but when they began more fully to know and proclaim the gospel, they were driven to find other platforms. The Reformation when yet a babe was like the newborn Christ, and had nowhere to lay its head, but a company of men comparable to the heavenly host proclaimed it under the open heavens, where shepherds and common people heard them gladly. Throughout England we have several trees remaining called "gospel oaks." There is one spot on the other side of the Thames known by the name of "Gospel Oak," and I have myself preached at Addlestone, in Surrey, under the far-spreading boughs of an ancient oak beneath which John Knox is said to have proclaimed the gospel during his sojourn in England. Full many a wild moor, and lone hillside, and secret spot in the forest have been consecrated in the same fashion, and traditions still linger over caves, and dells, and hilltops, where of old time the bands of the faithful met to hear the word of the Lord. Nor was it alone in solitary places that in days of yore the voice of the preacher was heard, for scarcely is there a market cross which has not served as a pulpit for itinerant gospellers. . . . To hear these heralds of the cross the country people flocked in great numbers, and the soldiers mingled with the crowd, ready to defend the preachers with their swords if any offered to molest them. . . .

In Germany and other continental countries the Reformation was greatly aided by the sermons delivered to the masses out-of-doors. We read of Lutheran preachers perambulating the country proclaiming the new doctrine to crowds in the market places, and burial grounds, and also on mountains and in meadows. . . .

From Dr. Wylie's *History of Protestantism* I borrow the following:

It is said that the first field-preaching in the Netherlands took place on the 14th of June, 1566, and was held in the neighborhood of Ghent. The preacher was Herman Modet, who had formerly been a monk, but was now the reformed pastor at Oudenard. . . . .

The second great field-preaching took place on the 23rd of July following, the people assembling in a large meadow in the vicinity of Ghent. The "Word" was precious in those days, and the people, eagerly thirsting to hear it, prepared to remain two days consecutively on the ground. Their arrangements more resembled an army pitching their camp than a peaceful multitude assembled for worship. Around the worshippers was a wall of barricades in the shape of carts and wagons. Sentinels were placed at all the entrances. A rude pulpit of planks was hastily run up and placed aloft on a cart. Modet was preacher, and around him were many thousands of persons, who listened with their pikes, hatchets, and guns lying by their sides, ready to be grasped on a sign from the sentinels who kept watch all around the assembly. In front of the entrances were erected stalls, whereat pedlars offered prohibited books to all who wished to buy. Along the roads running into the country were stationed certain persons, whose office it was to bid the casual passenger turn in and hear the gospel. . . . When the services were finished, the multitude would repair to other districts, where they encamped after the same fashion, and remained for the same space of time, and so passed through the whole of West Flanders. At these conventicles the Psalms of David, which had been translated into Low Dutch from the version of Clement Marot and Theodore Beza, were always sung. The odes of the Hebrew king, pealed forth by from five to ten thousand voices, and borne by the breeze over the woods and meadows, might be heard at great distances, arresting the ploughman as he turned the furrow, or the traveller as he pursued his way, and making him stop and wonder whence the ministrelsy proceeded.

. . . Where would the Reformation have been if its great preachers had confined themselves to churches and cathedrals? How would the common people have become indoctrinated with the gospel had it not been for those far-wandering evangelists, the colporteurs, and those daring innovators who found a pulpit on every heap of stones and an audience chamber in every open space near the abodes of men? . . .

We must not forget the regular out-of-doors ministry at Paul's Cross, under the eaves of the old cathedral. This was a famous institution, and enabled the notable preachers of the times to be heard by the citizens in great numbers. Kings and princes did not disdain to sit in the gallery built upon the cathedral wall, and listen to the preacher for the day. . . .

What the world would have been if there had not been preaching outside of walls, and beneath a more glorious roof than these rafters of fir, I am sure I cannot guess. It was a brave day for England when Whitefield began field preaching. When Wesley stood and preached a sermon on his father's grave, at Epworth, because the parish priest would not allow him admission within the (so-called) sacred edifice, Mr. Wesley writes: "I am well assured that I did far more good to my Lincolnshire parishioners by preaching three days on my father's tomb than I did by preaching three years in his pulpit." The same might be said of all the open-air preaching which followed, as compared with the regular discourses withindoors. "The thought of preaching in the open air was suggested to Whitefield by a crowd of a thousand people unable to gain admission to Bermondsey church, where he preached one Sunday afternoon. He met with no encouragement when he mentioned it to some of his friends; they thought it was a 'mad notion.' ". . . The chancellor of the diocese having put impediments in the way of Whitefield's preaching in the churches of Bristol on behalf of his Orphanhouse, he went to preach to the colliers at Kingswood "for the first time on a Saturday afternoon, taking his stand on Hannan Mount. He spoke on Matt. 5:1-3 to as many as came to hear; upwards of two hundred attended.". . . On the following day the journal relates:

> All the church doors being now shut, and if open not able to contain half that came to hear, at three in the afternoon I went to Kingswood among the colliers. . . . Hundreds and hundreds of them were soon brought under deep convictions, which (as the event proved) happily ended in a sound and thorough conversion. The change was visible to all, though numbers chose to impute it to anything rather than the finger of God. As the scene was quite new, and I had just begun to be an extempore preacher, it often occasioned many inward conflicts. Sometimes, when twenty thou-

sand people were before me, I had not, in my own apprehension, a word to say, either to God or them. But I was never totally deserted, and frequently knew by happy experience what our Lord meant when he said, "Out of his belly shall flow rivers of living water." The open firmament above me, the prospect of the adjacent fields, with the sight of thousands and thousands, some in coaches, some on horseback, and some on the trees, and, at times, all affected and drenched in tears together, to which sometimes was added the solemnity of the approaching evening, was almost too much for, and quite overcame, me.

Wesley writes in his journal:

Saturday, 31 (March, 1731). In the evening I reached Bristol, and met Mr. Whitefield there. I could scarce reconcile myself at first to this strange way of preaching in the fields, of which he set me an example on Sunday; having been all my life (till very lately) so tenacious of every point relating to decency and order, that I should have thought the saving of souls almost a sin, if it had not been done in a church.

Such were the feelings of a man who in after life became one of the greatest open-air preachers that ever lived! . . .

Glorious were those great gatherings in fields and commons which lasted throughout the long period in which Wesley and Whitefield blest our nation. Field-preaching was the wild note of the birds singing in the trees, in testimony that the true springtime of religion had come. Birds in cages may sing more sweetly, perhaps, but their music is not so natural, nor so sure a pledge of the coming summer. It was a blessed day when Methodists and others began to proclaim Jesus in the open air; then were the gates of hell shaken, and the captives of the devil set free by hundreds and by thousands. . . .

The great benefit of open-air preaching is that we get so many newcomers to hear the gospel who otherwise would never hear it. The gospel command is, "Go ye into all the world and preach the gospel to every creature," but it is so little obeyed that one would imagine that it ran thus: "Go into your own place of worship and preach the gospel to the few creatures who will come inside." "Go ye into the highways and hedges and compel them to come in," albeit it constitutes part of a parable, is worthy to be taken very literally, and in so doing its meaning will be best carried out. We ought actually to go into the streets and lanes and highways, for there are lurkers in the hedges, tramps on the highways, streetwalkers, and lane-haunters whom we shall never reach unless we pursue them into their own domains. Sportsmen must not stop at home and wait for the birds to come and be shot at, neither must fishermen throw their nets inside their boats and hope to take many fish. Traders *go* to the markets, they follow their customers and go out after business if it will not come to them; and so must we. Some of our brethren are prosing on and on, to empty pews and musty hassocks, while they might be conferring lasting benefit upon hundreds by quitting the old walls for a while, and seeking living stones for Jesus. Let them come out of Rehoboth and find room at the street corner, let them leave Salem and seek the peace of neglected souls, let them dream no longer at Bethel, but make an open space to be none other than the house of God, let them come down from Mount Zion, and up from Enon, and even away from Trinity, and St. Agnes, and St. Michael-and-All-Angels, and St. Margaret-Pattens, and St. Vedast, and St. Ethelburga, and all the rest of them, and try to find new saints among the sinners who are perishing for lack of knowledge.

I have known street preaching in London remarkably blest to persons whose character and condition would quite preclude their having been found in a place of worship. I know, for instance, a Jewish friend who, on coming from Poland, understood nothing whatever of the English language. In going about the streets on the Sunday he noticed the numerous groups listening to earnest speakers. He had never seen such a thing in his own country, where the Russian police would be alarmed if groups were seen in conversation, and he was therefore all the more interested. As he acquired a little English he became more and more constant in his attendance upon street speakers; indeed, it

was very much with the view of learning the language that he
listened at the first. I am afraid that the English which he acquired was not of the very best, which judgment I form as much
from what I have heard of open-air oratory as from having
listened to our Jewish friend himself, whose theology is better
than his English. However, that "Israelite indeed" has always
reason to commend the street preachers. How many other strangers
and foreigners may, by the same instrumentality, have become
fellow citizens with the saints and of the household of God we
cannot tell. Romanists also are met with in this manner more
frequently than some would suppose. . . . Infidels, also, are constantly yielding to the word of the Lord thus brought home to
them. The street evangelist, moreover, wins attention from those
eccentric people whose religion can neither be described nor
imagined. Such people hate the very sight of our churches and
meetinghouses, but will stand in a crowd to hear what is said,
and are often most impressed when they affect the greatest
contempt. . . .

Jonah in the streets of Nineveh was heard by multitudes who
would never have known of his existence if he had hired a hall;
John the Baptist by the Jordan awakened an interest which would
never have been aroused had he kept to the synagogue; and those
who went from city to city proclaiming everywhere the word of
the Lord Jesus would never have turned the world upside down if
they had felt it needful to confine themselves to iron rooms
adorned with the orthodox announcement, "The gospel of the
grace of God will (D.V.) be preached here next Lord's Day
evening."

I am quite sure, too, that if we could persuade our friends
in the country to come out a good many times in the year and
hold a service in a meadow, or in a shady grove, or on the hillside, or in a garden, or on a common, *it would be all the better
for the usual hearers.* The mere novelty of the place would
freshen their interest, and wake them up. The slight change of
scene would have a wonderful effect upon the more somnolent. . . .

After sitting a certain number of years in the same spot, where the pews, pulpit, galleries, and all things else are always the same, except that they get a little dirtier and dingier every week, where everybody occupies the same position for ever and for evermore, and the minister's face, voice, tone are much the same from January to December—you get to feel the holy quiet of the scene and listen to what is going on as though it were addressed to "the dull cold ear of death." As a miller hears his wheels as though he did not hear them, or a stoker scarcely notices the clatter of his engine after enduring it for a little time, or as a dweller in London never notices the ceaseless grind of the traffic, so do many members of our congregations become insensible to the most earnest addresses, and accept them as a matter of course. The preaching and the rest of it get to be so usual that they might as well not be at all. Hence a change of place might be useful, it might prevent monotony, shake up indifference, suggest thought, and in a thousand ways promote attention, and give new hope of doing good. A great fire which should burn some of our chapels to the ground might not be the greatest calamity which had ever occurred, if it only aroused some of those rivals of the seven sleepers of Ephesus who will never be moved so long as the old house and the old pews hold together. . . .

If I had my choice of a pitch for preaching, I should prefer to front a rising ground, or an open spot bounded at some little distance by a wall. Of course there must be sufficient space to allow of the congregation's assembling between the pulpit and the bounding object in front, but I like to see an end, and not to shout into boundless space. . . .

My friend Mr. Abraham once produced for me a grand cathedral in Oxfordshire. The remains of it are still called "Spurgeon's Tabernacle," and may be seen near Minster Lovell, in the form of a quadrilateral of oaks. Originally it was the *beau ideal* of a preaching place, for it was a cleared spot in the thick forest of Witchwood, and was reached by roads cut through the dense underwood.

. . . Here was a truly magnificent cathedral, with pillars and arches: a temple not made with hands, of which we might truly say,

> Father, thy hand
> Hath reared these venerable columns, thou
> Didst weave this verdant roof.

. . . Oh, sirs, it was grand indeed, to worship thus beneath the vaulted firmament, beyond the sound of city hum, where all around ministered to quiet fellowship with God. . . . I am still glad, like the Druids, to worship among the oak trees. This year a dove had built her nest just above my head, and she continued flying to and fro to feed her young, while the sermon proceeded. Why not? Where should she be more at home than where the Lord of Love and Prince of Peace was adored? It is true my arched cathedral is not waterproof, and other showers besides those of grace will descend upon the congregation, but this has its advantages, for it makes us the more grateful when the day is propitious, and the very precariousness of the weather excites a large amount of earnest prayer. . . .

Look well to the ground you select, that it is not swampy. I never like to see a man slip up to his knees in mire while I am preaching. . . . Always inconvenience yourself rather than your audience: your Master would have done so. Even in the streets of London a concern for the convenience of your hearers is one of the things which conciliates a crowd more than anything.

Avoid as your worst enemy the neighborhood of the Normandy poplar. These trees cause a perpetual hissing and rustling sound, almost like the noise of the sea. Every leaf of certain kinds of poplar is in perpetual motion, like the tongue of Talkative. The noise may not seem very loud, but it will drown the best of voices. "The sound of a going in the tops of the mulberry trees" is all very well, but keep clear of the noise of poplars and some other trees, or you will suffer for it. . . .

Practised preachers do not care to have the sun directly in their faces if they can help it, neither do they wish their hearers

to be distressed in like manner, and therefore they take this
item into consideration when arranging for a service. In London
we do not see that luminary often enough to be much concerned upon this point. Do not try to preach against the wind,
for it is an idle attempt. . . .

Get the people to *listen* outside that they may by-and-by
worship inside. You want no pulpit; a chair will do, or the
curb of the road. The less formality the better, and if you begin
by merely talking to the two or three around you and make no
pretence of sermonizing, you will do well. More good may be
done by personal talk to one than by a rhetorical address to fifty.
Do not purposely interfere with the thoroughfare, but if the crowd
should accumulate do not hasten away in sheer fright: the policeman will let you know soon enough. You are most wanted, however, where you will be in no danger of impeding passers-by,
but far more likely to be in danger yourself—I refer to those
central courts and blind alleys in our great cities which lie out
of the route of decency, and are known to nobody but the police,
and to them principally through bruises and wounds. Talk of
discovering the interior of Africa! We need explorers for Frying-
pan Alley and Emerald-Island Court; the Arctic regions are
well-nigh as accessible as Dobinson's Rents and Jack Ketch's
Warren. Heroes of the cross—here is a field for you more glorious
than the Cid ever beheld when with his brave right arm he smote
the paynim hosts. "Who will bring me into the strong city? Who
will lead me into Edom?" Who will enable us to win these slums
and dens for Jesus? Who can do it but the Lord? Soldiers of
Christ who venture into these regions must expect a revival of
the practices of the good old times, so far as brickbats are concerned, and I have known a flowerpot fall accidentally from an
upper window in a remarkably slanting direction. Still, if we
are born to be drowned we shall not be killed by flowerpots. . . .

I am somewhat pleased when I occasionally hear of a brother's
being locked up by the police, for it does him good, and it does
the people good also. It is a fine sight to see the minister of

the gospel marched off by the servant of the law! It excites sympathy for him, and the next step is sympathy for his message. Many who felt no interest in him before are eager to hear him when he is ordered to leave off, and still more so when he is taken to the station. The vilest of mankind respect a man who gets into trouble in order to do them good, and if they see unfair opposition excited they grow quite zealous in the man's defence.

I am persuaded that the more of open-air preaching there is in London the better. If it should become a nuisance to some it will be a blessing to others, if properly conducted. If it be the gospel which is spoken, and if the spirit of the preacher be one of love and truth, the results cannot be doubted: the bread cast upon the waters must be found again after many days. The gospel must, however, be preached in a manner worth the hearing, for mere noisemaking is an evil rather than a benefit. . . .

As to *style in preaching out-of-doors,* it should certainly be very different from much of that which prevails within, and perhaps if a speaker were to acquire a style adapted to a street audience, he would be wise to bring it indoors with him. A great deal of sermonizing may be defined as saying nothing at extreme length; but out-of-doors, verbosity is not admired: you must say something more, or your hearers will let you know. . . .

In the street, a man must keep himself alive, and use many illustrations and anecdotes, and sprinkle a quaint remark here and there. To dwell long on a point will never do. Reasoning must be brief, clear, and soon done with. The discourse must not be laboured or involved, neither must the second head depend upon the first, for the audience is a changing one, and each point must be complete in itself. . . .

Short sentences of words and short passages of thought are needed for out-of-doors. Long paragraphs and long arguments had better be reserved for other occasions. In quiet country crowds there is much force in an eloquent silence, now and then

interjected; it gives people time to breathe, and also to reflect.
Do not, however, attempt this in a London street; you must go
ahead, or someone else may run off with your congregation.
In a regular field sermon, pauses are very effective, and are
useful in several ways, both to speaker and listeners, but to
a passing company who are not inclined for anything like worship,
quick, short, sharp address is most adapted.

In the streets a man must from beginning to end be intense,
and for that very reason he must be condensed and concentrated in
his thought and utterance. . . . Shams and shows will have no
mercy from a street gathering. But have something to say, look
them in the face, say what you mean, put it plainly, boldly,
earnestly, courteously, and they will hear you. Never speak
against time or for the sake of hearing your own voice, or you
will obtain some information about your personal appearance
or manner of oratory which will probably be more true than
pleasing. "Crikey," says one, "wouldn't he do for an undertaker!
He'd make 'em weep." This was a compliment paid to a melancholy brother whose tone is peculiarly funereal. . . . The very
best speaker must be prepared to take his share of street wit,
and to return it if need be; but primness, demureness, formality,
sanctimonious longwindedness and the affection of superiority
actually invite offensive pleasantries, and to a considerable extent
deserve them. . . . A very great man in his own esteem will provoke immediate opposition, and the affectation of supernatural
saintliness will have the same effect. The less you are like a parson
the more likely you are to be heard; and, if you are known to be
a minister, the more you show yourself to be a man the better. . . .

The *action* of the street preacher should be of the very best.
It should be purely natural and unconstrained. No speaker should
stand up in the street in a grotesque manner, or he will weaken
himself and invite attack. . . . Some good men are grotesque
by nature, and others take great pains to make themselves so.
The wicked Londoners say, "What a cure!" I only wish I knew
of a cure for the evil. . . .

It will be very desirable to speak so as to be heard, but there is no use in incessant bawling. The best street preaching is not that which is done at the top of your voice, for it must be impossible to lay the proper emphasis upon telling passages when all along you are shouting with all your might. . . . A quiet, penetrating, conversational style would seem to be the most telling. Men do not bawl and halloa when they are pleading in deepest earnestness; they have generally at such times less wind and a little more rain: less rant and a few more tears. . . . Be wise now, therefore, O ye who would succeed in declaring your Master's message among the multitude, and use your voices as common sense would dictate.

In a tract published by that excellent society The Open-Air Mission, I notice the following:

QUALIFICATIONS FOR OPEN-AIR PREACHERS

1. A good voice.
2. Naturalness of manner.
3. Self-possession.
4. A good knowledge of Scripture and of common things.
5. Ability to adapt himself to any congregation.
6. Good illustrative powers.
7. Zeal, prudence, and common sense.
8. A large, loving heart.
9. Sincere belief in all he says.
10. Entire dependence on the Holy Spirit for success.
11. A close walk with God by prayer.
12. A consistent walk before men by a holy life.

If any man has all these qualifications, the Queen had better make a bishop of him at once, yet there is none of these qualities which could well be dispensed with. . . .

Certain characters, if they find that preaching is going on, will interrupt by hook or by crook. They go on purpose, and if answered once and again they still persevere. One constant rule is to be always courteous and good tempered, for if you become cross or angry it is all over with you. Another rule is to keep

to your subject, and never be drawn into side issues. Preach Christ
or nothing: don't dispute or discuss except with your eye on the
cross. If driven off for a moment always be on the watch to get
back to your sole topic. Tell them the old, old story, and if they
will not hear *that,* move on. Yet be adroit, and take them with
guile. Seek the one object by many roads. A little mother wit is
often the best resource and will work wonders with a crowd.
Bonhommie is the next best thing on such occasions. . . .

Christ is to be preached whether men will believe in him or
no. Our own experience of his power to save will be our best
reasoning, and earnestness our best rhetoric. The occasion will
frequently suggest the fittest thing to say, and we may also fall
back on the Holy Spirit, who will teach us in the selfsame hour
what we shall speak. The open-air speaker's calling is as honorable as it is arduous, as useful as it is laborious. God alone can
sustain you in it, but with him at your side you will have nothing
to fear. If ten thousand rebels were before you and a legion of
devils in every one of them, you need not tremble. More is he
that is for you than all they that be against you. . . .

> "By all hell's host withstood,
>   We all hell's host o'erthrow;
> And conquering them through Jesus' blood,
>   We still to conquer go."

12

The Faculty of Impromptu Speech

. . We are now to speak of extemporaneous speech in its truest and most thorough form—speech impromptu, without special preparation, without notes or immediate forethought.

Our first observation shall be that *we would not recommend any man to attempt preaching in this style as a general rule.* If he did so, he would succeed, we think, most certainly, in producing a vacuum in his meetinghouse; his gifts of dispersion would be clearly manifested. Unstudied thoughts coming from the mind without previous research, without the subjects in hand having been investigated at all, must be of a very inferior quality even from the most superior men; and as none of us would have the effrontery to glorify ourselves as men of genius or wonders of erudition, I fear that our unpremeditated thoughts upon most subjects would not be remarkably worthy of attention. Churches are not to be held together except by an instructive ministry; a mere filling up of time with oratory will not suffice. Everywhere men ask to be fed, really fed. Those newfangled religionists, whose public worship consists of the prelections of any brother who chooses to jump up and talk, notwithstanding their flattering inducements to the ignorant and garrulous, usually dwindle away, and die out; because even men with the most violently crotchety views, who conceive it to be the mind of the Spirit that every member of the body should be a mouth, soon grow impatient of hearing other people's nonsense, though de-lighted to dispense their own. . . . The method of unprepared ministrations is practically a failure, and theoretically unsound. The Holy Spirit has made no promise to supply spiritual food to the saints by an impromptu ministry. He will never do for us what we can do for ourselves. If we can study, and do not, if we can have a studious ministry and will not, we have no right to call in a divine agent to make up the deficits of our idleness or eccentricity. The God of providence has promised to feed his people with temporal food; but if we came together to a banquet, and no one had prepared a single dish, because all had faith in the Lord that food would be given in the selfsame hour, the festival would not be eminently satisfactory, but folly would be rebuked by hunger. . . . All sermons ought to be well considered and prepared by the preacher; and, as much as possible, every minister should, with much prayer for heavenly guidance, enter fully into his subject, exert all his mental faculties in original thinking, and gather together all the information within his reach. Viewing the whole matter from all quarters, the preacher should think it out, get it well masticated and digested; and having first fed upon the word himself should then prepare the like nutriment for others. Our sermons should be our mental lifeblood —the outflow of our intellectual and spiritual vigour; or, to change the figure, they should be diamonds well cut and well set— precious intrinsically, and bearing the marks of labour. God forbid that we should offer to the Lord that which costs us nothing.

Very strongly do I warn all of you against reading your sermons, but I recommend, as a most healthful exercise, and as a great aid towards attaining extemporizing power, the frequent writing of them. Those of us who write a great deal in other forms, for the press, et cetera, may not so much require that exercise; but if you do not use the pen in other ways, you will be wise to write at least some of your sermons, and revise them with great care. Leave them at home afterwards, but still write them out, that you may be preserved from a slipshod style. . . .

We do not recommend the plan of learning sermons by heart, and repeating them from memory; that is both a wearisome exercise of an inferior power of the mind and an indolent neglect of other and superior faculties. The most arduous and commendable plan is to store your mind with matter upon the subject of discourse, and then to deliver yourself with appropriate words which suggest themselves at the time. This is not extemporaneous preaching; the words are extemporal, as I think they always should be, but the thoughts are the result of research and study. Only thoughtless persons think this to be easy; it is at once the most laborious and the most efficient mode of preaching, and it has virtues, of its own of which I cannot now speak particularly since it would lead us away from the point in hand. . . . Brethren, covet earnestly this good gift, and go about to win it.

You are all convinced that the ability which we are considering must be a priceless possession for a minister. Did we hear a single heart whisper, "I wish I had it for then I should have no need to study so arduously"? Ah! then you must not have it, for you are unworthy of the boon, and unfit to be trusted with it. If you seek this gift as a pillow for an idle head, you will be much mistaken; for the possession of this noble power will involve you in a vast amount of labour in order to increase and even to retain it. . . .

Occasionally one has heard or read of men agreeing, by way of bravado, to preach upon texts given them at the time in the pulpit, or in the vestry: such vainglorious displays are disgusting, and border on profanity. As well might we have exhibitions of juggling on the Sabbath as such mountebankism of oratory. Our talents are given us for far other ends. . . .

The power of impromptu speech is invaluable, because it enables a man on the spur of the moment, in an emergency, to deliver himself with propriety. These emergencies will arise. Accidents will occur in the best-regulated assemblies. Singular events may turn the premeditated current of your thoughts quite aside. You will see clearly that the subject selected would be inopportune, and you will as a wise man drift into something else without demur. When the old road is closed, and there is no help for it but to make a new way for the chariot, unless you are qualified to drive the horses over a ploughed field as well as along the macadamized road on which you hoped to travel, you will find yourself off the coachbox, and mischief will befall the company. It is a great acquisition to be able at a public meeting, when you have heard the speeches of your brethren, and believe that they have been too frivolous, or it may be, on the other hand, too dull, without any allusions to them, quietly to counteract the mischief, and lead the assembly into a more profitable line of thought. This gift may be of the utmost importance in the church meeting, where business may arise which it would be difficult to foresee. . . . In some churches certain noisy men will rise and speak, and when they have done so, it is of great importance that the pastor should readily and convincingly reply, lest bad impressions should remain. A pastor who goes to the church meeting in the spirit of his Master, feeling sure that in reliance upon the Holy Spirit he is quite able to answer any untoward spirit, sits at ease, keeps his temper, rises in esteem on each occasion, and secures a quiet church; but the unready brother is flurried, probably gets into a passion, commits himself, and inherits a world of sorrow.

Besides this, a man may be called upon to preach at a moment's notice, through the non-arrival of the expected minister, or his sudden sickness; at a public meeting one may feel stirred to speak where silence had been resolved upon; and at any form of religious exercise emergencies may arise which will render impromptu speech as precious as the gold of Ophir. The gift is valuable—how is it to be obtained? The question leads us to remark that *some men will never obtain it*. There must be a natural adaptedness for extemporaneous speech, even as for the poetic art: a poet is born, not made. "Art may develop and perfect the talent of a speaker, but cannot produce it." All the rules of rhetoric and all the artifices of oratory cannot make a man eloquent; it is a gift from heaven, and where it is withheld it cannot be obtained. . . .

If a man would speak without any present study, he must usually study much. This is a paradox, perhaps, but its explanation lies upon the surface. If I am a miller, and I have a sack brought to my door, and am asked to fill that sack with good fine flour within the next five minutes, the only way in which I can do it is by keeping the flour-bin of my mill always full, so that I can at once open the mouth of the sack, fill it, and deliver it. I do not happen to be grinding at that time, and so far the delivery is extemporary; but I have been grinding before, and so have the flour to serve out to the customer. So, brethren, you must have been grinding, or you will not have the flour. You will not be able to extemporize good thinking unless you have been in the habit of thinking and feeding your mind with abundant and nourishing food. Work hard at every available moment. Store your minds very richly, and then, like merchants with crowded warehouses, you will have goods ready for your customers, and having arranged your good things upon the shelves of your mind, you will be able to hand them down at any time without the laborious process of going to market, sorting, folding, and preparing. I do not believe that any man can be successful in continuously maintaining the gift of extemporaneous speech, except by ordinarily using far more labour than is usual with those who write and commit their discourses to memory. Take it as a rule without exception, that to be able to overflow spontaneously you must be full.

The collection of a fund of ideas and expressions is exceedingly helpful. There is a wealth and poverty in each of these respects. He who has much information, well arranged and thoroughly understood, with which he is intimately familiar, will be able like some prince of fabulous wealth to scatter gold right and left among the crowd. To you, gentlemen, an intimate acquaintance with the Word of God, with the inward spiritual life, with the great problems of time and eternity, will be indispensable. Out of the abundance of the heart the mouth speaketh. Accustom yourselves to heavenly meditations, search the Scriptures, delight yourselves in the law of the Lord, and you need not fear to speak of things which you have tasted and handled of the good word of God. . . . Ignorance of theology is no rare thing in our pulpits, and the wonder is not that so few men are extempore speakers, but that so many are, when theologians are so scarce. We shall never have great preachers till we have great divines. You cannot build a man-of-war out of a currant bush, nor can great soul-moving preachers be formed out of superficial students. If you would be fluent, that is to say flowing, be filled with all knowledge, and especially the knowledge of Christ Jesus your Lord.

But we remarked that a fund of expressions would be also of much help to the extempore speaker; and, truly, second only to a store of ideas is a rich vocabulary. . . . You must be masters of words, they must be your genii, your angels, your thunder-bolts, or your drops of honey. Mere word-gatherers are hoarders of oyster shells, bean husks, and apple parings; but to a man who has wide information and deep thought, words are baskets of silver in which to serve up his apples of gold. See to it that you have a good team of words to draw the wagon of your thoughts.

I think, too, that a man who would speak well, extemporan-eously, *must be careful to select a topic which he understands.* . . . It is of no use to rise before an assembly, and hope to be inspired upon subjects of which you know nothing; if you are so unwise, the result will be that as you know nothing you will probably say it, and the people will not be edified. But I do not see why a man cannot speak extemporaneously upon a subject which he fully understands. Any tradesman, well versed in his line of business, could explain it to you without needing to retire for meditation; and surely we ought to be equally familiar with the first principles of our holy faith; we ought not to feel at a loss when called upon to speak upon topics which constitute the daily bread of our souls. I do not see what benefit is gained in such a case, by the mere manual labour of writing before speaking; because in so doing, a man would write extemporaneously, and extemporaneous writing is likely to be even feebler than extemporaneous speech. The gain of the writing lies in the opportunity of careful revision; but as able writers are able to express their thoughts correctly at the first, so also may able speakers. The thought of a man who finds himself upon his legs, dilating upon a theme with which he is familiar, may be very far from being his first thought; it may be the cream of his meditations warmed by the glow of his heart. He, having studied the subject well before, though not at that moment, may deliver himself most powerfully; whereas another man, sitting down to write, may only be penning his first ideas, which may be vague and vapid. Do not attempt to be impromptu then, unless you have well studied the theme—this paradox is a counsel of prudence. I remember to have been tried rather sharply upon one occasion, and had I not been versed in impromptu address, I know not how it would have sped with me. I was expected to preach in a certain chapel, and there was a crowded congregation, but I was not in time, being delayed by some blockade upon the railroad; so another minister went on with the service, and when I reached the place, all breathless with running, he was already preaching a sermon. Seeing me appear at the front door and pass up the aisle, he stopped and said, "There he is," and looking at me, he added, "I'll make way for you; come up and finish the sermon"; I asked him what was the text and how far he had gone with it. He told me what the text was, and said he had just passed through the first head; without hesitation I took up the discourse at that point and finished the sermon, and I should be ashamed of any man here who could not have done the same, the circumstances being such as to make the task a remarkably easy one. In the first place the minister was my grandfather, and, in the second place, the text was: "By grace are ye saved, through faith, and that not of yourselves, it is the gift of God." He must have been a more foolish animal than that which Balaam rode, if, at such a juncture, he had not found a tongue. "By grace are ye saved," had been spoken of as indicating *the source* of salvation; who could not follow by describing the next clause—"through faith," as *the channel?* One did not need to study much to show that salvation is received by us through faith. . . .

The acquisition of another language affords a fine drilling for the practice of extempore speech. Brought into connection with the roots of words, and the rules of speech, and being compelled to note the differentia of the two languages, a man grows by degrees to be much at home with parts of speech, moods, tenses, and inflections; like a workman he becomes familiar with his tools, and handles them as everyday companions. I know of no better exercise than to translate with as much rapidity as possible a portion of Virgil or Tacitus, and then with deliberation to amend one's mistakes. Persons who know no better, think all time thrown away which is spent upon the classics, but if it were only for the usefulness of such studies to the sacred orator, they ought to be retained in all our collegiate institutions. Who does not see that the perpetual comparison of the terms and idioms of two languages must aid facility of expression? Who does not see moreover that by this exercise the mind becomes able to appreciate refinements and subleties of meaning, and so acquires the power of distinguishing between things that differ—a power essential to an expositor of the Word of God, and an extempore declarer of his truth. Learn, gentlemen, to put together and unscrew all the machinery of language; mark every cog, and wheel, and bolt, and rod, and you will feel the more free to drive the engine, even at an express speed should emergencies demand it.

Every man who wishes to acquire this art must practise it. It was by slow degrees, as Burke says, that Charles Fox became the most brilliant and powerful debater that ever lived. He attributed his success to the resolution which he formed when very young, of speaking well or ill, at least once every night. "During five whole seasons," he used to say, "I spoke every night but one, and I regret only that I did not speak on that night too." At first he may do so with no other auditory than the chairs and books of his study, imitating the example of a gentleman who, upon applying for admission to this college, assured me that he had for two years practised himself in extempore preaching in his own room. Students living together might be of great mutual assistance by alternately acting the part of audience and speaker, with a little friendly criticism at the close of each attempt. Conversation, too, may be of essential service, if it be a matter of principle to make it solid and edifying. Thought is to be linked with speech, that is the problem; and it may assist a man in its solution, if he endeavours in his private musings to think aloud. So has this become habitual to me that I find it very helpful to be able, in private devotion, to pray with my voice; reading aloud is more beneficial to me than the silent process; and when I am mentally working out a sermon, it is a relief to me to speak to myself as the thoughts flow forth. Of course this only masters half the difficulty, and you must practise in public, in order to overcome the trepidation occasioned by the sight of an audience; but halfway is a great part of a journey. Good impromptu speech is just the utterance of a practised thinker—a man of information, meditating on his legs, and allowing his thoughts to march through his mouth into the open air. Think aloud as much as you can when you are alone, and you will soon be on the high road to success in this matter. . . .

In addition to the practice commended, I must urge upon you the necessity of being *cool and confident.* . . . This is not to be easily acquired by the young speaker. Cannot you young speakers sympathize with Blondin, the ropewalker? Do you not sometimes feel when you are preaching as though you are walking on a rope high in the air, and do you not tremble and wonder whether you will reach the other end in safety? Sometimes when you have been flourishing that beautiful balancing pole, and watching the metaphorical spangles which flash poetry upon your audience, have you not been half regretful that you ever exposed yourself to such risks of sudden descent, or, to drop the figure, have you not wondered whether you would be able to conclude the sentence, or find a verb for the nominative, or an accusative for the verb? Everything depends upon your being cool and unflurried. Forebodings of failure, and fear of man, will ruin you. Go on, trusting in God, and all will be well. If you have made a blunder in grammar, and you are half inclined to go back to correct it, you will soon make another, and your hesitation will involve you as in a net. Let me whisper—for it is meant for your ear alone—it is always a bad thing to go back. If you make a verbal blunder, go on, and do not notice it. My father gave me a very good rule when I was learning to write, which I think of equal utility in learning to speak. He used to say, "When you are writing, if you make a mistake by misspelling a word, or by writing a wrong word, do not cross it out and make a mess of it, but see how you can in the readiest way alter what you were going to say so as to bring in what you have written, and leave no trace of mistake." So in speaking, if the sentence will not finish in the best way, conclude it in another. It is of very little use to go back to amend, for you thus call attention to the flaw which perhaps few had noticed, and you draw off the mind from your subject to your language, which is the last thing which the preacher should do. If, however, your *lapsus linguae* should be noticed, all persons of sense will forgive a young beginner, and they will rather admire you than otherwise for attaching small importance to such slips, and pressing on with your whole heart towards your main design. A novice at public speaking is like a rider unused to horseback; if his horse stumbles he fears he will be down and throw him over his head, or if it be a little fresh, he feels assured that it will run away; and the eye of a friend, or the remark of a little boy, will make him as wretched as if he were lashed to the back of the great red dragon. But when a man is well used to mount he knows no dangers, and he meets with none, because his courage prevents them. When a speaker feels, "I am master of the situation," he usually is so. His confidence averts the disasters which trembling would be sure to create. . . .

When you are able to feel at home in the pulpit, and can look round and speak to the people as a brother talking to brethren, then you will be able to extemporize, but not till then. Bashfulness and timidity, which are so beautiful in our younger brethren, will be succeeded by that true modesty which forgets self, and is not careful as to its own reputation so long as Christ is preached in the most forcible manner at command.

In order to the holy and useful exercise of extemporal speech, the Christian minister must cultivate a childlike *reliance upon the immediate assistance of the Holy Spirit.* "I believe in the Holy Ghost," says the Creed. It is to be feared that many do not make this a real article of belief. To go up and down all the week wasting time, and then to cast ourselves upon the Spirit's aid, is wicked presumption, an attempt to make the Lord minister to our sloth and self-indulgence; but in an emergency the case is widely different. When a man finds himself unavoidably called upon to speak without any preparation, then he may with fullest confidence cast himself upon the Spirit of God. The divine mind beyond a doubt comes into contact with the human intellect, lifts it out of its weakness and distraction, makes it soaring and strong, and enables it both to understand and to express divine truth in a manner far beyond its unaided powers. . . . His Spirit will be ever with us, but especially under severe stress of service. Earnestly as I advise you not to try purely impromptu speaking more than you are obliged to do, till you have become somewhat matured in your ministry, I yet exhort you to speak in that manner whenever compelled to do so, believing that in the selfsame hour it shall be given you what you shall speak. . . .

You must continually practise extemporizing, and if to gain suitable opportunities you should frequently speak the word in cottages, in the schoolrooms of our hamlets, or to two or three by the wayside, your profiting shall be known unto all men. . . .

Above all things beware of letting your tongue outrun your brains. Guard against a feeble fluency, a garrulous prosiness,

a facility of saying nothing. . . . Elongated nonsense, para-
phrastic platitude, wire-drawn commonplace, or sacred rodomontade
are common enough, and are the scandal and shame of extemporizing. Even when sentiments of no value are beautifully expressed, and neatly worded, what is the use of them? Out of
nothing comes nothing. Extemporary speech without study is a
cloud without rain, a well without water, a fatal gift, injurious
equally to its possessor and his flock. . . . The sermons of such
preachers are like Snug the Joiner's part when he acted the lion:
"You may do it extempore, for it is nothing but roaring." Better
to lose, or rather never to possess, the gift of ready utterance,
than to degrade ourselves into mere noisemakers, the living rep-
resentations of Paul's sounding brass and tinkling cymbal. . . .

13

Sermons: Their Matter

Sermons should have real teaching in them, and their doctrine should be solid, substantial, and abundant. We do not enter the pulpit to talk for talk's sake; we have instructions to convey important to the last degree, and we cannot afford to utter pretty nothings. Our range of subjects is all but boundless, and we cannot, therefore, be excused if our discourses are threadbare and devoid of substance. If we speak as ambassadors for God, we need never complain of want of matter, for our message is full to overflowing. The entire gospel must be presented from the pulpit; the whole faith once delivered to the saints must be proclaimed by us. The truth as it is in Jesus must be instructively declared, so that the people may not merely hear, but *know,* the joyful sound. We serve not at the altar of "the unknown God," but we speak to the worshippers of him of whom it is written, "They that know thy name will put their trust in thee." . . . The true minister of Christ knows that the true value of a sermon must lie, not in its fashion and manner, but in the truth which it contains. Nothing can compensate for the absence of teaching; all the rhetoric in the world is but as chaff to the wheat, in contrast to the gospel of our salvation. However beautiful the sower's basket it is a miserable mockery if it be without seed. The grandest discourse ever delivered is an ostentatious failure if the doctrine of the grace of God be absent from it; it sweeps over men's heads like a cloud, but it distributes no rain upon the thirsty earth; and therefore the remembrance of it to souls taught wisdom by an experience of pressing need is one of disappointment, or worse. . . .

Sound information on scriptural subjects your hearers crave for, and must have. Accurate explanations of Holy Scripture they are entitled to, and if you are "an interpreter, one of a thousand," a real messenger of heaven, you will yield them plenteously. Whatever else may be present, the absence of edifying, instructive truth, like the absence of flour from bread, will be fatal. Estimated by their solid contents rather than their superficial area, many sermons are very poor specimens of godly discourse. . . . Brethren, if you are not theologians you are in your pastorates just nothing at all. You may be fine rhetoricians, and be rich in polished sentences; but without knowledge of the gospel, and aptness to teach it, you are but sounding brass and a tinkling cymbal. Verbiage is too often the fig leaf which does duty as a covering for theological ignorance. Sounding periods are offered instead of sound doctrine, and rhetorical flourishes in the place of robust thought. Such things ought not to be. . . .

We insist upon it, that there must be abundance of matter in sermons, and next, that *this matter must be congruous to the text*. The discourse should spring out of the text as a rule, and the more evidently it does so the better; but at all times, to say the least, it should have a very close relationship thereto. In the matter of spiritualizing and accommodation very large latitude is to be allowed; but liberty must not degenerate into license. . . . Some brethren have done with their text as soon as they have read it. Having paid all due honor to that particular passage by announcing it, they feel no necessity further to refer to it. They touch their hats, as it were, to that part of Scripture, and pass on to fresh fields and pastures new. Why do such men take a text at all? Why limit their own glorious liberty? Why make Scripture a horsing-block by which to mount upon their unbridled Pegasus? Surely the words of inspiration were never meant to be boot-hooks to help a Talkative to draw on his seven-leagued boots in which to leap from pole to pole.

The surest way to maintain variety is to keep to the mind of the Holy Spirit in the particular passage under consideration.

No two texts are exactly similar; something in the connection or drift of the passage gives to each apparently identical text a shade of difference. Keep to the Spirit's track and you will never repeat yourself or be short of matter: his paths drop fatness. . . .

Brethren, if you are in the habit of keeping to the precise sense of the Scripture before you, I will further recommend you to hold to the *ipsissima verba,* the very words of the Holy Ghost. . . . Let your matter, then, be copious, and let it grow out of the inspired word, as violets and primroses spring up naturally from the sod, or as the virgin honey drops from the comb.

Take care that your deliverances are always weighty, and full of really important teaching. Build not with wood, hay, and stubble, but with gold, silver, and precious stones. . . . We are on peril of our souls bound to deal with the solemnities of eternity and with no earthborn topics. There are, however, other and more inviting methods of wood and hay building, and it behooves you not to be duped by them. This remark is necessary, especially to those gentlemen who mistake high-flying sentences for eloquence, and latinized utterances for great depth of thought. . . . I remember a sermon by a would-be profound writer which quite stunned the reader with grenadier words of six-foot length, but which, when properly boiled down, came to as much essence of meat as this: Man has a soul, his soul will live in another world, and therefore he should take care that it occupies a happy place. No one can object to the teaching, but it is not so novel as to need a blast of trumpets and a procession of bedizened phrases to introduce it to public attention. . . . It is infamous to ascend your pulpit and pour over your people rivers of language, cataracts of words, in which mere platitudes are held in solution like infinitesimal grains of homeopathic medicine in an Atlantic of utterance. Better far give the people masses of unprepared truth in the rough, like pieces of meat from a butcher's block, chopped off anyhow, bone and all, and even dropped down in the sawdust, than ostentatiously hand them out upon a china dish a delicious slice of nothing at all, decorated with the parsley of poetry, and flavoured with the sauce of affectation.

It will be a happy circumstance if you are so guided by the Holy Spirit as to *give a clear testimony to all the doctrines which constitute or lie around the gospel.* No truth is to be kept back. . . . Harmony requires that the voice of one doctrine should not drown the rest, and it also demands that the gentler notes shall not be omitted because of the greater volume of other sounds. Every note appointed by the great minstrel must be sounded, each note having its own proportionate power and emphasis; the passage marked with forte must not be softened, and those with piano must not be rolled out like thunder, but each must have its due hearing. All revealed truth in harmonious proportion must be your theme.

Brethren, if you resolve in your pulpit utterances to deal with important verities, *you must not forever hover around the mere angles of truth.* Those doctrines which are not vital to the soul's salvation, nor even essential to practical Christianity, are not to be considered upon every occasion of worship. Bring in all the features of truth in due proportion, for every part of Scripture is profitable, and you are not only to preach the truth, but the whole truth. Do not insist perpetually upon one truth alone. A nose is an important feature in the human countenance, but to paint a man's nose alone is not a satisfactory method of taking his likeness: a doctrine may be very important, but an exaggerated estimate of it may be fatal to a harmonious and complete ministry. Do not make minor doctrines main points. Do not paint the details of the background of the gospel picture with the same heavy brush as the great objects in the foreground of it. For instance, the great problems of sublapsarianism and supralapsarianism, the trenchant debates concerning eternal filiation, the earnest dispute concerning the double procession, and the pre- or postmillenarian schemes, however important some may deem them, are practically of very little concern to that godly widow woman, with seven children to support by her needle, who wants far more to hear of the loving-kindness of the God of providence than of these mysteries profound; if you preach to her on the faithfulness of God to his people, she will be cheered and helped in the battle of life; but difficult questions will perplex her or send her to sleep. She is, however, the type of hundreds of those who most require your care. Our great master theme is the good news from heaven; the tidings of mercy through the atoning death of Jesus, mercy to the chief of sinners upon their believing in Jesus.

We must throw all our strength of judgment, memory, imagination, and eloquence into the delivery of the gospel, and not give to the preaching of the cross our random thoughts while wayside topics engross our deeper meditations. . . . There is such a thing as meanness of mental occupation unbecoming the rank of an ambassador of heaven. . . .

Do not overload a sermon with too much matter. All truth is not to be comprised in one discourse. Sermons are not to be bodies of divinity. There is such a thing as having too much to say, and saying it till hearers are sent home loathing rather than longing. . . . One thought fixed on the mind will be better than fifty thoughts made to flit across the ear. One tenpenny nail driven home and clenched will be more useful than a score of tin-tacks loosely fixed, to be pulled out again in an hour.

Our matter should be well arranged according to the true rules of mental architecture: not practical inferences at the basis and doctrines as the topstones, not metaphors in the foundations and propositions at the summit, not the more important truths first and the minor teachings last, after the manner of an anticlimax; but the thought must climb and ascend, one stair of teaching leading to another, one door of reasoning conducting to another, and the whole elevating the hearer to a chamber from whose windows truth is seen gleaming in the light of God. In preaching, have a place for everything, and everything in its place. . . .

Your doctrinal teaching should be clear and unmistakable. . . . Some men think in smoke and preach in a cloud. Your people

do not want a luminous haze, but the solid terra firma of truth.
. . . Let a minister keep clear of mystifying himself, and then
he is on the road to becoming intelligible to his people. No
man can hope to be felt who cannot make himself understood.
If we give our people refined truth, pure scriptural doctrine
and all so worded as to have no needless obscurity about it, we
shall be true shepherds of the sheep, and the profiting of our
people will soon be apparent. . . .

Let your teachings grow and advance; let them deepen with
your experience, and rise with your soul-progress. I do not mean,
preach new truths; for, on the contrary, I hold that man happy
who is so well taught from the first that, after fifty years of
ministry, he has never had to recant a doctrine or to mourn an
important omission; but I mean, let our depth and insight continually increase, and where there is spiritual advance it will
be so. . . . Our earliest productions must be surpassed by those
of our riper years. . . .

The word "sermon" is said to signify "a thrust," and, therefore, in sermonizing it must be our aim to *use the subject in
hand with energy and effect, and the subject must be capable of
such employment.* To choose mere moral themes will be to use a
wooden dagger; but the great truths of revelation are as sharp
swords. Keep to doctrines which stir the conscience and the heart.
. . . Hence I urge you to keep to the old-fashioned gospel, and
to that only, for assuredly it is the power of God unto salvation.

Of all I would wish to say this is the sum: my brethren, preach
CHRIST, always and evermore. He is the whole gospel. His
person, offices, and work must be our one great, all-compre-
hending theme. The world needs still to be told of its Saviour,
and of the way to reach him. Justification by faith should be,
far more than it is, the daily testimony of Protestant pulpits;
and if with this master-truth there should be more generally
associated the other great doctrines of grace, the better for our
churches and our age. . . . We are not called to proclaim
philosophy and metaphysics, but the simple gospel. Man's fall,

his need of a new birth, forgiveness through an atonement, and salvation as the result of faith—these are our battle-axe and weapons of war. We have enough to do to learn and teach these great truths, and accursed be that learning which shall divert us from our mission, or that wilful ignorance which shall cripple us in its pursuit. More and more am I jealous lest any views upon prophecy, church government, politics, or even systematic theology should withdraw one of us from glorying in the cross of Christ. . . . Blessed is that ministry of which CHRIST IS ALL.

14

To Workers with Slender Apparatus

. . . A good library should be looked upon as an indispensable part of church furniture; and the deacons, whose business it is "to serve tables," will be wise if, without neglecting the table of the Lord, or of the poor, and without diminishing the supplies of the minister's dinner-table, they give an eye to his study-table, and keep it supplied with new works and standard books in fair abundance. It would be money well laid out, and would be productive far beyond expectation. Instead of waxing eloquent upon the declining power of the pulpit, leading men in the church should use the legitimate means for improving its power. . . .

Give over expecting to receive instructive sermons from men who are shut out of the storehouse of knowledge. . . .

If a man can purchase but very few books, my first advice to him would be, *let him purchase the very best.* If he cannot spend much, let him spend well. The best will always be the cheapest. Leave mere dilutions and attenuations to those who can afford such luxuries. Do not buy milk and water, but get condensed milk, and put what water you like to it yourself. . . . Prefer books which abound in what James Hamilton used to call "Bibline," or the essence of books. You require accurate, condensed, reliable, standard books, and should make sure that you get them. . . .

The next rule I shall lay down is, *master those books you have.* Read them thoroughly. Bathe in them until they saturate you. Read and re-read them, masticate them, and digest them.

Let them go into your very self. Peruse a good book several times, and make notes and analyses of it. A student will find that his mental constitution is more affected by one book thoroughly mastered than by twenty books which he has merely skimmed, lapping at them, as the classic proverb puts it, "As the dogs drink of Nilus." Little learning and much pride come of hasty reading. Books may be piled on the brain till it cannot work. Some men are disabled from thinking by their putting meditation away for the sake of much reading. . . .

In reading books let your motto be, "Much, not many." Think as well as read, and keep the thinking always proportionate to the reading, and your small library will not be a great misfortune.

There is very much sound sense in the remark of a writer in the *Quarterly Review* many years back.

> Give us the *one* dear book, cheaply picked from the stall by the price of the dinner, thumbed and dog-eared, cracked in the back and broken in the corner, noted on the flyleaf and scrawled on the margin, sullied and scorched, torn and worn, smoothed in the pocket and grimed on the hearth, damped by the grass and dusted among the cinders, over which you have dreamed in the grove and dozed before the embers, but read again, again, and again, from cover to cover. It is by this one book, and its three or four single successors, that more cultivation has been imparted than by all the myriads which bear down the mile-long, bulging, bending shelves of the Bodleian.

But if you feel you must have more books, *I recommend to you a little judicious borrowing*. . . . I specially advise you, in order to borrow again, to return whatsoever is lent, promptly, and in good condition. I hope there is not so much need that I should say much about returning books, as there would have been a few months ago, for I have lately met with a statement by a clergyman, which has very much raised my opinion of human nature; for he declares that he has a personal acquaintance with three gentlemen who have actually returned borrowed umbrellas! I am sorry to say that he moves in a more favored circle than I

do, for I have personal acquaintance with several young men
who have borrowed books and never returned them. . . .

In case the famine of books should be sore in the land, *there
is one book which you all have, and that is your Bible;* and a
minister with his Bible is like David with his sling and stone,
fully equipped for the fray. No man may say that he has no well
to draw from while the Scriptures are within reach. In the Bible
we have a perfect library, and he who studies it thoroughly will
be a better scholar than if he had devoured the Alexandrian
library entire. To understand the Bible should be our ambition;
we should be familiar with it, as familiar as the housewife with
her needle, the merchant with his ledger, the mariner with his
ship. We ought to know its general run, the contents of each
book, the details of its histories, its doctrines, its precepts, and
everything about it. Erasmus, speaking of Jerome, asks, "Who
but he ever learned by heart the whole Scripture? or imbibed,
or meditated on it as he did?" . . . That may have been a feat
of memory, but the study needful to it must have been highly
profitable. . . .

The Scriptures will be sweeter than honey to our taste, and
will make us "wiser than the ancients." We shall never be short
of holy matter if we are continually studying the inspired volume;
nay, it is not only matter that we shall find there, but illustration too; for the Bible is its own best illustrator. If you want
anecdote, simile, allegory, or parable, turn to the sacred page.
Scriptural truth never looks more lovely than when she is adorned
with jewels from her own treasury. I have lately been reading
the Books of the Kings and the Chronicles, and I have become
enamoured of them; they are as full of divine instruction as the
Psalms or prophets, if read with opened eyes. I think it was
Ambrose who used to say, "I adore the infinity of Scripture."
I hear that same voice which sounded in the ear of Augustine,
concerning the Book of God, *"Tolle, lege;* Take, read." It may
be you will dwell in retirement in some village, where you will
find no one who is above your own level, and where you will meet

with very few books worth your reading; then read and meditate in the law of the Lord both day and night, and you shall be "as a tree planted by the rivers of water." Make the Bible the man of your right hand, the companion of every hour, and you will have little reason to lament your slender equipment in inferior things.

I would earnestly impress upon you the truth, that a man who is short of apparatus can *make up for it by much thought.* Thinking is better than possessing books. Thinking is an exercise of the soul which both develops and educates. A little girl was once asked whether she knew what her soul was, and, to the surprise of all, she said, "Sir, my soul is my think." If this be correct, some persons have very little soul. Without thinking, reading cannot benefit the mind, but it may delude the man into the idea that he is growing wise. . . . Thought is the backbone of study, and if more ministers would think, what a blessing it would be! Only, we want men who will think about the revealed will of God, and not dreamers who evolve religions out of their own consciousness. Nowadays we are pestered with a set of fellows who must needs stand on their heads and think with their feet. Romancing is their notion of meditation. Instead of considering revealed truth, they excogitate a mess of their own, in which error, and nonsense, and conceit appear in about equal parts; and they call this broth "modern thought." We want men who will try to think straight, and yet think deep, because they think God's thoughts. Far be it from me to urge you to imitate the boastful thinkers of this age, who empty their meetinghouses, and then glory that they preach to the cultivated and intellectual. It is miserable cant. Earnest thought upon things which are assuredly believed among us is quite another matter, and to that I urge you. Personally I owe much to many hours, and even days, spent alone, under an old oak tree, by the river Medway. Happening to be somewhat indisposed at the time when I was leaving school, I was allowed considerable leisure, and, armed with an excellent fishing rod, I caught a few small fishes, and enjoyed many daydreams, intermingled with searchings of heart, and much ruminating of knowledge acquired. If boys would think, it would be well to give them less classwork and more opportunity for thought. All cram and no digestion makes flesh destitute of muscle, and this is more deplorable mentally than physically. If your people are not numerous enough to supply you with a library, they will make fewer demands on your time, and, in having time for meditation, you will be even better off than your brethren with many books and little space for contemplation.

Without books *a man may learn much by keeping his eyes open*. Current history, incidents which transpire under his own nose, events recorded in the newspaper, matters of common talk—he may learn from them all. The difference between eyes and no eyes is wonderful. If you have no books to try your eyes, keep them open wherever you go, and you will find something worth looking at. Can you not learn from nature? Every flower is waiting to teach you. "Consider the lilies," and learn from the roses. Not only may you go to the ant, but every living thing offers itself for your instruction. There is a voice in every gale, and a lesson in every grain of dust it bears. Sermons glisten in the morning on every blade of grass, and homilies fly by you as the sere leaves fall from the trees. A forest is a library, a cornfield is a volume of philosophy, the rock is a history, and the river at its base a poem. Go, thou who hast thine eyes opened, and find lessons of wisdom everywhere, in heaven above, in the earth beneath, and in the waters under the earth. Books are poor things compared with these.

Moreover, however scant your libraries, *you can study yourself*. This is a mysterious volume, the major part of which you have not read. If any man thinks that he knows himself thoroughly, he deceives himself; for the most difficult book you will ever read is your own heart. I said to a doubter the other day, who seemed to be wandering in a maze, "Well, really I cannot understand you; but I am not vexed, for I never could understand myself"; and I certainly meant what I said. Watch the twists and turns and singularities of your own mind, and the strangeness of your own experience; the depravity of your heart, and the work of divine grace; your tendency to sin, and your capacity for holiness; how akin you are to a devil, and yet how allied to God himself! Note how wisely you can act when taught of God, and how foolishly you behave when left to yourself. You will find the study of your heart to be of immense importance to you as a watcher over the souls of others. A man's own experience should be to him the laboratory in which he tests the medicines which he prescribes for others. Even your own faults and failures will instruct you if you bring them to the Lord. Absolutely sinless men would be unable to sympathize with imperfect men and women. Study the Lord's dealings with your own souls, and you will know more of his ways with others.

Read other men; they are as instructive as books. Suppose there should come up to one of our great hospitals a young student so poor that he could not purchase surgical books: it would certainly be a great detriment to him; but if he had the run of the hospital, if he saw operations performed, and watched cases from day to day, I should not wonder but what he might turn out as skilful a surgeon as his more favoured companions. . . . Now, much that a minister needs to know he must learn by actual observation. All wise pastors have walked the hospitals spiritually, and dealt with inquirers, hypocrites, backsliders, the despairing, and the presumptuous. A man who has had a sound practical experience in the things of God himself, and watched the hearts of his fellows, other things being equal, will be a far more useful man than he who knows only what he has read. . . . We should have practical familiarity with men's souls; and if we have much of it, the fewness of our books will be a light affliction. . . .

Learn from experienced saints. What deep things some of them can teach to us younger men! What instances God's poor people can narrate of the Lord's providential appearances for them; how they glory in his upholding grace and his faithfulness to his covenant! What fresh light they often shed upon the

promises, revealing meanings hidden from the carnally wise, but
made clear to simple hearts! . . .

As for the inquirer, how much is to be gathered from him!
I have seen very much of my own stupidity while in conversation
with seeking souls. I have been baffled by a poor lad while
trying to bring him to the Saviour; I thought I had him fast, but
he has eluded me again and again with perverse ingenuity of
unbelief. Sometimes inquirers who are really anxious surprise me
with their singular skill in battling against hope; their arguments are endless and their difficulties countless. They put us
to a *non plus* again and again. The grace of God at last enables
us to bring them to the light, but not until we have seen our own
inefficiency. In the strange perversities of unbelief, the singular
constructions and misconstructions which the desponding put
upon their feelings and upon scriptural statements, you will often
find a world of instruction. I would sooner give a young man an
hour with inquirers and the mentally depressed than a week in
the best of our classes, so far as practical training for the pastorate is concerned.

Once more, be much at death-beds; they are illuminated
books. There shall you read the very poetry of our religion, and
learn the secrets thereof. What spendid gems are washed up by
the waves of Jordan! What fair flowers grow on its banks! The
everlasting fountains in the glory-land throw their spray aloft,
and the dewdrops fall on this side the narrow stream! I have
heard humble men and women, in their departing hours, talk as
though they were inspired, uttering strange words, aglow with
supernal glory. These they learned from no lips beneath the
moon; they must have heard them while sitting in the suburbs of
the New Jerusalem. God whispers them in their ears amid their
pain and weakness, and then they tell us a little of what the
Spirit has revealed. . . .

Is not this enough upon our subject? If you desire more, it
is time I remember the sage saying, that it is better to send away
an audience longing than loathing; and, therefore, Adieu!

15

The Blind Eye and the Deaf Ear

Having often said in this room that a minister ought to have one blind eye and one deaf ear, I have excited the curiosity of several brethren, who have requested an explanation; for it appears to them, as it does also to me, that the keener eyes and ears we have the better. Well, gentlemen, since the text is somewhat mysterious, you shall have the exegesis of it.

A part of my meaning is expressed in plain language by Solomon, in the book of Ecclesiastes (7:21): "Also take no heed unto all words that are spoken; lest thou hear thy servant curse thee." The margin says, "Give not thy heart to all words that are spoken"—do not take them to heart or let them weigh with you, do not notice them, or act as if you heard them. You cannot stop people's tongues, and therefore the best thing is to stop your own ears and never mind what is spoken. There is a world of idle chitchat abroad, and he who takes note of it will have enough to do. He will find that even those who live with him are not always singing his praises, and that when he has displeased his most faithful servants they have, in the heat of the moment, spoken fierce words which it would be better for him not to have heard. Who has not, under temporary irritation, said that of another which he has afterwards regretted? It is the part of the generous to treat passionate words as if they had never been uttered. When a man is in an angry mood it is wise to walk away from him, and leave off strife before it be meddled with; and if we are compelled to hear hasty language, we must endeavour to obliterate it from the memory, and say with David, "But I, as a deaf man, heard not . . . I was as a man that heareth not, and in whose mouth are no reproofs." . . . We would say of the general gossip of the village, and of the unadvised words of angry friends—do not hear them, for you also have talked idly and angrily in your day, and would even now be in an awkward position if you were called to account for every word that you have spoken, even about your dearest friend. . . .

In enlarging upon my text, let me say first—when you commence your ministry make up your mind to begin with a clean sheet; *be deaf and blind to the long standing differences which may survive in the church.* As soon as you enter upon your pastorate you may be waited upon by persons who are anxious to secure your adhesion to their side in a family quarrel or church dispute; be deaf and blind to these people, and assure them that bygones must be bygones with you, and that as you have not inherited your predecessor's cupboard you do not mean to eat his cold meat. If any flagrant injustice has been done, be diligent to set it right, but if it be a mere feud, bid the quarrelsome party cease from it, and tell him once for all that you will have nothing to do with it. . . . Know nothing of parties and cliques, but be the pastor of all the flock, and care for all alike. Blessed are the peacemakers, and one sure way of peacemaking is to let the fire of contention alone. Neither fan it, nor stir it, nor add fuel to it, but let it go out of itself. Begin your ministry with one blind eye and one deaf ear. . . .

The blind eye and the deaf ear will come in exceedingly well in connection with the gossips of the place. Every church, and, for the matter of that, every village and family, is plagued with certain Mrs. Grundys, who drink tea and talk vitriol. They are never quiet, but buzz around to the great annoyance of those who are devout and practical. No one needs to look far for perpetual motion; he has only to watch their tongues. At tea-meetings, Dorcas meetings and other gatherings, they practise

vivisection upon the characters of their neighbours, and of course
they are eager to try their knives upon the minister, the minister's
wife, the minister's children, the minister's wife's bonnet, the
dress of the minister's daughter, and how many new ribbons she
has worn for the last six months, and so on ad infinitum. . . .
Let the creatures buzz, and do not even hear them, unless indeed
they buzz so much concerning one person that the matter threatens
to be serious; then it will be well to bring them to book and
talk in sober earnestness to them. Assure them that you are
obliged to have facts definitely before you, that your memory is
not very tenacious, that you have many things to think of, that
you are always afraid of making any mistake in such matters, and
that if they would be good enough to write down what they have
to say the case would be more fully before you, and you could
give more time to its consideration. Mrs. Grundy will not do
that; she has a great objection to making clear and definite statements; she prefers talking at random.

I heartily wish that by any process we could put down gossip,
but I suppose that it will never be done so long as the human
race continues what it is. . . . What can't be cured must be
endured, and the best way of enduring it is not to listen to it.
Over one of our old castles a former owner has inscribed these
lines—

> THEY SAY.
> WHAT DO THEY SAY?
> LET THEM SAY.

Thin-skinned persons should learn this motto by heart. . . .

Above all, never join in talebearing yourself, and beg your
wife to abstain from it also. Some men are too talkative by
half, and remind me of the young man who was sent to Socrates
to learn oratory. On being introduced to the philosopher he
talked so incessantly that Socrates asked for double fees. "Why
charge me double?" said the young fellow. "Because," said the
orator, "I must teach you two sciences: the one how to hold

your tongue and the other how to speak." The first science is the more difficult, but aim at proficiency in it, or you will suffer greatly, and create trouble without end.

Avoid with your whole soul that spirit of suspicion which sours some men's lives, and *to all things from which you might harshly draw an unkind inference turn a blind eye and deaf ear.* Suspicion makes a man a torment to himself and a spy towards others. Once begin to suspect, and causes for distrust will multiply around you, and your very suspiciousness will create the major part of them. Many a friend has been transformed into an enemy by being suspected. Do not, therefore, look about you with the eyes of mistrust, nor listen as an eavesdropper with the quick ear of fear. . . . When nothing is to be discovered which will help us to love others, we had better cease from the inquiry, for we may drag to light that which may be the commencement of years of contention. I am not, of course, referring to cases requiring discipline, which must be thoroughly investigated and boldly dealt with, but I have upon my mind mere personal matters where the main sufferer is yourself; here it is always best not to know, nor to wish to know, what is being said about you, either by friends or foes. Those who praise us are probably as much mistaken as those who abuse us, and the one may be regarded as a set-off to the other, if indeed it be worthwhile taking any account at all of man's judgment. If we have the approbation of our God, certified by a placid conscience, we can afford to be indifferent to the opinions of our fellow men, whether they commend or condemn. If we cannot reach this point we are babes and not men.

Some are childishly anxious to know their friend's opinion of them, and if it contain the smallest element of dissent or censure, they regard him as an enemy forthwith. Surely we are not popes, and do not wish our hearers to regard us as infallible! We have known men become quite enraged at a perfectly fair and reasonable remark, and regard an honest friend as an opponent who delighted to find fault; this misrepresentation on the one

side has soon produced heat on the other, and strife has ensued.
How much better is gentle forbearance! You must be able to bear
criticism, or you are not fit to be at the head of a congregation; and you must let the critic go without reckoning him among
your deadly foes, or you will prove yourself a mere weakling.
It is wisest always to show double kindness where you have been
severely handled by one who thought it his duty to do so, for
he is probably an honest man and worth winning. He who in
your early days hardly thinks you fit for the pastorate may yet
become your firmest defender if he sees that you grow in grace,
and advance in qualification for the work; do not, therefore, regard him as a foe for truthfully expressing his doubts—does not
your own heart confess that his fears were not altogether ground-
less? Turn your deaf ear to what you judge to be his harsh
criticism, and endeavour to preach better. . . .

Where I have known that there existed a measure of disaffec-
tion to myself, I have not recognized it, unless it has been forced
upon me, but have, on the contrary, acted towards the opposing
person with all the more courtesy and friendliness, and I have
never heard any more of the matter. If I had treated the good
man as an opponent, he would have done his best to take the
part assigned him, and carry it out to his own credit: but I felt
that he was a Christian man, and had a right to dislike me if
he thought fit, and that if he did so I ought not to think un-
kindly of him; and therefore I treated him as one who was a
friend to my Lord, if not to me, gave him some work to do which
implied confidence in him, made him feel at home, and by degrees
won him to be an attached friend as well as a fellow worker. . . .
Never make a brother remember that he once uttered a hard
speech in reference to yourself. If you see him in a happier mood,
do not mention the former painful occasion: if he be a man of
right spirit he will in future be unwilling to vex a pastor who
has treated him so generously, and if he be a mere boor it is a
pity to hold any argument with him. . . .

It would be better to be deceived a hundred times than to

live a life of suspicion. It is intolerable. The miser who traverses his chamber at midnight and hears a burglar in every falling leaf is not more wretched than the minister who believes that plots are hatching against him, and that reports to his disadvantage are being spread. . . . Nor is suspicion merely a source of disquietude; it is a moral evil, and injures the character of the man who harbors it. Suspicion in kings creates tyranny, in husbands jealousy, and in ministers bitterness; such bitterness as in spirit dissolves all the ties of the pastoral relation, eating like a corrosive acid into the very soul of the office and making it a curse rather than a blessing. When once this terrible evil has curdled all the milk of human kindness in a man's bosom, he becomes more fit for the detective force than for the ministry; like a spider, he begins to cast out his lines, and fashions a web of tremulous threads, all of which lead up to himself and warn him of the least touch of even the tiniest midge. There he sits in the centre, a mass of sensation, all nerves and raw wounds, excitable and excited, a self-immolated martyr drawing the blazing faggots about him, and apparently anxious to be burned. The most faithful friend is unsafe under such conditions. The most careful avoidance of offence will not secure immunity from mistrust, but will probably be construed into cunning and cowardice. . . .

Brethren, shun this vice by renouncing the love of self. Judge it to be a small matter what men think or say of you, and care only for their treatment of your Lord. If you are naturally sensitive do not indulge the weakness, nor allow others to play upon it. Would it not be a great degradation of your office if you were to keep an army of spies in your pay to collect information as to all that your people said of you? And yet it amounts to this if you allow certain busybodies to bring you all the gossip of the place. Drive the creatures away. Abhor those mischief-making, tattling handmaidens of strife. Those who will fetch will carry, and no doubt the gossips go from your house and report every observation which falls from your lips, with plenty of garnishing of their own. Remember that, as the receiver is as bad as the thief, so the hearer of scandal is a sharer in the guilt of it. If there were no listening ears, there would be no talebearing tongues. While you are a buyer of ill wares the demand will create the supply, and the factories of falsehood will be working full time. No one wishes to become a creator of lies, and yet he who hears slanders with pleasure and believes them with readiness will hatch many a brood into active life. . . .

Learn to disbelieve those who have no faith in their brethren. Suspect those who would lead you to suspect others. . . .

Need I say a word or two about the wisdom of *never hearing what was not meant for you?* The eavesdropper is a mean person, very little if anything better than the common informer, and he who says he *overheard* may be considered to have heard over and above what he should have done. . . .

It is a well-worn proverb that listeners seldom hear any good of themselves. Listening is a sort of larceny, but the goods stolen are never a pleasure to the thief. Information obtained by clandestine means must, in all but extreme cases, be more injury than benefit to a cause. . . . Ours is a mission of grace and peace; we are not prosecutors who search out condemnatory evidence, but friends whose love would cover a multitude of offences. . . .

To opinions and remarks about yourself turn also as a general rule the blind eye and the deaf ear. Public men must expect public criticism, and as the public cannot be regarded as infallible, public men may expect to be criticised in a way which is neither fair nor pleasant. To all honest and just remarks we are bound to give due measure of heed, but to the bitter verdict of prejudice, the frivolous faultfinding of men of fashion, the stupid utterances of the ignorant, and the fierce denunciations of opponents, we may very safely turn a deaf ear. We cannot expect those to approve of us whom we condemn by our testimony against their favorite sins; their commendation would show that we had missed our mark. We naturally look to be approved by our own people, the members of our churches, and the adherents of our congregations, and when they make observations which show that they are not very great admirers, we may be tempted to discouragement if not to anger: herein lies a snare. . . . If the people should happen to agree with your verdict, it will only feed your pitiful vanity, and if they think otherwise your fishing for their praise will injure you in their esteem. In any case it is all about yourself, and this is a poor theme to be anxious about; play the man, and do not demean yourself by seeking compliments like little children when dressed in new clothes, who say, "See my pretty frock." Have you not by this time discovered that flattery is as injurious as it is pleasant? It softens the mind and makes you more sensitive to slander. In proportion as praise pleases you censure will pain you. Besides, it is a crime to be taken off from your great object of glorifying the Lord Jesus by petty considerations as to your little self, and, if there were no other reason, this ought to weigh much with you. Pride is a deadly sin, and will grow without your borrowing the parish water cart to quicken it. Forget expressions which feed your vanity, and if you find yourself relishing the unwholesome morsels confess the sin with deep humiliation. . . . Knowing something myself of those secret whippings which our good Father administers to his servants when he sees them unduly exalted, I heartily add my own solemn warnings against your pampering the flesh by listening to the praises of the kindest friends you have. They are injudicious, and you must beware of them.

A sensible friend who will unsparingly criticise you from week to week will be a far greater blessing to you than a thousand undiscriminating admirers if you have sense enough to bear his treatment, and grace enough to be thankful for it. When I was preaching at the Surrey Gardens, an unknown censor of great ability used to send me a weekly list of my mispronunciations and other slips of speech. He never signed his name, and that was my only cause of complaint against him, for he left me in a

debt which I could not acknowledge. I take this opportunity
of confessing my obligations to him, for with genial temper,
and an evident desire to benefit me, he marked down most
relentlessly everything which he supposed me to have said in-
correctly. Concerning some of these corrections he was in error
himself, but for the most part he was right, and his remarks
enabled me to perceive and avoid many mistakes. I looked for
his weekly memoranda with much interest, and I trust I am all
the better for them. If I had repeated a sentence two or three
Sundays before, he would say, "See same expression in such a
sermon," mentioning number and page. He remarked on one
occasion that I too often quote the line "Nothing in my hands I
bring," and, he added, "we are sufficiently informed of the vacuity
of your hands." . . . No money can purchase outspoken honest
judgment, and when we can get it for nothing let us utilize it to
the fullest extent. The worst of it is that of those who offer
their judgments few are qualified to form them, and we shall be
pestered with foolish, impertinent remarks, unless we turn to
them all the blind eye and the deaf ear.

*In the case of false reports against yourself, for the most
part use the deaf ear.* Unfortunately liars are not yet extinct,
and you may be accused of crimes which your soul abhors. Be
not staggered thereby, for this trial has befallen the very best
of men, and even your Lord did not escape the envenomed tongue
of falsehood. In almost all cases it is the wisest course to let
such things die a natural death. A great lie, if unnoticed, is
like a big fish out of water; it dashes and plunges and beats
itself to death in a short time. To answer it is to supply it
with its element, and help it to a longer life. Falsehoods
usually carry their own refutation somewhere about them, and
sting themselves to death. Some lies especially have a peculiar
smell which betrays their rottenness to every honest nose. If
you are disturbed by them, the object of their invention is partly
answered, but your silent endurance disappoints malice and gives
you a partial victory, which God in his care of you will soon

turn into a complete deliverance. Your blameless life will be
your best defence, and those who have seen it will not allow you
to be condemned so readily as your slanderers expect. Only abstain from fighting your own battles, and in nine cases out of
ten your accusers will gain nothing by their malevolence but
chagrin for themselves and contempt from others. To prosecute
the slanderer is very seldom wise. I remember a beloved servant
of Christ who in his youth was very sensitive, and, being falsely
accused, proceeded against the person at law. An apology was
offered, it withdrew every iota of the charge, and was most
ample, but the good man insisted upon its being printed in the
newspapers, and the result convinced him of his own unwisdom.
Multitudes, who would otherwise have never heard of the libel,
asked what it meant, and made comments thereon, generally
concluding with the sage remark that he must have done something imprudent to provoke such an accusation. . . . Standing as
we do in a position which makes us choice targets for the devil
and his allies, our best course is to defend our innocence by
our silence and leave our reputation with God. Yet there are
exceptions to this general rule. When distinct, definite, public
charges are made against a man he is bound to answer them, and
answer them in the clearest and most open manner. To decline
all investigation is in such a case practically to plead guilty,
and whatever may be the mode of putting it, the general public
ordinarily regard a refusal to reply as a proof of guilt. . . .
In every instance counsel should be sought of the Lord as to how
to deal with slanderous tongues, and in the issue innocence will
be vindicated and falsehood convicted. . . .

Once more, my brethren, the blind eye and the deaf ear will
be useful to you *in relation to other churches and their pastors.*
I am always delighted when a brother in meddling with other
people's business burns his fingers. Why did he not attend to his
own concerns and not episcopize in another's diocese? I am
frequently requested by members of churches to meddle in their
home disputes; but unless they come to me with authority,

officially appointing me to be umpire, I decline. . . . Internal dissensions in our churches are very like quarrels between man and wife: when the case comes to such a pass that they must fight it out, the interposing party will be the victim of their common fury. . . .

We are recommended by one of the world's proverbs to wash our dirty linen at home, and I will add another line to it, and advise that we do not call on our neighbours while their linen is in the suds. This is due to our friends, and will best promote peace. . . . Many a trifling difference within a church has been fanned into a great flame by ministers outside who had no idea of the mischief they were causing. . . . My counsel is that we join the "Know-nothings," and never say a word upon a matter till we have heard both sides; and, moreover, that we do our best to avoid hearing either one side or the other if the matter does not concern us.

Is not this a sufficient explanation of my declaration that I have one blind eye and one deaf ear, and that they are the best eye and ear I have?

16

The Minister's Fainting Fits

. . . The strong are not always vigorous, the wise not always ready, the brave not always courageous, and the joyous not always happy. . . .

It is not necessary by quotations from the biographies of eminent ministers to prove that seasons of fearful prostration have fallen to the lot of most, if not all of them. The life of Luther might suffice to give a thousand instances, and he was by no means of the weaker sort. His great spirit was often in the seventh heaven of exultation, and as frequently on the borders of despair. . . . Instead of multiplying cases, let us dwell upon the reasons why these things are permitted; why it is that the children of light sometimes walk in the thick darkness; why the heralds of the daybreak find themselves at times in tenfold night. . . .

It is of need be that we are sometimes in heaviness. Good men are promised tribulation in this world, and ministers may expect a larger share than others, that they may learn sympathy with the Lord's suffering people, and so may be fitting shepherds of an ailing flock. Disembodied spirits might have been sent to proclaim the word, but they could not have entered into the feelings of those who, being in this body, do groan, being burdened; angels might have been ordained evangelists, but their celestial attributes would have disqualified them from having compassion on the ignorant; men of marble might have been fashioned, but their impassive natures would have been a sarcasm upon our feebleness, and a mockery of our wants. Men, and men subject to human passions, the all-wise God has chosen to be his vessels of grace; hence these tears, hence these perplexities and castings down.

Moreover, *most of us are in some way or other unsound physically.* Here and there we meet with an old man who could not remember that ever he was laid aside for a day; but the great mass of us labour under some form or other of infirmity, either in body or mind. . . . As to mental maladies, is any man altogether sane? Are we not all a little off the balance? Some minds appear to have a gloomy tinge essential to their very individuality; of them it may be said, "Melancholy marked them for her own"—fine minds withal, and ruled by noblest principles, but yet most prone to forget the silver lining, and to remember only the cloud. . . . These infirmities may be no detriment to a man's career of special usefulness; they may even have been imposed upon him by divine wisdom as necessary qualifications for his peculiar course of service. Some plants owe their medicinal qualities to the marsh in which they grow; others to the shades in which alone they flourish. There are precious fruits put forth by the moon as well as by the sun. Boats need ballast as well as sail; a drag on the carriage wheel is no hindrance when the road runs downhill. Pain has, probably, in some cases developed genius, hunting out the soul which otherwise might have slept like a lion in its den. Had it not been for the broken wing, some might have lost themselves in the clouds, some even of those choice doves who now bear the olive branch in their mouths and show the way to the ark. But where in body and mind there are predisposing causes to lowness of spirit, it is no marvel if in dark moments the heart succumbs to them; the wonder in many cases is—and if inner lives could be written, men would see it so—how some ministers keep at their work at all, and still wear a smile upon their countenances. . . . "Blessed are they that mourn," said the Man of Sorrows, and let none account themselves otherwise when their tears are salted with grace. We have the treasure of the gospel in earthen vessels, and if there be a flaw in the vessel here and there, let none wonder.

Our work, when earnestly undertaken, lays us open to attacks in the direction of depression. Who can bear the weight of souls without sinking to the dust? Passionate longings after men's conversion, if not fully satisfied (and when are they?), consume the soul with anxiety and disappointment. To see the hopeful turn aside, the godly grow cold, professors abusing their privileges, and sinners waxing more bold in sin—are not these sights enough to crush us to the earth? . . . How can we be otherwise than sorrowful, while men believe not our report, and the divine arm is not revealed? All mental work tends to weary and to depress, for much study is a weariness of the flesh; but ours is more than mental work—it is heart work, the labour of our inmost soul. . . . It is our duty and our privilege to exhaust our lives for Jesus. We are not to be living specimens of men in fine preservation, but living *sacrifices,* whose lot is to be consumed; we are to spend and to be spent, not to lay ourselves up in lavender, and nurse our flesh. Such soul-travail as that of a faithful minister will bring on occasional seasons of exhaustion, when heart and flesh will fail. Moses' hands grew heavy in intercession, and Paul cried out, "Who is sufficient for these things?" Even John the Baptist is thought to have had his fainting fits, and the apostles were once amazed, and were sore afraid.

Our position in the church will also conduce to this. A minister fully equipped for his work will usually be a spirit by himself, above, beyond, and apart from others. The most loving of his people cannot enter into his peculiar thoughts, cares, and temptations. In the ranks, men walk shoulder to shoulder, with many comrades, but as the officer rises in rank, men of his standing are fewer in number. There are many soldiers, few captains, fewer colonels, but only one commander-in-chief. So, in our churches, the man whom the Lord raises as a leader becomes, in the same degree in which he is a superior man, a solitary man. . . . Men of God who rise above their fellows into nearer communion with heavenly things, in their weaker moments feel the lack of human sympathy. Like their Lord in Gethsemane, they look in vain for comfort to the disciples sleeping around them; they are shocked at the apathy of their little band of brethren, and return to their secret agony with all the heavier burden pressing upon them, because they have found their dearest companions slumbering. No one knows, but he who has endured it, the solitude of a soul which has outstripped its fellows in zeal for the Lord of hosts: it dares not reveal itself, lest men count it mad; it cannot conceal itself, for a fire burns within its bones; only before the Lord does it find rest. Our Lord's sending out his disciples by two and two manifested that he knew what was in men; but for such a man as Paul, it seems to me that no helpmeet was found; Barnabas, or Silas, or Luke, were hills too low to hold high converse with such a Himalayan summit as the apostle of the Gentiles. This loneliness, which if I mistake not is felt by many of my brethren, is a fertile source of depression; and our ministers' fraternal meetings, and the cultivation of holy intercourse with kindred minds, will, with God's blessing, help us greatly to escape the snare.

There can be little doubt that sedentary habits have a tendency to create despondency in some constitutions. Burton, in his *Anatomy of Melancholy*, has a chapter upon this cause of sadness; and, quoting from one of the myriad authors whom he lays under contribution, he says:

> Students are negligent of their bodies. Other men look to their tools; a painter will wash his pencils; a smith will look to his hammer, anvil, forge; a husbandman will mend his plough-irons, and grind his hatchet if it be dull; a falconer or huntsman will have an especial care of his hawks, hounds, horses, dogs, etc.; a musician will string and unstring his lute; only scholars neglect that instrument (their brain and spirits I mean) which they daily use.

. . . To sit long in one posture, poring over a book, or driving a quill, is in itself a taxing of nature; but add to this a badly ventilated chamber, a body which has long been without muscular

exercise, and a heart burdened with many cares, and we have all
the elements for preparing a seething cauldron of despair, especially in the dim months of fog—

> When a blanket wraps the day,
> When the rotten woodland drips,
> And the leaf is stamped in clay.

Let a man be naturally as blithe as a bird, he will hardly be
able to bear up year after year against such a suicidal process;
he will make his study a prison and his books the warders of a
gaol, while nature lies outside his window calling him to health
and beckoning him to joy. He who forgets the humming of the
bees among the heather, the cooing of the wood pigeons in the
forest, the song of birds in the woods, the rippling of rills among
the rushes, and the sighing of the wind among the pines, need
not wonder if his heart forgets to sing and his soul grows heavy.
A day's breathing of fresh air upon the hills, or a few hours'
ramble in the beechwoods' umbrageous calm, would sweep the
cobwebs out of the brain of scores of our toiling ministers who
are now but half alive. A mouthful of sea air, or a stiff walk
in the wind's face, would not give grace to the soul, but it would
yield oxygen to the body, which is next best.

> Heaviest the heart is in a heavy air,
> Ev'ry wind that rises blows away despair.

The ferns and the rabbits, the streams and the trout, the fir
trees and the squirrels, the primroses and the violets, the farmyard, the new-mown hay, and the fragrant hops—these are the
best medicines for hypochondriacs, the surest tonics for the declining, the best refreshments for the weary. For lack of opportunity, or inclination, these great remedies are neglected, and
the student becomes a self-immolated victim.

The times most favorable to fits of depression, so far as I
have experienced, may be summed up in a brief catalogue. First
among them I mention *the hour of great success.* When at last a

long-cherished desire is fulfilled, when God has been glorified greatly by our means, a great triumph achieved, then we are apt to faint. It might be imagined that amid special favours our soul would soar to heights of ecstasy, and rejoice with joy unspeakable, but it is generally the reverse. The Lord seldom exposes his warriors to the perils of exultation over victory; he knows that few of them can endure such a test, and therefore dashes their cup with bitterness. . . . While the trial lasts, the strength is equal to the emergency; but when it is over, natural weakness claims the right to show itself. Secretly sustained, Jacob can wrestle all night, but he must limp in the morning when the contest is over, lest he boast himself beyond measure. . . . Men cannot bear unalloyed happiness. . . . Whirled from off our feet by a revival, carried aloft by popularity, exalted by success in soul-winning, we should be as the chaff which the wind driveth away, were it not that the gracious discipline of mercy breaks the ships of our vainglory with a strong east wind, and casts us shipwrecked, naked, and forlorn upon the Rock of Ages.

Before any great achievement, some measure of the same depression is very usual. Surveying the difficulties before us, our hearts sink within us. . . . Such was my experience when I first became a pastor in London. My success appalled me; and the thought of the career which it seemed to open up, so far from elating me, cast me into the lowest depth, out of which I uttered my *miserere* and found no room for a *gloria in excelsis.* Who was I that I should continue to lead so great a multitude? I would betake me to my village obscurity, or emigrate to America, and find a solitary nest in the backwoods, where I might be sufficient for the things which would be demanded of me. It was just then that the curtain was rising upon my lifework, and I dreaded what it might reveal. I hope I was not faithless, but I was timorous and filled with a sense of my own unfitness. I dreaded the work which a gracious providence had prepared for me. . . . This depression comes over me whenever the Lord is preparing a larger blessing for my ministry. . . .

In the midst of a long stretch of unbroken labour, the same affliction may be looked for. The bow cannot be always bent without fear of breaking. Repose is as needful to the mind as sleep to the body. Our Sabbaths are our days of toil, and if we do not rest upon some other day we shall break down. . . . Rest time is not waste time. It is economy to gather fresh strength. Look at the mower in the summer's day, with so much to cut down ere the sun sets. He pauses in his labour—is he a sluggard? He looks for his stone, and begins to draw it up and down his scythe, with *rink-a-tink rink-a-tink, rink-a-tink.* Is that idle music—is he wasting precious moments? How much he might have mowed while he has been ringing out those notes on his scythe! But he is sharpening his tool, and he will do far more when once again he gives his strength to those long sweeps which lay the grass prostrate in rows before him. Even thus a little pause prepares the mind for greater service in the good cause. Fishermen must mend their nets, and we must every now and then repair our mental waste and set our machinery in order for future service. To tug the oar from day to day, like a galley-slave who knows no holidays, suits not mortal men. Millstreams go on and on for ever, but we must have our pauses and our intervals. Who can help being out of breath when the race is continued without intermission? Even beasts of burden must be turned out to grass occasionally; the very sea pauses at ebb and flood; earth keeps the Sabbath of the wintry months; and man, even when exalted to be God's ambassador, must rest or faint; must trim his lamp or let it burn low; must recruit his vigour or grow prematurely old. It is wisdom to take occasional furlough. In the long run, we shall do more by sometimes doing less. On, on, on, for ever, without recreation, may suit spirits emancipated from this "heavy clay," but while we are in this tabernacle, we must every now and then cry halt, and serve the Lord by holy inaction and consecrated leisure. Let no tender conscience doubt the lawfulness of going out of harness for a while, but learn from the experience of others the necessity and duty of taking timely rest.

One crushing stroke has sometimes laid the minister very low. The brother most relied upon becomes a traitor. Judas lifts up his heel against the man who trusted him, and the preacher's heart for the moment fails him. We are all too apt to look to an arm of flesh, and from that propensity many of our sorrows arise. . . . Strife, also, and division, and slander, and foolish censures, have often laid holy men prostrate, and made them go "as with a sword in their bones." Hard words wound some delicate minds very keenly. Many of the best of ministers, from the very spirituality of their character, are exceedingly sensitive—too sensitive for such a world as this. . . . By experience the soul is hardened to the rough blows which are inevitable in our warfare; but at first these things utterly stagger us, and send us to our homes wrapped in a horror of great darkness. The trials of a true minister are not few, and such as are caused by ungrateful professors are harder to bear than the coarsest attacks of avowed enemies. Let no man who looks for ease of mind and seeks the quietude of life enter the ministry; if he does so he will flee from it in disgust. . . .

This evil will also come upon us, we know not why, and then it is all the more difficult to drive it away. Causeless depression is not to be reasoned with, nor can David's harp charm it away by sweet discoursings. As well fight with the mist as with this shapeless, undefinable, yet all-beclouding hopelessness. One affords himself no pity when in this case, because it seems so unreasonable, and even sinful to be troubled without manifest cause; and yet troubled the man is, even in the very depths of his spirit. If those who laugh at such melancholy did but feel the grief of it for one hour, their laughter would be sobered into compassion. Resolution might, perhaps, shake it off, but where are we to find the resolution when the whole man is unstrung? The physician and the divine may unite their skill in such cases, and both find their hands full, and more than full. The iron bolt which so mysteriously fastens the door of hope and holds our spirits in gloomy prison, needs a heavenly hand to push it back; and when that hand is seen we cry with the apostle, "Blessed be God, even the Father of our Lord Jesus Christ, the Father of mercies, and the God of all comfort; Who comforteth us in all our tribulation, that we may be able to comfort them which are in any trouble, by the comfort wherewith we ourselves are comforted of God" (II Cor. 1:3-4). . . . When we are ridden with horrible fears, and weighed down with an intolerable incubus, we need but the Sun of Righteousness to rise, and the evils generated of our darkness are driven away; but nothing short of this will chase away the nightmare of the soul. . . .

If it be inquired why the valley of the shadow of death must so often be traversed by the servants of King Jesus, the answer is not far to find. All this is promotive of the Lord's mode of working, which is summed up in these words: "Not by might nor by power, but my Spirit, saith the Lord." Instruments shall be used, but their intrinsic weakness shall be clearly manifested; there shall be no division of the glory, no diminishing the honour due to the Great Worker. The man shall be emptied of self, and then filled with the Holy Ghost. In his own apprehension he shall be like a sere leaf driven of the tempest, and then shall be strengthened into a brazen wall against the enemies of truth. To hide pride from the worker is the great difficulty. Uninterrupted success and unfading joy in it would be more than our weak heads could bear. Our wine must needs be mixed with water, lest it turn our brains. My witness is, that those who are honoured of their Lord in public, have usually to endure a secret chastening, or to carry a peculiar cross, lest by any means they exalt themselves, and fall into the snare of the devil. . . .

By all the castings down of his servants God is glorified, for they are led to magnify him when again he sets them on their feet, and even while prostrate in the dust their faith yields him praise. They speak all the more sweetly of his faithfulness, and

are the more firmly established in his love. Such mature men
as some elderly preachers are, could scarcely have been produced
if they had not been emptied from vessel to vessel, and made to
see their own emptiness and the vanity of all things round about
them. Glory be to God for the furnace, the hammer, and the file.
Heaven shall be all the fuller of bliss because we have been
filled with anguish here below, and earth shall be better tilled
because of our training in the school of adversity.

The lesson of wisdom is, *be not dismayed by soul-trouble.*
Count it no strange thing, but a part of ordinary ministerial
experience. Should the power of depression be more than ordinary,
think not that all is over with your usefulness. Cast not away
your confidence, for it hath great recompense of reward. Even
if the enemy's foot be on your neck, expect to rise and over-
throw him. Cast the burden of the present, along with the sin
of the past and the fear of the future, upon the Lord, who for-
saketh not his saints. Live by the day—ay, by the hour. Put no
trust in frames and feelings. Care more for a grain of faith
than a ton of excitement. Trust in God alone, and lean not on
the reeds of human help. Be not surprised when friends fail you:
it is a failing world. Never count upon immutability in man:
inconstancy you may reckon upon without fear of disappointment.
The disciples of Jesus forsook him; be not amazed if your adherents wander away to other teachers: as they were not your all
when with you, all is not gone from you with their departure.
Serve God with all your might while the candle is burning, and
then when it goes out for a season, you will have the less to
regret. Be content to be nothing, for that is what you are. When
your own emptiness is painfully forced upon your consciousness, chide yourself that you ever dreamed of being full, except
in the Lord. Set small store by present rewards; be grateful for
earnests by the way, but look for the recompensing joy here-
after. Continue with double earnestness to serve your Lord when
no visible result is before you. . . . In nothing let us be turned

aside from the path which the divine call has urged us to pursue. Come fair or come foul, the pulpit is our watchtower, and the ministry our warfare; be it ours, when we cannot see the face of our God, to trust under the shadow of his wings.

17

The Minister's Ordinary
Conversation

OUR subject is to be the minister's common conversation
when he mingles with men in general, and is supposed to be
quite at his ease. How shall he order his speech among his fellow
men? First and foremost, let me say, *let him give himself no ministerial airs,* but avoid everything which is stilted, official, fussy,
and pretentious. "The Son of Man" is a noble title; it was given
to Ezekiel, and to a greater than he: let not the ambassador of
heaven be other than a son of man. In fact, let him remember
that the more simple and unaffected he is, the more closely
will he resemble that child-man, the holy child Jesus. There is
such a thing as trying to be too much a minister, and becoming
too little a man; though the more of a true man you are, the
more truly will you be what a servant of the Lord should be.
Schoolmasters and ministers have generally an appearance peculiarly their own; in the wrong sense, they "are not as other men
are." They are too often speckled birds, looking as if they were not
at home among the other inhabitants of the country, but awkward and peculiar. When I have seeen a flamingo gravely stalk-
ing along, an owl blinking in the shade, or a stork demurely
lost in thought, I have been irresistibly led to remember some
of my dignified brethren of the teaching and preaching fraternity,
who are so marvellously proper at all times that they are just
a shade amusing. Their very respectable, stilted, dignified, important, self-restrained manner is easily acquired; but is it worth
acquiring?

225

. . . I know brethren who, from head to foot, in garb, tone, manner, necktie, and boots, are so utterly "parsonic" that no particle of manhood is visible. One young sprig of divinity must needs go through the streets in a gown, and another of the High Church order has recorded it in the newspapers with much complacency that he traversed Switzerland and Italy, wearing in all places his biretta; few boys would have been so proud of a fool's cap. None of us are likely to go as far as that in our apparel; but we may do the like by our mannerism. Some men appear to have a white cravat twisted round their souls; their manhood is throttled with that starched rag. Certain brethren maintain an air of superiority which they think impressive, but which is simply offensive, and eminently opposed to their pretensions as followers of the lowly Jesus. . . . "Stand aside, I am holier than thou," is written across their foreheads.

A well-known minister was once rebuked by a sublime brother for his indulgence in a certain luxury, and the expense was made a great argument. "Well, well," he replied, "there may be something in that; but remember, I do not spend half so much upon my weakness as you do in starch." That is the article I am deprecating, that dreadful ministerial starch. If you have indulged in it, I would earnestly advise you to "go and wash in Jordan seven times," and get it out of you, every particle of it. I am persuaded that one reason why our workingmen so universally keep clear of ministers is because they abhor their artificial and unmanly ways. If they saw us, in the pulpit and out of it, acting like real men, and speaking naturally, like honest men, they would come around us. . . . The vice of the ministry is that ministers will parsonificate the gospel. We must have humanity along with our divinity if we would win the masses. Everybody can see through affectations, and people are not likely to be taken in by them. Fling away your stilts, brethren, and walk on your feet; doff your ecclesiasticism, and array yourselves in truth.

Still a minister, wherever he is, is a minister, and should recollect that he is on duty. A policeman or a soldier may be off duty, but a minister never is. Even in our recreations we should still pursue the great object of our lives; for we are called to be diligent "in season and out of season." . . . A minister should be like a certain chamber which I saw at Beaulieu, in the New Forest, in which a cobweb is never seen. . . . Our minds should be equally clear of idle habits.

On our public rests for porters in the City of London you may read the words, "Rest, but do not loiter," and they contain advice worthy of our attention. . . . When the mind gets fatigued and out of order, to rest it is no more idleness than sleep is idleness; and no man is called lazy for sleeping the proper time. It is far better to be industriously asleep than lazily awake. Be ready to do good even in your resting times and in your leisure hours; and so be really a minister, and there will be no need for you to proclaim that you are so.

The Christian minister out of the pulpit should be a sociable man. . . . Keep aloof from others, and how can you benefit them? Our Master went to a wedding, and ate bread with publicans and sinners, and yet was far more pure than those sanctimonious Pharisees, whose glory was that they were separate from their fellow men. Some ministers need to be told that they are of the same species as their hearers. It is a remarkable fact, but we may as well state it, that bishops, canons, archdeacons, prebendaries, rural deans, rectors, vicars, and even archbishops, are only men after all; and God has not railed off a holy corner of the earth to serve as a chancel for them, to abide therein by themselves.

It would not be amiss if there could be a revival of holy talk in the churchyard and the meeting-yard. I like to see the big yew trees outside our ancient churches with seats all round them. They seem to say: "Sit down here, neighbour, and talk upon the sermon; here comes the pastor, he will join us, and we shall have a pleasant, holy chat." It is not every preacher we would care to talk with; but there are some whom one would give a fortune to converse with for an hour. I love a minister whose face invites me to make him my friend—a man upon whose door-step you read, *Salve,* "Welcome"; and feel that there is no need of that Pompeian warning, *Cave Canem,* "Beware of the dog." Give me the man around whom the children come, like flies around a honeypot: they are first-class judges of a good man. . . . So you will find that children have their instincts, and discover very speedily who is their friend; and depend upon it the children's friend is one who will be worth knowing. Have a good word to say to each and every member of the family—the big boys, and the young ladies, and the little girls, and everybody. No one knows what a smile and a hearty sentence may do. A man who is to do much with men must love them, and feel at home with them. An individual who has no geniality about him had better be an undertaker, and bury the dead, for he will never succeed in influencing the living. . . . A man must have a great heart if he would have a great congregation. His heart should be as capacious as those noble harbours along our coast, which contain sea room for a fleet. When a man has a large, loving heart, men go to him as ships to a haven, and feel at peace when they have anchored under the lee of his friendship. Such a man is hearty in private as well as in public; his blood is not cold and fishy, but he is warm as your own fireside. No pride and selfishness chill you when you approach him; he has his doors all open to receive you, and you are at home with him at once. Such men I would persuade you to be, every one of you.

The Christian minister should also be very cheerful. I don't believe in going about like certain monks whom I saw in Rome, who salute each other in sepulchral tones, and convey the pleasant information, "Brother, we must die"; to which lively salutation each lively brother of the order replies, "Yes, brother, we must die." I was glad to be assured upon such good authority that all these lazy fellows are about to die; upon the whole, it is about the best thing they can do; but till that event occurs, they might use some more comfortable form of salutation.

No doubt there are some people who will be impressed by the very solemn appearance of ministers. I have heard of one who felt convinced that there must be something in the Roman Catholic religion, from the extremely starved and pinched appearance of a certain ecclesiastic. . . . Certainly, I have never met with a text which mentions prominence of bone as an evidence of grace. . . . Some of the biggest rogues in the world have been as mortified in appearance as if they had lived on locusts and wild honey. It is a very vulgar error to suppose that a melancholy countenance is the index of a gracious heart. I commend cheerfulness to all who would win souls; not levity and frothiness, but a genial, happy spirit. There are more flies caught with honey than with vinegar, and there will be more souls led to heaven by a man who wears heaven in his face than by one who bears Tartarus in his looks.

Young ministers, and, indeed, all others, when they are in company, *should take care not to engross all the conversation.* They are quite qualified to do so, no doubt—I mean from their capacity to instruct, and readiness of utterance—but they must remember that people do not care to be perpetually instructed; they like to take a turn in the conversation themselves. Nothing pleases some people so much as to let them talk, and it may be for their good to let them be pleased. I spent an hour one evening with a person who did me the honour to say that he found me a very charming companion, and most instructive in conversation; yet I do not hesitate to confess that I said scarcely anything at all, but allowed him to have the talk to himself. By exercising patience I gained his good opinion, and an opportunity to address him on other occasions. A man has no more right at table to talk all than to eat all. We are not to think ourselves Sir Oracle, before whom no dog must open his mouth. No; let all the company contribute of their stores, and they will think all the better of the godly words with which you try to season the discourse.

There are some companies into which you will go, especially

when you are first settled, where everybody will be awed by the majesty of your presence, and people will be invited because the new minister is to be there. . . . Hero-worship is a kind of idolatry, and must not be encouraged. . . . Ministers will not have to do it long; for their foolish admirers are very apt to turn round upon them, and if they do not stone them nearly to death, they will go as far as they dare in unkindness and contempt.

While I say, "Do not talk all, or assume an importance which is mere imposture," still, *do not be a dummy*. People will form their estimate of you and your ministry by what they see of you in private as well as by your public deliverances. Many young men have ruined themselves in the pulpit by being indiscreet in the parlor, and have lost all hope of doing good by their stupidity or frivolity in company. Don't be an inanimate log. . . .

Try to turn the conversation to profitable use. Be sociable and cheerful and all that, but labour to accomplish something. Why should you sow the wind, or plough a rock? Consider yourself, after all, as being very much responsible for the conversation which goes on where you are. . . . therefore, steer it into a good channel. Do this without roughness or force. . . . If your heart is in it and your wits are awake, this will be easy enough, especially if you breathe a prayer for guidance.

. . . To be a holy talker for Jesus might be almost as fruitful an office as to be a faithful preacher. . . .

Here, perhaps, I may insert a canon, which nevertheless I believe to be quite needless, in reference to each one of the honourable brethren whom I am now addressing. *Do not frequent rich men's tables to gain their countenance, and never make yourself a sort of general hanger-on at tea-parties and entertainments.* Who are you that you should be dancing attendance upon this wealthy man and the other, when the Lord's poor, his sick people, and his wandering sheep require you? . . . Deliciously sarcastic was that famous letter "from an old and beloved minister to his dear son" upon his entrance into the ministry, the following extract from which hits our present point:

. . . Keep also a watchful eye on all likely persons, especially wealthy or influential, who may come to your town; call upon them, and attempt to win them over by the devotions of the drawing room to your cause. Thus you may most efficiently serve the Master's interests. People need looking after, and the result of a long experience goes to confirm my conviction, long cherished, that the power of the pulpit is trifling compared with the power of the parlor. We must imitate and sanctify, by the Word of God and prayer, the exercises of the Jesuits. They succeeded not by the pulpit so much as by the parlor. In the parlor you can whisper— you can meet people on all their little personal private ideas. The pulpit is a very unpleasant place; of course it is the great power of God, and so on, but it is the parlor that tells, and a minister has not the same chance of success if he be a good preacher as if he is a perfect gentleman; nor in cultivated society has any man a legitimate prospect of success if he is not, whatever else he may be, a gentleman. I have always admired Lord Shaftesbury's character of St. Paul in his "Characteristics"—that he was a fine gentleman. And I would say to you, be a gentleman. Not that I need to say so, but I am persuaded that only in this way can we hope for the conversion of our growing, wealthy middle classes. We must show that our religion is the religion of good sense and good taste; that we disapprove of strong excitements and strong stimulants; and oh, my dear boy, if you would be useful, often in your closet make it a matter of earnest prayer that you may be proper. If I were asked what is your first duty, *be proper;* and your second, *be proper;* and your third, *be proper.*

. . . In all probability, sensible conversation will sometimes drift into controversy, and here many a good man runs upon a snag. *The sensible minister will be particularly gentle in argument.* He, above all should not make the mistake of fancying that there is force in temper, and power in speaking angrily. A heathen who stood in a crowd in Calcutta, listening to a missionary disputing with a Brahmin, said he knew which was right though he did not understand the language—he knew that he was in the wrong who lost his temper first. For the most part, that is a very accurate way of judging. Try to avoid debating with people. State your opinion and let them state theirs. If you see that a stick is crooked, and you want people to see how crooked it is, lay a straight rod down beside it; that will be quite enough. But if you are drawn into controversy, use very hard arguments and very soft words. Frequently you cannot convince a man by tugging at his reason, but you can persuade him by winning his affections. . . .

And lastly, with all his amiability, *the minister should be firm for his principles, and bold to avow and defend them in all companies.* When a fair opportunity occurs, or he has managed to create one, let him not be slow to make use of it. Strong in his principles, earnest in his tone, and affectionate in heart, let him speak out like a man and thank God for the privilege. There need be no reticence—there should be none. The maddest romances of Spiritualists, the wildest dreams of Utopian reformers, the silliest chitchat of the town, and the vainest nonsense of the frivolous word, demand a hearing and get it. And shall not Christ be heard? Shall his message of love remain untold, for fear we should be charged with intrusion or accused of cant? Is religion to be tabooed—the best and noblest of all themes forbidden? If this be the rule of any society, we will not comply with it. If we cannot break it down, we will leave the society to itself, as men desert a house smitten with leprosy. We cannot consent to be gagged. There is no reason why we should be. We will go to no place where we cannot take our Master with us. While others take liberty to sin, we shall not renounce our liberty to rebuke and warn them.

Wisely used, our common conversation may be a potent means for good. Trains of thought may be started by a single sentence which may lead to the conversion of persons whom our sermons have never reached. . . .

Be it ours to sow, not only on the honest and good soil, but on the rock and on the highway, and at the last great day to reap a glad harvest. May the bread which we cast upon the waters in odd times and strange occasions be found again after many days.

█

18

Attention!

OUR subject is one which I find scarcely ever noticed in any books upon homiletics—a very curious fact, for it is a most important matter, and worthy of more than one chapter. . . . That overlooked topic is, *how to obtain and retain the attention of our hearers.* Their attention must be gained, or nothing can be done with them: and it must be retained, or we may go on word-spinning, but no good will come of it.

Over the head of military announcements our English officers always place the word "ATTENTION!" in large capitals, and we need some such word over all our sermons. We need the earnest, candid, wakeful, continued attention of all those who are in the congregation. If men's minds are wandering far away they cannot receive the truth, and it is much the same if they are inactive. . . . There are preachers who care very little whether they are attended to or not; so long as they can hold on through the allotted time it is of very small importance to them whether their people hear for eternity, or hear in vain: the sooner such ministers sleep in the churchyard and preach by the verse on their gravestones the better. Some brethren speak up the ventilator, as if they sought the attention of the angels; and others look down upon their book as if they were absorbed in thought, or had themselves for an audience, and felt much honoured thereby. Why do not such brethren preach on the prairie and edify the stars? If their preaching has no reference to their hearers they might do so with evident propriety; if a sermon be a soliloquy, the more lonely the performer the better. To a rational preacher (and not all are rational) it must seem essential to interest all his audience, from the eldest to the youngest. We ought not to make even children inattentive. "Make them inattentive," say you, "who does that?" I say that most preachers do; and when children are not quiet in a meeting it is often as much our fault as theirs.

Can you not put in a little story or parable on purpose for the little ones? Can you not catch the eye of the boy in the gallery, and the little girl downstairs, who have begun to fidget, and smile them into order? I often talk with my eyes to the orphan boys at the foot of my pulpit. We want all eyes fixed upon us and all ears open to us. To me it is an annoyance if even a blind man does not look at me with his face. If I see anybody turning round, whispering, nodding, or looking at his watch, I judge that I am not up to the mark, and must by some means win these minds. Very seldom have I to complain, and when I do, my general plan is to complain of myself, and own that I have no right to attention unless I know how to command it.

Now, there are some congregations whose attention you do not readily gain; they do not care to be interested. It is useless to scold them; that will be like throwing a bush at a bird to catch it. The fact is, that in most cases there is another person whom you should scold, and that is yourself. It may be their duty to attend, but it is far more your duty to make them do so. You must attract the fish to your hook, and if they do not come you should blame the fisherman and not the fish. Compel them to stand still awhile and hear what God the Lord would speak to their souls. . . . Recollect that to some of our people it is not so easy to be attentive; many of them are not interested in the matter, and they have felt not enough of any gracious operation on their hearts to make them confess that the gospel is of any special value to them. . . . Many of them have through the week been borne down by the press of business cares. They ought to roll their burden on the Lord; but do *you* always do so? Do *you* always find it easy to escape from anxieties? Are *you* able to forget the sick wife and the ailing children at home? There is no doubt whatever that many come into the house of God loaded heavily with the thoughts of their daily avocations. The farmer recollects the fields that are to be ploughed or to be sown; it is a wet Sunday, and he is reflecting upon the yellow look of the young wheat. The merchant sees that dishonoured bill fluttering before his eyes, and the tradesman counts over his bad debts. I should not wonder if the colours of the ladies' ribbons and the creak of the gentlemen's boots disturb many. . . . You must have sufficient leverage in your discourse and its subject to lift them right up from the earth to which they cleave, and to elevate them a little nearer heaven.

Frequently it is very difficult for congregations to attend, because of the place and the atmosphere. For instance, if the place is like this room at present, sealed against the pure air, with every window closed, they have enough to do to breathe, and cannot think of anything else: when people have inhaled over and over again the air which has been in other people's lungs, the whole machinery of life gets out of gear, and they are more likely to feel an aching head than a broken heart. The next best thing to the grace of God for a preacher is oxygen. Pray that the windows of heaven may be opened, but begin by opening the windows of your meetinghouse. . . .

Sometimes the manners of our people are inimical to attention; they are not in the habit of attending; they attend the chapel but do not attend to the preacher. They are accustomed to look round at every one who enters the place, and they come in at all times, sometimes with much stamping, squeaking of boots, and banging of doors. I was preaching once to a people who continually looked around, and I adopted the expedient of saying, "Now, friends, as it is so very interesting to you to know who comes in, and it disturbs me so very much for you to look around, I will, if you like, describe each one as he comes in, so that you may sit and look at me, and keep up at least a show of decency." I described one gentleman who came in, who happened to be a friend whom I could depict without offence, as "a very respectable gentleman who had just taken his hat off," and so on; and after that one attempt I found it was not necessary to describe any more, because they felt shocked at what I was doing, and I assured them that I was much more shocked that they should render it necessary for me to reduce their conduct to such absurdity. It cured them for the time being, and I hope for ever, much to their pastor's joy.

. . . *In order to get attention, the first golden rule is, always say something worth hearing.* Most persons possess an instinct which leads them to desire to hear a good thing. They have a similar instinct, also, which you had better take note of, namely, that which prevents their seeing the good of attentively listening to mere words. It is not a severe criticism to say that there are ministers whose words stand in a very large proportion to their thoughts. In fact, their words hide their thoughts, if they have any. They pour out heaps of chaff, and, perhaps, there may be somewhere or other an oat or two, but it would be hard to say where. . . .

Give your hearers something which they can treasure up and remember; something likely to be useful to them, the best matter from the best of places, solid doctrine from the Divine Word. Give them manna fresh from the skies, not the same thing over and over again, in the same form ad nauseam, like workhouse bread cut into the same shape all the year round. Give them something striking, something that a man might get up in the middle of the night to hear, and which is worth his walking fifty miles to listen to. You are quite capable of doing that. *Do it,* brethren. Do it continually, and you will have all the attention you can desire.

Let the good matter which you give them be very clearly arranged. There is a great deal in that. It is possible to heap up a vast mass of good things all in a muddle. Ever since the day I was sent to shop with a basket, and purchased a pound of tea, a quarter-of-a-pound of mustard, and three pounds of rice, and on my way home saw a pack of hounds and felt it necessary to follow them over hedge and ditch (as I always did when I was a boy), and found when I reached home that all the goods were amalgamated—tea, mustard, and rice—into one awful mess, I have understood the necessity of packing up my subjects in good stout parcels, bound round with the thread of my discourse; and this makes me keep to firstly, secondly, and thirdly, however unfashionable that method may now be. People will not drink your mustardy tea, nor will they enjoy muddled-up sermons, in which you cannot tell head from tail, because they have neither, but are like Mr. Bright's Skye terrier, whose head and tail were both alike. Put the truth before men in a logical, orderly manner, so that they can easily remember it, and they will the more readily receive it.

Be sure, moreover, to speak plainly, because, however excellent your matter, if a man does not comprehend it, it can be of no use to him; you might as well have spoken to him in the language of Kamtchatka as in your own tongue, if you use phrases that are quite out of his line, and modes of expression which are not suitable to his mind. Go up to his level if he is a poor man; go down to his understanding if he is an educated person. You smile at my contorting the terms in that manner, but I think there is more going up in being plain to the illiterate than there is in being refined for the polite; at any rate, it is the more difficult of the two, and the most like the Saviour's mode of speech. It is wise to walk in a path where your auditors can accompany you, and not to mount the high horse and ride over their heads. Our Lord and Master was the King of preachers, and he never was above anybody's comprehension, except so far as the grandeur and glory of his matter were concerned; his words and utterances were such that he spake like "the holy child Jesus." Let your hearts indite a good matter, clearly arranged and plainly put, and you are pretty sure to gain the ear, and so the heart.

Attend also to your manner of address; aim in that at the promotion of attention. And here I should say, as a rule do not read your sermons. . . . The best reading I have ever heard has tasted of paper, and has stuck in my throat. I have not relished it, for my digestion is not good enough to dissolve foolscap. . . .

Here let me say, *if you would be listened to, do not extemporize in the emphatic sense,* for that is as bad as reading, or perhaps worse (unless the manuscript was written extemporaneously); I mean without previous study. Do not go into the pulpit and say the first thing that comes to hand, for the uppermost thing with most men is mere froth. Your people need discourses which have been prayed over and laboriously prepared. People do not want raw food; it must be cooked and made ready for them. We must give out of our very souls, in the words which naturally suggest themselves, the matter which has been as thoroughly prepared by us as it possibly could have been by a sermon-writer; indeed, it should be even better prepared, if we would speak well. The best method is, in my judgment, that in which the man does not extemporize the matter, but extemporizes the words; the language comes to him at the moment, but the theme has been well thought out. . . .

In order to get attention, make your manner as pleasing as it can possibly be. Do not, for instance, indulge in monotones. Vary your voice continually. Vary your speed as well—dash as rapidly as a lightning flash, and anon, travel forward in quiet majesty. Shift your accent, move your emphasis, and avoid singsong. Vary the tone; use the bass sometimes, and let the thunders roll within; at other times speak as you ought to do generally— from the lips, and let your speech be conversational. Anything for a change. . . . I shall not, however, dwell much upon this, because preachers have been known to arouse and sustain attention by their matter alone, when their mode of speech has been very imperfect. . . .

We may remember that Mosees was slow of speech, and yet every ear was attent to his words: probably Paul also laboured under a similar infirmity, for his speech was said to be contemptible; of this, however, we are not sure, for it was only the criticism of his enemies. Paul's power in the churches was very great, and yet he was not always able to maintain attention when his sermon was long, for at least one hearer went to sleep under him with serious result. Manner is not everything. Still, if you have gathered good matter, it is a pity to convey it meanly: a king should not ride in a dustcart; the glorious doctrines of grace should not be slovenly delivered. Right royal truths should ride in a chariot of gold. Bring forth the noblest of your milk-white steeds, and let the music sound forth melodiously from the silver trumpets, as truth rides through the streets. If people do not attend, do not let them find excuses in our faulty utterance. If, however, we cannot mend in this respect let us be the more diligent to make up for it by the richness of our matter, and on all occasions let us do our very best.

As a rule, do not make the introduction too long. It is always a pity to build a great porch to a little house. An excellent Christian woman once heard John Howe, and, as he took up an hour in his preface, her observation was, that the dear good man was so long a time in laying the cloth, that she lost her appetite; she did not think there would be any dinner after all. Spread your table quickly, and have done with the clatter of the knives and plates. . . . I prefer to make the introduction of my sermon very like that of the town crier, who rings his bell and cries, "Oh, yes! This is to give notice," merely to let people know that he has news for them and wants them to listen. To do that, the introduction should have something striking in it. It is well to fire a startling shot as the signal gun to clear the decks for action. Do not start at the full pitch and tension of your mind, but yet in such way that all will be led to expect a good time. Do not make your exordium a pompous introduction into nothing, but a step to something better still. Be alive at the very commencement.

In preaching, *do not repeat yourselves.* I used to hear a divine who had a habit, after he had uttered about a dozen sentences, of saying, "As I have already observed," or, "I repeat what I before remarked." Well, good soul, as there was nothing particular in what he had said, the repetition only revealed the more clearly the nakedness of the land. If it was very good, and you said it forcibly, why go over it again? And if it was a feeble affair, why exhibit it a second time? Occasionally, of course, the repetition of a few sentences may be very telling; anything may be good occasionally, and yet be very vicious as a habit. Who wonders that people do not listen the first time when they know it is all to come over again?

Yet further, do not repeat the same idea over and over again in other words. Let there be something fresh in each sentence. Be not for ever hammering away at the same nail: yours is a large Bible; permit the people to enjoy its length and breadth. And, brethren, do not think it necessary or important every time you preach to give a complete summary of theology, or a formal digest of doctrines. . . . I know a divine whose sermons whenever they are printed read like theological summaries, more fitted for a classroom than for a pulpit—they fall flat on the public ear. Our hearers do not want the bare bones of definition, but meat and flavour. Definitions and differences are all very well; but when they are the staple of a sermon they remind us of the young man whose discourse was made up of various important distinctions. Upon this performance an old deacon observed, that there was one distinction which he had omitted, namely, the distinction between meat and bones. If preachers do not make that distinction, all their other distinctions will not bring them much distinction

In order to maintain attention, *avoid being too long*. An old preacher used to say to a young man who preached an hour, "My dear friend, I do not care what else you preach about, but I wish you would always preach *about* forty minutes." We ought seldom to go much beyond that—forty minutes, or say, three-quarters of an hour. If a fellow cannot say all he has to say in that time, when will he say it? But somebody said he liked "to do justice to his subject." Well, but ought he not to do justice to his people, or, at least, have a little mercy upon them, and not keep them too long? The subject will not complain of you,

but the people will. In some country places, in the afternoon
especially, the farmers have to milk their cows, and one farmer
bitterly complained to me about a young man—I think from this
College—"Sir, he ought to have given over at four o'clock,
but he kept on till half-past, and there were all my cows waiting
to be milked! *How would he have liked it if he had been a cow?*"
There was a great deal of sense in that question. The Society
for the Prevention of Cruelty to Animals ought to have prosecuted
that young sinner. How can farmers hear to profit when they have
cows-on-the-brain? The mother feels morally certain during that
extra ten minutes of your sermon that the baby is crying, or the
fire is out, and she cannot and will not give her heart to your
ministrations. You are keeping her ten minutes longer than she
bargained for, and she looks upon it as a piece of injustice on
your part. There is a kind of moral compact between you and your
congregation that you will not weary them more than an hour and
a half, and if you keep them longer, it amounts to an infraction
of a treaty and a piece of practical dishonesty of which you ought
not to be guilty. Brevity is a virtue within the reach of all of
us; do not let us lose the opportunity of gaining the credit which
it brings. If you ask me how you may shorten your sermons, I
should say, *study them better.* Spend more time in the study that
you may need less in the pulpit. We are generally longest when
we have least to say. A man with a great deal of well-prepared
matter will probably not exceed forty minutes; when he has less to
say he will go on for fifty minutes, and when he has absolutely
nothing he will need an hour to say it in. Attend to these minor
things and they will help to retain attention. . . .

Our whole life must be such as to add weight to our words,
so that in after years we shall be able to wield the invincible
eloquence of a long-sustained character, and obtain, not merely
the attention, but the affectionate veneration of our flock. If
by our prayers and tears and labours our people become spiritually
healthy, we need not fear that we shall lose their attention. A
people hungering after righteousness, and a minister anxious to

feed their souls, will act in sweetest harmony with each other when their common theme is the word of the Lord.

If you need another direction for winning attention, I should say, *be interested yourself,* and you will interest others. . . . Your subject must weigh so much upon your own mind that you dedicate all your faculties at their best to the deliverance of your soul concerning it; and then when your hearers see that the topic has engrossed you, it will by degrees engross them.

Do you wonder that people do not attend to a man who does not feel that he has anything important to say? Do you wonder that they do not listen with all their ears when a man does not speak with all his heart? Do you marvel that their thoughts ramble to subjects which are real to them when they find that the preacher is wasting time over matters which he treats as if they were fictions? . . . At the same time, you cannot hold men's minds in rapt attention by mere earnestness if you have nothing to say. People will not stand at their doors for ever to hear a fellow beat a drum; they will come out to see what he is at, but when they find that it is much ado about nothing, they will slam the door and go in again, as much as to say, "You have taken us in and we do not like it." Have something to say, and say it earnestly, and the congregation will be at your feet.

It may be superfluous to remark that for the mass of our people it is well that *there should be a goodly number of illustrations in our discourses.* We have the example of our Lord for that: and most of the greatest preachers have abounded in similes, metaphors, allegories, and anecdotes. But beware of overdoing this business . . . . If you tell anecdotes let them have some degree of freshness and originality; keep your eyes open, and gather flowers from the garden and the field with your own hands; they will be far more acceptable than withered specimens borrowed from other men's bouquets, however beautiful those may once have been. . . . Real instruction must be given and solid doctrine taught, or you will find your imagery pall upon your hearers, and they will pine for spiritual meat.

In your sermons *cultivate what Father Taylor calls "the surprise power."* There is a great deal of force in that for winning attention. Do not say what everybody expected you would say. Keep your sentence out of ruts. If you have already said, "Salvation is all of grace" do not always add, "and not by human merit," but vary it and say, "Salvation is all of grace; self-righteousness has not a corner to hide its head in." . . . I sat last year about this time on the beach at Mentone by the Mediterranean Sea. The waves were very gently rising and falling, for there is little or no tide, and the wind was still. The waves crept up languidly one after another, and I took little heed of them, though they were just at my feet. Suddenly, as if seized with a new passion, the sea sent up one far-reaching billow, which drenched me thoroughly. Quiet as I had been before, you can readily conceive how quickly I was on my feet, and how speedily my daydreaming ended. I observed to a ministering brother at my side, "This shows us how to preach; to wake people up we must astonish them with something they were not looking for." Brethren, take them at unawares. Let your thunderbolt drop out of a clear sky. When all is calm and bright let the tempest rush up, and by contrast make its terrors all the greater. Remember, however, that nothing will avail if you go to sleep yourself while you are preaching. Is that possible? Oh, possible! It is done every Sunday. Many ministers are more than half asleep all through the sermon; indeed, they never were awake at any time, and probably never will be unless a cannon should be fired off near their ear: tame phrases, hackneyed expressions, and dreary monotones make the staple of their discourses, and they wonder that the people are so drowsy: I confess I do not.

A very useful help in securing attention is *a pause.* Pull up short every now and then, and the passengers on your coach will wake up. The miller goes to sleep while the mill wheels revolve; but if by some means or other the grinding ceases, the good man starts and cries, "What now?" On a sultry summer's day, if nothing will keep off the drowsy feeling, be very short, sing more than usual, or call on a brother or two to pray. A minister who saw that the people would sleep, sat down and observed, "I saw you were all resting, and I thought I would rest too." . . . Know how to pause. . . . Speech is silver, but silence is golden when hearers are inattentive. Keep, on, on, on, on, on, with common-place matter and monotonous tone, and you are rocking the cradle, and deeper slumbers will result; give the cradle a jerk, and sleep will flee.

I suggest again that in order to secure attention all through a discourse, we must *make the people feel that they have an interest in what we are saying to them*. . . . I have heard of some very strange things, but I never did hear of a person going to sleep while a will was being read in which he expected a legacy; neither have I heard of a prisoner going to sleep while the judge was summing up, and his life was hanging in jeopardy. Self-interest quickens attention. Preach upon practical themes, pressing, present, personal matters, and you will secure an earnest hearing.

It will be well to *prevent attendants traversing the aisles* to meddle with gas or candles, or to distribute plates for collections, or to open windows. Deacons and sextons trotting over the place are a torture never to be patiently endured, and should be kindly, but decidedly, requested to suspend their perambulations.

Late attendance, also, needs remedying, and our gentlest reasonings and expostulations must be brought to bear upon it. . . .

I give you a golden rule for securing attention at the commencement, namely, always say something worth hearing; I will now give you a diamond rule, and conclude. *Be yourself* clothed with the Spirit of God, and then no question about attention or non-attention will arise. . . . When God speaks men must listen; and though he may speak through a poor feeble man like themselves, the majesty of the truth will compel them to regard his voice. Supernatural power must be your reliance. We say to you, perfect yourselves in oratory, cultivate all the fields of knowledge, make your sermon mentally and rhetorically all it ought to be (you ought to do no less in such a service), but at the same time remember, "It is not by might, nor by power," that men are regenerated or sanctified, but "by my Spirit, saith the Lord." Are you not conscious sometimes of being clad with zeal as with a cloak, and filled to the full with the Spirit of God? At such times you have had a hearing people, and erelong, a believing people; but if you are not thus endowed with power from on high, you are to them no more than a musician who plays upon a goodly instrument, or sings a sweet song with a clear voice, reaching the ear but not the heart. . . .

In fine, beloved brethren, by any means, by all means, labour to glorify God by conversions, and rest not till your heart's desire is fulfilled.

Marks of Faith

*"Then said Jesus unto him, Except ye see signs
and wonders, ye will not believe."*—John 4:48.

YOU will remember that Luke, in his letter to Theophilus,
speaks of things which Jesus began both *to do* and *to teach,* as if
there was a connection between his doings and his teachings.
In fact, there *was* a relation of the most intimate kind. His
teachings were the explanation of his doings; his doings con-
firmations of his teachings. Jesus Christ had never occasion to
say, "Do as I say, but not as I do." His words and his actions
were in perfect harmony with one another. You might be sure
that he was honest in what he *said,* because what he *did* forced that
conviction upon your mind. Moreover, you were led to see that
what he taught you must be true, because he spoke with authority—
an authority proved and demonstrated by the miracles he wrought.

Oh, my brethren in Christ! When our biographies shall come
to be written at last, God grant that they may not be all sayings,
but that they may be a history of our sayings and doings! And
may the good Spirit so dwell in us, that at last it may be seen
that our doings did not clash with our sayings! It is one thing
to preach, but another thing to practise; and unless preaching and practice go together, the preacher is himself condemned,
and his ill practice may be the means of condemning multitudes
through his leading them astray. If you make a profession of
being God's servant, live up to that profession; and if you
think it necessary to exhort others to virtue, take care that you

set the example. You can have no right to teach, if you have not yourself learned the lesson which you would teach to others.

Thus much by way of preface; and now concerning the subject itself. The narrative before us seems to me to suggest three points, and those points each of them triplets. I shall notice in this narrative, first, the three stages of faith; in the second place, the three diseases to which faith is subject; and, in the third place, three questions about your faith.

I.   To begin, then, with *faith in three of its stages.*

Doubtless, the history of faith might with propriety be divided just as accurately into five or six different states of growth; but our narrative suggests a threefold division, and therefore we stand to that this morning.

There is a nobleman living at Capernaum; he hears a rumour that a celebrated prophet and preacher is continually going through the cities of Galilee and Judea, and is given to understand that this mighty preacher does not merely charm every hearer by his eloquence, but wins the hearts of men by singularly benevolent miracles which he works as a confirmation of his mission. He stores these things in his heart, little thinking that they will ever be of any practical service to him. It comes to pass on a certain day that his son falls sick—perhaps his only son, one very dear to his father's heart. The sickness, instead of diminishing, gradually increases. Fever breathes its hot breath upon the child, and seems to dry up all the moisture in his body, and to blast the bloom from his cheek. The father consults every physician within his reach; they look upon the child and candidly pronounce him hopeless. No cure can possibly be wrought. That child is at the point of death; the arrow of death has almost sunk into his flesh; it has well-nigh penetrated his heart; he is not near death merely, but at death's very point; he has been forced by disease upon the barbed arrows of that insatiate archer. The father now bethinks himself, and calls to recollection the stories he has heard of the cures wrought by Jesus of

Nazareth. There is a little faith in his soul; though but a little, still enough to make him use every endeavour to test the truth of what he has heard.

Jesus Christ has come to Cana again; it is some fifteen or twenty miles. The father travels with all speed; he arrives at the place where Jesus is. His faith has got to such a stage that, as soon as he sees the Master, he begins to cry, "Lord, come down ere my child die." The Master, instead of giving him an answer which might console him, rebukes him for the littleness of his faith, and tells him, "Except ye see signs and wonders, ye will not believe." The man, however, pays little regard to the rebuke, for there is a desire which has absorbed all the powers of his soul. "Sir," says he, "come down ere my child die." His faith has now arrived at such a stage that he pleads in prayer, and earnestly importunes the Lord to come and heal his son. The Master looks upon him with an eye of ineffable benevolence, and says to him, "Go thy way; thy son liveth." The father goes his way cheerfully, quickly, contentedly, trusting in the word which as yet no evidence has confirmed. He has now come to the second stage of his faith, he has come out of the seeking stage into the relying stage. He no more cries and pleads for a thing he has not; he trusts and believes that the thing is given to him, though as yet he has not perceived the gift. On his road home, the servants meet him with joyful haste; they say, "Master, thy son liveth." He enquires quickly at what hour the fever left him. The answer is given him—about the seventh hour the fever abated; nay, it stayed its course. Then he comes to the third stage. He goes home; he sees his child perfectly restored. The child springs into his arms and covers him with kisses; when he has held him up again and again to see if he is really the little one that lay so wan, and pale, and sick, he triumphs in a higher sense still. His faith has gone from reliance up to full assurance; and then his whole house believes as well as himself.

I have given you just these outlines of the narrative, that

you may see the three stages of faith. Let us now examine each more minutely.

When faith begins in the soul, it is but as a grain of mustard seed. God's people are not born giants. They are babes at first; and as they are babes in grace, so their graces are, as it were, in their infancy. Faith is but as a little child, when first God gives it; or to use another figure, it is not a fire, but a spark, a spark which seems as if it must go out, but which is nevertheless fanned and kept alive until it cometh to a flame, like unto the vehement heat of Nebuchadnezzar's furnace. The poor man in the narrative, when he had faith given him, had it but in a very small degree. It was seeking faith. That is the first stage of faith. Now just notice that this seeking faith excited his activity. As soon as ever God gives a man the seeking faith, he is no more idle about religion; he does not fold his arms with the wicked Antinomian, and cry, "If I am to be saved, I shall be saved, and I will sit still, for if I am to be damned, I shall be damned." He is not careless and indifferent, as he used to be, as to whether he should go up to the house of God or no. He has got seeking faith, and that faith makes him attend the means of grace, leads him to search the Word, leads him to be diligent in the use of every ordained means of blessing for the soul. There is a sermon to be heard: no matter that there are five miles to walk, seeking faith gives him strength to bear the uneasiness of his position, for, "Oh," he says, "if I *may* but hear the Word." See how he leans forward that he may not lose a syllable, for, "Perhaps," says he, "the sentence that I lose may be the very one that I want." How earnest he is that he may not only be sometimes in the house of God, but very often there. He becomes amongst the most enthusiastic of hearers, the most earnest of men that attend that place of worship. Seeking faith gives a man activity.

More than this, seeking faith, though it is very weak in some things, gives a man great power in prayer. How earnest was this nobleman: "Lord, come down ere my child die." Ay, and when seeking faith enters into the soul, it makes a man pray. He is not content now with muttering over a few words when he rises in the morning, and then, half asleep, ringing the same chimes at night when he goes to bed; but he gets away—he steals a quarter of an hour from his business if he can—that he may cry to God in secret. He has not the faith yet which enables him to say, "My sins are forgiven"; but he has faith enough to know that Christ *can* forgive his sins, and what he wants is that he may know that *his* sins are really cast behind Jehovah's back. Sometimes this man has no convenience for prayer, but seeking faith will make him pray in a garret, in a hayloft, in a sawpit, from behind a hedge, or even walking the street. Satan may throw a thousand difficulties in the way, but seeking faith will compel a man to knock at mercy's door. Now the faith that you have received doth not yet give you peace, it doth not put you where there is no condemnation, but yet it is such a faith, that if it grows it will come to that. It has but to be nourished, to be cherished, to be exercised, and the little one shall become mighty, seeking faith shall come to a higher degree of development, and you that knocked at mercy's gate shall enter in and find a welcome at Jesus' table.

And I would have you further notice, that the seeking faith in this man's case did not simply make him earnest in prayer, but importunate in it. He asked once, and the only answer he received was an apparent rebuff. He did not turn away offended, and say, "He rebukes me." No. "Sir," saith he, "come down ere my child die." I cannot tell you how he said it, but I have no doubt it was expressed in soul-moving terms, with tears starting from his eyes, with hands that were placed together in the attitude of entreaty. He seemed to say, "I cannot let thee go except thou come and save my child. Oh, do come. Is there anything I can say that can induce thee? Let a father's affection be my best argument; and if my lips be not eloquent, let the tears of my eyes supply the place of the words of my tongue. Come down, ere my child die." And oh, what mighty prayers those are which seeking faith will make a man pray! I have heard the seeker sometimes plead with God with all the power that Jacob ever could have had at Jabbok's brook. I have seen the sinner under distress of soul seem to take hold of the pillars of the gate of mercy, and rock them to and fro as though he would sooner pull them up from their deep foundations than go away without effecting an entrance. I have seen him pull and tug, and strive and fight, and wrestle, rather than not enter the kingdom of heaven, for he knew that the kingdom of heaven suffered violence, and the violent would take it by force. No wonder that you have not any peace, if you have been bringing before God your cold prayers. Heat them red-hot in the furnace of desire, or think not they will ever burn their way upwards to heaven. You that merely say in the chill form of orthodoxy, "God be merciful to me a sinner," will never find mercy. It is the man that cries in the burning anguish of heartfelt emotion, "God be merciful to *me* a sinner; save *me* or I perish," that gains his suit. It is he who concentrates his soul in every word, and flings the violence of his being into every sentence, that wins his way through the gates of heaven. Seeking faith, when once it is given, can make a man do this. Doubtless there are some here who have got as far as that already. I thought I saw the tears starting from many an eye, just now brushed away very hastily, but I could see it as an index that some said in their souls, "Ay, I know the meaning of that, and I trust God has brought me thus far."

One word I must say here with regard to the weakness of this seeking faith. It can do much, but it makes many mistakes. The fault of seeking faith is, that it knows too little, for you will observe that this poor man said, "Sir, *come down.*" Well, but he need not come down. The Lord can work the miracle without coming down. But our poor friend thought the Master could not save his son, unless he came and looked at him, and put his hand upon him, and knelt down perhaps upon him as Elijah did. "Oh, come down," saith he. So is it with you. You have been dictating to God how he shall save you. You want him to send you some terrible convictions, and then you think you could believe; or else, you want to have a dream or a vision, or to hear a voice speaking to you, saying, "Son, thy sins are forgiven thee." That is your fault, you see. Your seeking faith is strong enough to make you pray, but it is not strong enough to cast out of the mind your own silly fancies. You are wanting to see signs and wonders, or else you will not believe. Oh, nobleman, if Jesus chooses to speak the word and thy son is healed, will not that suit thee as well as his coming down? "Oh," saith he, "I never thought of that!" And so poor sinner, if Jesus chooses to give thee peace this morning in this hall, will not that suit thee as well as being a month under the whip of the law? If, as you pass out of these doors, you be enabled simply to trust in Christ, and so find peace, will not that be as good a salvation as though you should have to go through fire and through water, and all your sins should be made to ride over your head? Here, then, is the weakness of your faith. Though there is much excellence in it, because it makes you pray, there is some fault in it because it makes you imprudently prescribe to the Almighty how he shall bless you—makes you in effect to impugn his sovereignty, and leads you ignorantly to dictate to him in what form the promised boon shall come.

We will now pass on to the second stage of faith. The Master stretched out his hand, and said, "Go thy way, thy son liveth." Do you see the face of that nobleman? Those furrows that were there seem smoothed in a moment, all gone. Those eyes are full of tears, but they are of another sort now—they are tears of joy. He claps his hands, retires silently, his heart ready to burst with gratitude, his whole soul full of confidence. "Why are you so happy, sir?" "Why, my child is cured," saith he. "Nay, but you have not seen him cured." "But my Lord said he was, and I believe him." "But it may be that when you get home you will find your faith to be a delusion and your child a corpse." "Nay," saith he, "I believe in that man. Once I believed him and sought him, now I believe him and have found him." "But you have no evidence whatever that your child is

healed." "Nay," saith he, "I do not want any. The naked word
of that divine prophet is enough for me. He spake it, and I
know it is true. He told me to go my way, my son lived; I go
my way, and I am quite at peace and at ease." Now mark, when
your faith gets to a second stage in which you shall be able to
take Christ at his word, then it is you shall begin to know the
happiness of believing, and then it is your faith saves your
soul. Take Christ at his word, poor sinner. "He that believeth
on the Lord Jesus Christ shall be saved." "But," saith one, "I
feel no evidence." Believe it none the less for that. "But," says
another, "I do not feel enjoyment in my heart." Believe it,
be your heart never so gloomy, that enjoyment shall come afterwards. That is an heroic faith which believes Christ in the
teeth of a thousand contradictions. When the Lord gives you
that faith, you can say, "I consult not with flesh and blood. He
who said to me, 'Believe and be saved,' gave me grace to believe,
and I therefore am confident that I am saved. When I once cast
my soul, sink or swim, upon the love, and blood, and power of
Christ, though conscience give no witness to my soul, though
doubts distress me, and fears plague me, yet it is mine to honour
my Master by believing his Word, though it be contradictory to
sense, though reason rebel against it, and present feeling dare
to give it the lie." Oh! it is an honourable thing when a man has
a follower, and that follower believes that man implicitly. The
man propounds an opinion which is in contradiction to the received opinion of the universe; he stands up and addresses it to
the people, and they hiss and hoot, and scorn him—but that
man has one disciple, who says, "I believe my Master; what he
has said I believe is true." There is something noble in the
man who receives such homage as that. He seems to say, "Now
I am master of one heart, at least"; and when you, in the teeth
of everything that is conflicting, stand to Christ and believe
his words, you do him greater homage than cherubim and seraphim
before the throne. Dare to believe; trust Christ, I say, and thou
art saved.

In this stage of faith it is that a man begins to enjoy quietness and peace of mind. I am not quite certain as to the number of miles between Cana and Capernaum, but several excellent expositors say it is fifteen, some twenty. I suppose the miles may have altered in their length lately. It need not, however, have taken this good man long to get home to his son. It was at the seventh hour that the Master said, "Thy son liveth." It is evident from this text that he did not meet his servants till the next day, because they say, "Yesterday, at the seventh hour, the fever left him." What do you conclude from that? Why, I draw this inference: the nobleman was so sure that his child was alive and well that he was in no violent hurry to return. He did not go home immediately, as though he must be in time to get another doctor, if Christ had not succeeded, but he went his way leisurely and calmly, confident in the truth of what Jesus had said to him. Well, says an old father of the church, "He that believeth shall not make haste." In this case it was true. The man took his time. He was, it may be, twelve hours or more before he reached his home—though probably it was but fifteen miles for him to travel. He who takes the naked word of Christ to be the basis of his hope stands on a rock while all other ground is sinking sand. My brothers and sisters, some of you have got as far as this. You are now taking Christ at his word; it shall not be long before you will get to the third and best stage of faith. But if it should be ever so long, still stand here; still believe your Lord and Master; still trust him. If he does not take you into his banqueting house, still trust him. Nay, if he locks you up in the castle, or in the dungeon, still trust him. Say, "Though he slay me, yet will I trust in him." Should he let the arrows of affliction stick fast in your flesh, still trust him; and by-and-by your righteousness shall come forth as the light, your glory as a lamp that burneth.

We must now hurry on to the third and best stage of faith. The servants meet the nobleman—his son is healed. He arrives at home, clasps his child, and sees him perfectly restored. And

now, says the narrative, "Himself believed, and his whole house."
And yet, you will have noticed that in the fiftieth verse, it
says that he believed. "The man believed the word that Jesus
had spoken unto him." Now, some expositors have been greatly
puzzled, for they did not know when this man did believe. Good
Calvin says—and his remarks are always weighty, and always
excellent—Calvin says, this man had, in the first place, only a
faith which relied for one thing upon Christ. He believed the
word Christ had spoken. Afterwards he had a faith which took
Christ into his soul, to become his disciple, and trust him as
the Messiah. I think I am not wrong in using this as an illustration of faith in its highest state. He found his son healed at
the very hour when Jesus said he should be. "And now," he
says, "I believe"; that is to say, he believed with full assurance
of faith. His mind was so rid of all its doubts; he believed in
Jesus of Nazareth as the Christ of God, sure he was a prophet
sent from God, and doubts and misgivings no longer occupied his
soul. Ah! I know many poor creatures who want to get up to this
state, but they want to get there all at first. They are like a man
who wants to get up a ladder without going up the lowest rounds.
"Oh," they say, "if I had the full assurance of faith, then I
should believe I am a child of God." No, no; believe, trust in
Christ's naked word, and then you shall come afterwards to feel
in your soul the witness of the Spirit that you are born of God.
Assurance is a flower—you must plant the bulb first, the naked,
perhaps unseemly, bulb of faith—plant it in the grain, and you
shall have the flower by-and-by. The shrivelled seed of a little
faith springs upwards, and then you have the ripe corn in the
ear of full assurance of faith. But here I want you to notice,
that when this man came to full assurance of faith, it is said
his house believed too.

There is a text often quoted, and I do not think I have heard
it quoted rightly yet. By the way, there are some people who
know no more of authors than what they hear quoted, and some
who know no more of the Bible than what they hear quoted, too.

Now, there is that passage, "Believe on the Lord Jesus Christ, and thou shalt be saved." What have the last three words done that they should be cut off? "And thy house"; those three words seem to me to be as precious as the first. "Believe and thou shalt be saved, and thy house." Does the father's faith save the family? Yes! No! *Yes,* it does in some way; namely, that the father's faith makes him pray for his family, and God hears his prayer, and the family is saved. *No,* the father's faith cannot be a substitute for the faith of the children, they must believe too. In both senses of the word, I say, "Yes, or No." When a man has believed, there is hope that his children will be saved. Nay, there is a promise; and the father ought not to rest satisfied until he sees all his children saved. If he does, he has not believed right yet. There are many men who only believe for themselves. I like, if I get a promise, to believe it as broad as it is. Why should not my faith be as broad as the promise? Now, thus it stands: "Believe and thou shalt be saved, and thy house!" I have a claim on God for my little ones. When I go before God in prayer, I can plead, "Lord, I believe, and thou hast said I shall be saved, and my house; thou hast saved me, but thou has not fulfilled thy promise till thou hast saved my house too." . . .

II.   And now we come to the second department of our subject, the *three diseases to which faith is very subject,* and these three diseases break out in different stages.

First, with regard to seeking faith. The power of seeking faith lies in its driving a man to prayer. And here is the disease; for we are very likely, when we are seeking to begin, to suspend prayerfulness. How often does the devil whisper in a man's ear, "Do not pray, it is of no use. You know you will be shut out of heaven!" Or, when the man thinks he has got an answer to prayer, then Satan says, "You need not pray any more; you have got what you asked for." Or, if after a month of crying he has received a blessing, then Satan whispers, "Fool that thou art, to tarry at mercy's gate. Get gone! Get gone! That gate is nailed up and barred fast, and you will never be heard." Oh, my friends! If you are subject to this disease while seeking Christ, I bid you cry against it, and labour against it; never cease to pray. A man can never sink in the river of wrath so long as ever he can cry. So long as ever you can cry to God for mercy, mercy shall never withdraw itself from you.

Oh, let not Satan push you back from the closet door, but push in, whether he will or not! Give up prayer, and you seal your own damnation; renounce secret supplication, and you renounce Christ and heaven. Continue in prayer, and though the blessing tarry, it must come; in God's own time it must appear to you.

The disease which is most likely to fall upon those in the second stage—namely, those who are trusting implicitly in Christ—is the disease of wanting to see signs and wonders, or else they will not believe. In the early stages of my ministry, in the midst of a rural population, I used to meet continually with persons who thought they were Christians because, as they imagined, they had seen signs and wonders; and since then, stories the most ridiculous have been told me by earnest and sincere people, as reasons why they thought they were saved. I have heard a narrative something like this: "I believe my sins are put away." "Why?" "Well, sir, I was down in the back garden and I saw a great cloud, and I thought, now God can make that cloud go away if he pleases, and it did go away: and I thought the cloud and my sins were gone too, and I have not had a doubt since then." I thought, Well, you have good reason to doubt, for that is totally absurd. Were I to tell you the whims and fancies that some people get into their heads, you might smile, and that might not be to your profit. Certain it is, that men patch up any idle story, any strange fancy, in order to make them think that they may then trust Christ. Oh, my dear friends, if you have no better reason to believe you are in Christ than a dream or a vision, it is time you began again! I grant you there have been some who have been alarmed, convinced, and perhaps converted, by strange freaks of their imagination; but if you rely on these as being pledges from God, if you look on these as being evidences that you are saved, I tell you that you will be resting on a dream, a delusion. You may as well seek to build a castle in the air, or a house upon the sands.

No, he who believes Christ, believes Christ because he says it, and because here it is written in the Word; he does not believe it because he dreamed it, or because he heard a voice that might probably be a blackbird singing, or because he thought he saw an angel in the sky, which was just as likely to be mist of a peculiar shape as anything else. No, we must have done with this desire to see signs and wonders. If they come, be thankful; if they come not, trust simply in the Word, which says, "All manner of sin shall be forgiven unto men." I do not wish to say this to hurt any tender conscience, which conscience may perhaps have found some little comfort in such singular wonders; but I only say this honestly, lest any of you should be deceived. I do solemnly warn you to place no reliance whatever on any thing you think you have seen, or dreamed, or heard. *This* volume is the sure word of testimony, unto which ye do well if ye take heed, as unto a light which shineth in a dark place. Trust in the Lord; wait patiently for him; cast all thy confidence where he put all thy sins, namely upon Christ Jesus alone, and thou shalt be saved, with or without any of these signs and wonders.

I am afraid some Christians have fallen into the same error of wanting to see signs and wonders. They have been meeting together in special prayer meetings to seek for a revival; and because people have not dropped down in a fainting fit, and have not screamed and made a noise, perhaps they have thought the revival has not come. Oh, that we had but eyes to see God's gifts in the way God chooses to give them! We do not want the revival of the north of Ireland; we want the revival in its goodness, but not in that particular shape. If the Lord sends it in another, we shall be all the more glad to be without these exceptional works in the flesh. Where the Spirit works in the soul, we are always glad to see true conversion; and if he chooses to work in the body too, we shall be glad to see it. If men's hearts are renewed, what matters it though they do not scream out. If their consciences are quickened, what matters it though they do not fall into a fit; if they do but find Christ, who is to regret that they do not lie for five or six weeks motionless and senseless? Take it without the signs and wonders. For my part, I have no craving for them. Let me see God's work done in God's own way, a true and thorough revival—but the signs and wonders we can readily dispense with, for they are certainly not demanded by the faithful, and they will only be the laughing-stock of the faithless.

Having thus spoken of these two diseases, I will only just mention the other. There is a third, then, which lies in the way of our attaining the highest degree of faith—namely, full assurance—and that is want of observation. The nobleman in our text made careful inquiries about the day and the hour when his son was healed. It was by that he obtained his assurance. But we do not observe God's hand as much as we should. Our good puritanic forefathers, when it rained, used to say that God had unstopped the bottles of heaven. When it rains nowadays, we think the clouds have become condensed. If they had a field of hay cut, they used to plead of the Lord that he would bid the sun shine. We, perhaps, are wiser, as we think; and we consider it hardly worthwhile to pray about such things, thinking they will come in the course of nature. They believed that God was in every storm; nay, in every cloud of dust. They used to speak of a present God in everything; but we speak of such things as laws of nature, as if laws were ever anything, except there was someone to carry them out, and some secret power to set the whole machinery in motion. We do not get our assurance, because we do not observe enough. If you were to watch providential goodness day by day, if you noticed the answers to your prayers, if you would just put down somewhere in the book of your remembrance God's continued mercies toward *you,* I do think you would become like this father who was led to full assurance of faith, because he noticed that the very hour when Jesus spoke was the hour when the healing came. Be watchful, Christian. He that looks for providences will never lack a providence to look at.

Take heed then of these three diseases; of ceasing from prayer; waiting to see signs and wonders; and neglect of observing the manifest hand of God.

III.   And now I come to my third and last head, upon which solemnly, though briefly, there are *three questions to be addressed to you about your faith.*

First, then, thou sayest, "I have faith." Be it so. There be many a man who saith he hath gold that hath it not; there be many that think themselves rich and increased in goods, that are naked, and poor, and miserable. I say unto thee, therefore; in the first place, does thy faith make thee *pray?* Not the praying of the man who prates like a parrot the prayers he has learned; but dost thou cry the cry of a living child? Dost thou tell to God thy wants and thy desires? And dost thou *seek* his face, and *ask* his mercy? Man, if thou livest without prayer, thou art a Christless soul; thy faith is a delusion, and thy confidence which results from it is a dream that will destroy thee. Wake up out of thy deathlike slumbers; for as long as thou art dumb in prayer, God cannot answer thee. Thou shalt not live to God, if thou dost not live in the closet; he that is never on his knees on earth, shall never stand upon his feet in heaven; he that never wrestles with the angel here below, shall never be admitted into heaven by that angel above.

I know I speak to some today that are prayerless ones. You have plenty of time for your countinghouse, but you have none for your closet. Family prayer you have never had; but I will not talk to you about that. Private prayer you have neglected. Do you not sometimes rise in the morning so near the time when you must keep your appointments that—you do kneel it is true;

but where is the prayer? And as to any extra occasions of supplication, why, you never indulge yourselves in them. Prayer
with you is a sort of luxury too dear to indulge in often. Ah!
but he who has true faith in his heart, is praying all day long.
I do not mean that he is on his knees; but often when he is
bargaining, when he is in his shop, or in his countinghouse, his
heart finds a little space, a vacuum for a moment, and up it leaps
into the bosom of its God, and it is down again, refreshed to
go about its business and meet the face of man. Oh! those
ejaculatory prayers—not merely the filling the censer in the
morning with incense, but that casting in of little bits of cinna-
mon and frankincense all day long, so as always to keep it fresh
—that is the way to live, and that is the line of a true, genuine
believer. If your faith does not make you pray, have nothing to
do with it; get rid of it, and God help thee to begin again.

But thou sayest, "I have faith." I will ask thee a second
question. Does that faith make thee *obedient?* Jesus said to
the nobleman, "Go thy way," and he went without a word; however much he might have wished to stay and listen to the Master,
he obeyed. Does your faith make you obedient? In these days we
have specimens of Christians of the most sorry, sorry kind. I
have heard it observed by tradesmen that they know many men
that have not the fear of God before their eyes, that are most
just and upright men in their dealings; and on the other hand,
they know some professing Christians, who are not positively
dishonest, but they can back and hedge a little; they do not seem
to keep up to the time if they have a bill to pay; they are not
regular, they are not exact; in fact, sometimes—and who shall
hide what is true?—you catch Christians doing dirty actions, and
professors of religion defiling themselves with acts which merely
worldly men would scorn. Now, sirs, I bear my testimony this
morning as God's minister, too honest to alter a word to please
any man that lives, you are no Christian if you can act in business
beneath the dignity of an honest man. If God has not made you
honest, he has not saved your soul. Rest assured that if you can

go on, disobedient to the moral laws of God, if your life is inconsistent and lascivious, if your conversation is mixed up with things which even a worlding might reject, the love of God is not in you. I do not plead for perfection, but I do plead for honesty, and if your religion has not made you careful and prayerful in common life, if you are not in fact made a new creature in Christ Jesus—your faith is but an empty name, as sounding brass, or a tinkling cymbal.

I will ask you one more question about your faith, and I have done. Thou sayest, "I have faith." Has thy faith led thee to bless thy household? Good Rowland Hill once said, in his own quaint way, that when a man became a Christian, his dog and his cat ought to be the better for it; and I think it was Mr. Jay who always would say that a man, when he became a Christian, was better in every relation. He was a better husband, a better master, a better father than he was before, or else his religion was not genuine. Now, have you ever thought, my dear Christian brethren, about blessing your household? Do I hear one saying, "I keep my religion to myself." Do not be very anxious about its ever being stolen, then; you need not put it under lock and key—there is not enough to tempt the devil himself to come and take it from you. A man who can keep his godliness to himself has so small a proportion of it, I am afraid it will be no credit to himself, and no blessing to other people.

But you do sometimes, strange to say, meet with fathers that do not seem as if they interested themselves in their children's salvation, any more than they do about poor children in the back slums of St. Giles's. They would like to see the boy put out well, and they would like to see the girl married comfortably; but as to their being converted, it does not seem to trouble their heads. It is true the father occupies his seat in a house of worship, and sits down with a community of Christians; and he *hopes* his children may turn out well. They have the benefit of his hope—certainly a very large legacy: he will no doubt when he dies leave them his best wishes, and may they grow rich upon them! But he never seems to have made it a matter of anxiety of soul, as to whether they shall be saved or not. Out upon such a religion as that! Cast it on the dunghill; hurl it to the dogs; let it be buried like Koniah, with the burial of an ass; cast it without the camp, like an unclean thing. It is not the religion of God. He that careth not for his own household is worse than a heathen man and a publican.

Never be content, my brethren in Christ, till all your children are saved. Lay the promise before your God. The promise is unto you and unto your children. The Greek word does not refer to infants, but to children, grandchildren, and any descendants you may have, whether grown-up or not. Do not cease to plead till not only your children, but your great grandchildren, if you have such, are saved. I stand here today a proof that God is not untrue to his promise. I can cast my eye back through four or five generations, and see that God has been pleased to hear the prayers of our grandfather's grandfather, who used to supplicate with God that his children might live before Him to the last generation, and God has never deserted the house, but has been pleased to bring first one, and then another, to fear and love his name. So be it with you; and in asking this, you are not asking more than God is ready to give you. He cannot refuse unless he run back from his promise. He cannot refuse to give you both your own and your children's souls as an answer to the prayer of your faith. "Ah," says one, "but you do not know what children mine are." No, my dear friend, but I know that if you are a Christian, they are children that God has promised to bless. "Oh, but they are such unruly ones, they break my heart." Then pray God to break their hearts, and they will not break your heart any more. "But they will bring my grey hairs with sorrow to the grave." Pray God, then, that he may bring their eyes with sorrow to prayer, and to supplication, and to the cross, and then they will not bring you to the grave. "But," you say, "my children have such hard hearts." Look at your own. You think they cannot be saved: look at yourselves;

he that saved you can save them. Go to him in prayer, and say, "Lord, I will not let thee go except thou bless me"; and if thy child be at the point of death, and, as you think, at the point of damnation on account of sin, still plead like the nobleman, "Lord, come down ere my child perish, and save him for thy mercy's sake." And, oh, Thou that dwellest in the highest heavens thou wilt ne'er refuse thy people. Be it far from us to dream that thou wilt forget thy promise. In the name of all thy people, we put our hand upon thy Word most solemnly, and pledge thee to thy covenant. Thou hast said thy mercy is unto the children's children of them that fear thee and keep thy commandments. Thou hast said the promise is unto us and unto our children; Lord, thou wilt not deny thine own covenant; we challenge thy word by holy faith this morning—"Do as thou hast said." AMEN.

The Chaff Driven Away

{Sermon}

"The ungodly are not so: but are like the chaff which the wind driveth away."—Psalms 1:4.

AND who are the ungodly? Are they open and wilful sinners—men who take God's name in vain, and blaspheme—men who break the laws of man, the laws of the State—men who are scarcely to be trusted with liberty? Certainly these are included, but these are not mainly intended. While such men come under the category of "sinners" and "scorners," there is another class expressly aimed at by the term "ungodly." And who are the ungodly? Are they the men who deny God's existence, who neglect the outward forms of religion, who scoff at everything that is sacred, and make a jest of things at which angels tremble? These are included, most certainly, but neither are these the men specially aimed at. They are the scornful, the pestilent; these are the men whose iniquities have gone beforehand to judgment against them, and whose sins are clamouring before the throne for justice. Another class of men is intended under the term "ungodly." And who are they? Surely my brethren, the answer may well strike you with awe. I do trust there are not many in this hall who may be called scorners; and, perhaps, not very many who would come under the denomination of open profligates and rebels; but how large a proportion of all those who attend our places of worship may justly be ranked under the character of the ungodly! What does this exactly mean? Let me just show its differences once again, and then more precisely define it.

We sometimes call men irreligious; and, surely, to be irreligious is bad enough: but to be religious is not good enough. A man may be religious, yet not be godly. There are many who are religious; as touching the law outwardly they are blameless: Hebrews of the Hebrews, Pharisees of the straitest sect. They neglect no rubric, they break no law of their church, they are exceedingly precise in their religion; yet, notwithstanding this, they may rank under the class of the ungodly; for to be religious is one thing, and to be godly is quite another. To be godly, then, —to come at once to the mark—to be godly is to have a constant eye to God, to recognize him in all things, to trust him, to love him, to serve him. And the ungodly man is one who does not have an eye to God in his daily business, who lives in this world as if there were no God; while he attends to all the outward ceremonies of religion, he never goes to their core, never enters into their secret heart and their deep mysteries. He sees the sacraments, but he sees not God therein; he hears the preaching, he comes up to the house of prayer, into the midst of the great congregation, he bows his head, but there is no present Deity to him, there is no manifest God. There is no hearing of his voice, there is no bowing before his throne.

Doubtless, there are a large number here who must confess that they are not trusting in the blood of Christ, they are not influenced by the Holy Ghost, they do not love God; they cannot say that the bent and tenor of their lives is towards him. Why, you have been the last six days about your business, occupying all your time—and quite right is it to be diligent in business—but how many of you have forgotten God all the while? You have been trading for yourselves, not for God. The righteous man does everything in the name of God; at least, this is his constant desire. Whether he eats or drinks, or whatsoever he does, he desires to do all in the name of the Lord Jesus. But you have not recognized God in your shop. You have not acknowledged him in your dealings with your fellow men. You have acted towards them as if there had been no God whatever.

And, perhaps, even this day you must confess that your heart does not love the Lord. You have never gone into his company. You do not seek retirement. You do not relish private prayer. Now God's children cannot be happy without sometimes talking to their Father. They love to cling to him. They feel that he is their life, their love, their all. Their daily cry is, "Lord, draw me to thyself; come thou to me, or draw me up to thee." They pant to know more of God; they long to reflect more of his image; they seek to keep his law; and it is their desire that they may be pervaded with his Spirit. But such are not your desires. You have no such longings as these. It is true you are not addicted to strong drink, you do not swear, you are no thief, you are no harlot. In all these things you are blameless; yet are you ungodly, being without God in the world. He is not your friend; he is not your helper. You do not cleave to him with purpose of heart. You are not his child. You have not "the Spirit of adoption, whereby we cry, Abba, Father." You could do as well without a God as with one. In fact you feel that the thought of God, if you think of it solemnly, strikes you with terror, and excites in your breasts no emotions of delight. You are ungodly. Well then, mark, whatever I have to say this morning, belongs to you. Don't be looking round you and saying, I wonder how this will suit my neighbour. Do not I beseech you be thinking this of some thriftless loon who has spent his estate in extravagance and debauchery, but be thinking of yourself. If you are not born again, if you are not a partaker of the Spirit, if you are not reconciled to God, if your sins be not forgiven, if you are not this day a living member of the living church of Christ, all the curses that are written in this book belong to you, and that part of them in particular which it will be my solemn business to thunder out this morning. I pray God that this part may be applied to your soul, that you may be made to tremble before the Most High, and seek him who will certainly be found of you, if you seek him with all your hearts.

You will readily perceive that my text may be divided into

three parts. You have, first a fearful negative—"The ungodly are *not* so." You have in the next place a terrible comparison—"They are *like the chaff*." Then you have, thirdly, an awful prophecy—"which the *wind driveth away*."

First, then, you have *a fearful negative*. The Vulgate Latin version, the Arabic and Septuagint, read this first sentence thus: "Not so the ungodly, not so," for according to their version there is a double negative here—"Not so the ungodly, not so." Now in order to understand what is meant by this negative you must read the third verse. The righteous man is said to be "like a tree planted by the rivers of water, that bringeth forth his fruit in his season; his leaf also shall not wither; and whatsoever he doeth shall prosper."—"Not so the ungodly, not so."

The ungodly are not like a "tree planted." If they may be compared to a tree at all, they are as trees "twice dead, plucked up by the roots," or if they are to be compared to anything that hath life, then are they like the tree in the desert which is planted there by a chance hand, which hath naught to nourish it. It is the peculiar characteristic of the Christian man that he is like "a tree planted." That is to say, there is a special providence exercised in his position and in his culture. You all know the difference between a tree that is planted and a tree that is self-sown. The tree that is planted in the garden is visited by the husbandman. He digs about it; he dungs it; he trims it, prunes it, and looks for its fruit. It is an object of property and of special care. The wild tree in the forest, the tree which is self-sown upon the plain, no one owns: no one watches over it; no heart will sigh if the lightning flash shall shiver it; no tear will be wept if the blast should light upon it, and all its leaves should wither. It is no man's property. It shelters no man's roof. No man careth for it. Let it die; why doth it stand there to suck nourishment from the soil and yield none again.

The ungodly are, it is true, the subjects of a general providence,

even as everything is ordered of God; but the righteous have
a special providence over them. They are trees planted. Everything which takes place works together for their good. The
Lord their God is their guardian. He watches the earth that it
should bring forth for them its fruit. The precious things of the
heavens, the dew, and the deep that coucheth beneath, and the
precious fruits brought forth by the sun, and the precious things
put forth by the moon—these are their heritage. He watcheth
everything round about them. If pestilence stalk through the
land, he permitteth not one of its shafts to hit, unless he seeth
it is for good. If war ariseth, behold he stretches his aegis
over his children; and if famine comes, they shall be fed, and
in the days of scarcity they shall be satisfied. Is it not a glorious
thing for the Christian to know that the very hairs of his head
are all numbered, that the angels of God keep watch and ward
over him; that the Lord is his shepherd, and therefore, he shall
not want? I know this is a doctrine that often comforts me.
Let what will happen, if I can but fall back upon the thought
that there is a providence in everything, what do I need? A
providence in the great and in the little there assuredly is to
every child of God. It may be said of every tree of the Lord's
right hand planting, "I the Lord do keep it; I will water it
every moment; lest any hurt it, I will watch it night and day."
Upon the righteous there are not only ten eyes, but there are all
the eyes of the Omniscient ever fixed both by night and day.
The Lord knoweth the way of the righteous. They are like the
planted tree. Not so ye that are ungodly; there is no special
providence for you. To whom will ye carry your troubles? Where
is your shelter in the day of wrath? Where is your shield in
the hour of battle? Who shall be your sun when darkness shall
gather about you? Who shall comfort you when your troubles
shall encompass you round? You have no eternal arm to lean upon.
You have no compassionate heart to beat for you. You have no
loving eye to watch you. You are left alone! alone! alone! like
the heath in the desert, or like the forest tree which no man

regardeth, until the time comes when the sharpened axe shall be lifted up, and the tree must fall. "Not so," then, "the ungodly, not so." 'Tis a fearful negative: the ungodly man is not the object of the special providence of God.

The righteous man is like a tree planted by the "rivers of water." Now, a tree that is planted by the rivers of water sends out its roots, and they soon draw sufficient nourishment. The tree that is planted far away upon the arid desert hath its times of drought; it depends upon the casual thundercloud that weeps over it, and distils the scanty drops of rain. But this tree planted by rivers of water hath a perennial supply. It knows no drought, no time of scarcity. Its roots have but to suck up the nourishment which pours itself lavishly there. "Not so the ungodly, not so." They have no such rivers from which to suck their joy, their comfort, and their life. As for the believer, come what may, he can say: if earth shall fail him, then will he look to heaven. If man forsake him, then he looks to the divine man Christ Jesus. If the world should shake, his inheritance is on high. If everything should pass away, he hath a portion that can never be dissolved. He is planted not by brooks that may be dried up, far less in a desert, which only hath a scanty share, but by the rivers of water. Oh, my beloved brethren, you and I know something about what this means. We know what it is to drink of the rivers of Christ's fulness. We know what it is to partake and satisfy ourselves as with marrow and fatness. Well may we rejoice with joy unspeakable and full of glory, for our storehouse is inexhaustible, our riches can never be spent. We have a wealth that cannot be counted, a treasury that never can be drained. This is our glory, that we have a something to rely upon which can never fail us. We are trees planted by the rivers of water.

Ah! but not so you that are ungodly, not so. Your days of drought shall come. You may rejoice now, but what will you do upon the bed of sickness, when fever shall make you toss from side to side, when head and heart shall be racked with anguish,

when death shall stare upon you, and shall glaze your eyes?
What will ye do when ye come into the swellings of Jordan? You
have joys today, but where will be your joys then? You have
wells now, but what will you do when these are all stopped up,
when these shall all fail, when your skin-bottles are dried, when
your broken cisterns have emptied themselves of their last drop—
what will ye do then, ye ungodly? Surely this negative is full
of awful threatenings to you. You may have a little mirth and
merriment now, you may enjoy a little excitement at present, but
what will ye do when the hot wind comes upon you—the wind of
tribulation? And above all, what will you do when the chilling
blast of death shall freeze your blood? Ah, where, oh where will
you then look? You will look no longer to friends, nor to the
comforts of home. You cannot find in the hour of death consolation on the bosom of the most loving wife; you will be quite
unable then to find peace in all your riches or your treasures.
As for your past life, however good it may seem, if you are
ungodly, you will find no comfort in the retrospect; and as for
the future, you will find no comfort in the prospect; for there
will be for you nothing but "a fearful looking for of judgment
and fiery indignation." Oh, my ungodly friends, I beseech you,
think upon this matter, for if there were nothing worse, the
first sentence of my text sounds like the trumpets of doom,
and hath in it bitterness like the vials of the Revelation.

It is said of the righteous man that he "bringeth forth his
fruit in his season." "Not so the ungodly, not so"; they bring
forth no fruit—or if there be here and there a shrivelled grape
upon the vine, it is brought forth in the wrong season, when
the genial heat of the sun cannot ripen it, and therefore it is
sere and worthless. Many people imagine that if they do not
commit positive sin, they are all right. Now let me give you a
little sermon in the midst of my sermon. Here is the text:
"Curse ye Meroz, said the angel of the Lord, curse ye bitterly
the inhabitants thereof; because they came not to the help of the
Lord, to the help of the Lord against the mighty." First, what

has Meroz done? Nothing. Secondly, is Meroz cursed? Yes,
cursed bitterly. What for?—for doing nothing? Yes, for doing
nothing. "Curse ye bitterly the inhabitants thereof," for what
they did not do, "because they came not to the help of the Lord,
to the help of the Lord against the mighty." Did Meroz fight
against God? No. Did Meroz put on a buckler and lay hold on
shield and spear and go forth against the Most High? No. What
did Meroz do? Nothing. And is it cursed? Yes, cursed bitterly,
with the inhabitants thereof, "because they came not to the help
of the Lord, to the help of the Lord against the mighty." Preach
that sermon to yourselves when you get home. Draw it out at
length, and perhaps while you are sitting down you will say,
"Meroz! Why, that is myself. I don't fight against God, I am no
enemy to Christ, I do not persecute his people; in fact I even
love his ministers. I love to go up and hear the Word preached.
I should not be happy if I spent my Sunday anywhere but in God's
house. But still that must mean me, for I do not go up 'to the
help of the Lord against the mighty.' I do nothing. I am a
fruitless tree." Ah, then, remember you are cursed, and cursed
bitterly, too. Not for what you do, but for what you don't do.

So here it is, one of the sad curses of the ungodly—that they
bring forth no fruit in their season. Why, look at many of you.
What is the good of you in this world? With regard to your
families, you are their mainstay and prop. God bless you in
your work, and may you train up your children well. But as to
the church, what good are you? You occupy a seat, you have had
it these years; how do you know but that you have been occupying
a seat which might have been the place where some other sinner
would have been converted had he been there? It is true you sit
and hear the sermon; yes, but what of that, if that sermon shall
add to your condemnation? It is true that you make one among
many, but what if you should be a black sheep in the midst of
the flock! What are you doing for Christ? Of what value are
you? Have you added one stone to his spiritual temple? Have
you done as much as the poor woman who broke the alabaster box

upon his head? You have done nothing for him. He has nourished you and brought you up, and you have done nothing for him. "The ox knoweth his owner, and the ass his master's crib," but you do not know, you do not consider. Behold, the Lord hath a controversy with you this day, not for what you have done, but for what you have not done. He has sent you the ministry; you are invited every Sabbath-day. You are hearing the Word continually; you are enjoying privileges. God is feeding you in his providence, clothing you in his compassion, and you are doing nothing for him. You are a cumberer of the ground, bringing forth no fruit at all. Oh, my dear hearer, I beseech thee lay this to heart, for this is a curse as well as a sign to you. It is not only a bad trait in thy character, but it is a curse from God. Thou are ungodly, and therefore fruitless. Thou lovest him not, therefore thou art not like the tree which "bringeth forth his fruit in his season."

"His leaf also shall not wither. Not so the ungodly, not so." The ungodly man's leaf *shall* wither. I see before me this day many proofs that God's promise is verified to his people. Look round, and behold what a large number of grey-headed men assemble every Lord's day to hear the Word. There are many of them who loved Christ in their youth. Then they had "a joy unspeakable and full of glory" in making a profession of his dear name, and now they have come into what men call the sere and yellow leaf of life, but they do not find it so, for they still bring forth fruit in old age; they are still fat and flourishing to show that the Lord is upright. Their leaf has not withered; they are just as active in the cause of Christ as ever they were, and perhaps ten times more happy. Instead of bringing forth no fruit, they bring forth richer and more luscious clusters than ever they did before. Walking in the midst of the younger ones, they shine as lights in the midst of the world; or, to return to the simile, they are like trees whose branches hang down by reason of the abundance of their fruit, even as their heads bow down by reason of the abundance of their years. What a mercy it is, dear brethren, to have Christ for your portion in youth, and such a Christ too as will last us all our life long. To see good old Rowland Hill preaching when he was tottering on the borders of the grave and talking of the faithfulness of Christ—what a glorious sight! There was a proof! That leaf did not wither. Was there ever a tree like this that would maintain its greenness eighty years and yet not wither? Was there ever a religion like this that would make the old men youthful and make their tottering feet leap for joy? And yet this is the religion of Christ. Our leaf withers not.

But oh, "not so the ungodly, not so." Your leaf shall wither— at least when they that look out of the windows are darkened, when the grinders fail because they are few, when your days of old age shall come upon you and the grasshopper shall be a burden, if not before, shall your leaf wither. But how many there are whose leaves do wither! There comes a blight from God, and the tree which once looked green becomes brown and dead, and at last it blackens and has to be removed. We have seen such in our lives—men that seemed to be getting on in this world, rich and happy, and respected by almost everybody, but they had no solid background, they had no rock to stand on, no God to trust to. I have seen them spreading themselves like a green bay tree, and I have often envied them as the Psalmist did, but "I looked, and lo they were not;" I passed by and lo there was not so much as a stump of them left; God had cursed their habitation; as a dream when one awaketh, their image had been despised; as the wax before the fire, they had melted away; like the fat of rams had they been consumed; into smoke did they consume away. "Not so the ungodly, not so," says the text, and surely experience proves it: the ungodly man's leaf must and shall wither. And then it is added concerning the righteous man, "Whatsoever he doeth shall prosper." Godly men, it is true, have many tribulations, but I am not sure that they have more than the wicked. I do think that when a man is converted he will find it to be true that religion's "ways are ways of pleasantness, and all her paths are peace," and he has a better hope of even worldly prosperity when he becomes a Christian, than the ungodly man has.

Christian habits are the best business habits, if men would but believe it. When a man mixes his religion with his business, and allows every act of his life to be guided by it, he stands the best chance in this world, if I may be allowed such a secular expression, for "honesty is the best policy" after all, and Christianity is the best honesty. The sharp, cutting competition of the times may be called honesty; it is only called so *down here,* it is not called so *up there,* for there is a good deal of cheating in it. Honesty in the highest sense—Christian honesty—will be found, after all, to be the best policy in everything, and there will ordinarily be a prosperity, even worldly prosperity, attending a good man in the patient, industrious pursuit of his calling. But if he does not have that success he craves, still there is one thing he knows: he would have it if it were best for him. I often hear Christian men talk in this fashion: "Well, I do but very little business," says one, "but I have enough coming in to live upon comfortably and happily. I never cared much for push and competition; I never felt that I was fit for it, and I sometimes thank God that I never thrust myself out into the rough stream, but that I was content to keep along shore." And I have marked this one thing—and, as a matter of fact, I know it cannot be disproved—that many such humble-minded men are the very best of Christians, they live the happiest lives, and whatsoever they do certainly does prosper, for they get what they expected, though they did not expect much, and they get what they want, though their wants are not very large. They are not going in for anything very great, and therefore they do not come out plucked and empty-handed, but they just hold on their way, looking to Providence constantly for their supplies, and they have all they require; and whatsoever they do prospers. But they can say, too, that even if they had lost their all, if they had been brought to poverty, they would have felt poverty itself was the best prosperity, for God would have made their souls prosperous, even though their outward estates had become less.

"Not so the ungodly, not so." Whatever an ungodly man gets, be it little or be it much, is loss to him. He puts his money into a bag that is full of holes. If he saves it, it corrupts and rusts. If he spends it, it does him little service. The man that hath no God, hath no prosperity. Is he fat—he fattens for the slaughter! Is he in adversity—behold, the first drops of the fated storm have begun to fall on him. To the ungodly man there is nothing good in this life. The sweet that he tasteth is the sweetness of poison. That which looketh fair is but as paint upon the harlot's face, beneath there is loathsomeness and disease. There may be a greenness and a verdure upon the mound, but within there lies the rotting carcass, the loathsomeness of corruption. Whatsoever the believer doth, it shall prosper. "Not so the ungodly, not so." Surely this first part of my text is quite bad enough—to have the gate of blessedness shut against you, to have the promises denied to you, to be without the blessing which is given to the godly—this punishment of the lost surely were enough to make us start in dismay.

Listen awhile to the *terrible comparison.*

"The ungodly are like the chaff." They are not like the wild tree, for that hath life, and they are dead in sin. They are not compared here even to the dead tree plucked up by the roots, for that may be of some service. As it floats down the stream, the hand of poverty may recall it from the water, and kindle a fire and relieve the cold. They are not even like the heath in the desert, for it hath some uses, and tends to cheer the arid waste. They are like nothing that hath life, nothing that is of any value. They are here said to be like chaff which the wind driveth away. Now you will at once see how terrible is this figure, if you look at it a moment. They are like chaff. Chaff envelops good corn, but when the wheat is cut down and carried into the barn, the corn alone is useful, the grain alone is looked

at, and that chaff which has grown side by side with the good
living wheat, is now become utterly useless, and is to be separated
and driven away. And the wicked are compared to chaff—think for
a moment, of two or three reasons.

First, because they are sapless and fruitless. Chaff hath no
sap of life in itself. It is of no use, of no service. Men do but
desire to get rid of it. They take the fan into their hands that
they may thoroughly purge their floor. They cast up the wheat
before the wind with the winnowing shovel, that the breath of
the air may blow away the chaff, and leave the wheat pure.
All that they care for the chaff is that they may get rid of
it, that it may be blown away to waste, for it is sapless and
fruitless. Then, again, you notice that it is light and unstable.
The wind sweeps through the wheat, the wheat remains un-
moved, the chaff flies away. When cast up in the shovel, the
wheat soon finds its place, and returns to the spot from which it
has been lifted up; but the chaff is light, it has no stability.
Every eddying wind, every breath moves it and carries it away.
So are the ungodly. They have nothing stable; they are light,
they are but as the froth upon the water; they are but as a bubble
on the breaker, seen today and gone, here and there, and then
carried away forever.

Again, the wicked are compared to chaff because it is base
and worthless. Who will buy it? Who cares for it? In the East,
at least, no use whatever can be made of it. They are content
to burn it up and get rid of it, and the sooner they get rid of
it, the better pleased are they. So is it with the wicked. They
are good for nothing, useless in this world, useless in the world
to come. They are the dross, the offal of all creation. The man
who is ungodly, however much he may value himself, is as
nothing in the estimation of God. Put a gold chain round his
neck, put a star upon his breast, put a crown upon his head, and
what is he but a crowned heap of dust, useless, perhaps worse than
useless. Base in God's sight, who tramples them beneath his feet.
The potter's vessel hath some service, and even the broken potsherd

might be used. Some Job might scrape himself with it. But what shall be done with the chaff? It is of no use anywhere, and no one careth for it.

See, then, your value, my hearers, if you fear not God. Cast up your accounts and look at yourselves in the right light. You think, perhaps, that you are good for much, but God saith you are good for nothing. You are "like the chaff which the wind driveth away." I linger no more upon this comparison, but choose, rather, to dwell upon the third head, which was this:

The *awful prophecy* contained in the verse "They are like the chaff which the wind driveth away."

How near the chaff is to the grain! It is, in fact, its envelop; they grow together. My hearers, I wish to speak now very pointedly and personally. How nearly related are the ungodly to the righteous! One of you, it may be, now present, an ungodly man, is the father of a godly child. You have been to that child what the chaff is to the wheat; you have nourished the child—cherished it in your bosom; you have been wrapt about it like the chaff about the grain. Is it not an awful thing for you to think that you should have been in such close relationship to a child of God, but that in the great day of division you must be separated from it? The chaff cannot be taken into heaven with the wheat. I point to another. You are the son of a godly mother; you have grown up at her knee. She taught you, when you were but a little one, to say your little prayer, and to sing the little hymn "Gentle Jesus, meek and mild, look upon a little child." That mother looked upon you as her joy and her comfort. She is gone now. But you were once to her what the chaff is to the wheat. You grew, as it were, upon the same stock, you were of the same family, and her heart was wholly wrapt up in you. You were her joy and her comfort here below. Does it not cause you one pang of regret that, dying as you are, you must everlastingly be separated from her? Where she is you can never come.

Mayhap, too, I have here a mother who has lost several infants; she has been to those infants what the chaff is to the wheat—wrapt up in her bosom, for a little while she fondled them; and they, God's good wheat, have been gathered into the garner, and there they are now in Jesus' floor. There are their little spirits rejoicing before the throne of the Most High. The mother who is left thinks not of it, but she is the mother of angels, and, perhaps, herself a child of hell. Ah, mother! what think you of this? Is this separation from your child eternal? Will you be content to be found at God's great winnowing-day the chaff, and will you be driven from your children? Shall you see them in heaven—them in heaven, and yourselves then cast out forever? Can you bear the thought? Has your heart become brutish? Is your soul harder than a nether millstone? Surely, if it be no, the thought of your present intimate connection with God's people, and of your sure separation, will make you tremble. And, oh! my hearers, here are some of you sitting side by side with the godly. You sing as they sing, you hear as they hear. Perhaps you assist the outward wants of the Church. You are to the church just what the chaff is to the wheat. You are the outward husk, the congregation which surrounds the inner living nucleus of the church. And must it be—must you be separated from us? Are you content to go from the songs of the saints to the shrieks of the doomed? Will you go from the great convocation of the righteous to the last general assembly of the destroyed and cursed? The thought checks my voice. I must speak slowly on this matter for a while.

Well, dear brethren, well I know that this thought used to be dreadful to me. My mother said to me once, after she had long prayed for me, and had come to the conviction that I was hopeless, "Ah," said she, "my son, if at the last great day you are condemned, remember your mother will say amen to your condemnation." That stung me to the quick. Must the mother that brought me forth, and that loved me, say "Amen" to my being condemned at last? Yet such things must be. Doth not the wheat say amen to the chaff being blown into fire unquenchable? Think,

my dear hearers, think again. And must it be—must I bid farewell to her I love—who served the Lord in spirit. Must I see her
body committed to the grave, and as I stand there, must I bid
her a last, a final farewell? Must I be forever separated from
her, because I fear not God, neither regard him, and therefore
cannot have a portion among the Lord's chosen ones? What, have
you lost your relatives forever? Are your pious fathers and mothers
buried in a "sure and certain hope" to which you are strangers?
Will you never sing the song of rejoicing with them in heaven?
Is there never to be another salutation? Is death a gulf that
cannot be bridged to you?

Oh, I hope it is the joy of some of us to know we shall meet
many of our kindred above; and as we have lost one after
another, this has been our sweet consolation: they are gone and
we shall soon follow them; they are not lost, but gone before;
they are buried as to their flesh, but their souls are in Paradise,
and we shall be there also; and, when we have seen our Saviour's
face, and rejoiced in that glorious vision, then shall we see
them also, and have deeper and purer fellowship with them than
we ever had before in all the days of our lives. Well, here is a
sad prophecy! The wicked are "like the chaff which the wind
driveth away."

But you will remark that the awful character of my text
does not appear upon the surface. They "are like the chaff which
the wind *driveth away.*" Where—where—where? Where are they
driven? The man is in health, the sun shines, the sky is calm,
the world is still about him. Suddenly there is seen a little
cloud the size of a man's hand. A little signal overtakes him.
The hurricane begins to rise, but first it is but a faint breath.
The wicked man feels the cold air blowing on him, but he
screens it with the physician, and he thinks that surely he shall
live. The storm is on. God hath decreed it, and man cannot
stay it. The breath becomes a wind, the wind a storm, the storm
a howling hurricane. His soul is swept away. To go to heaven
on angel's wings is a glorious thing; but to be swept out of this

world with the wicked, is an awful thing—to be carried, not
on wings of cherubs, but on the eagle wings of the wind; to be
borne, not by yon songsters up to their celestial seats, but to be
carried away in the midst of a howling tempest, by grim friends.
The wicked are like the chaff which the wind driveth away. I
do not know how to bring out the fulness of its poetry—the
great storm sweeping man from the place on which he stands.
He is driven away. And now cannot your thoughts go further
on, while I again repeat the question, Whither is he driven?
Ah! Whither is he driven?

I cannot tell you into what state that soul at once enters;
that is to say, I cannot tell you by any guess of my own—that
were frivolous, and were to play with a solemn matter—but I can
tell you one thing, Jesus Christ himself hath said it: "He will
burn up the chaff with unquenchable fire." You die, but you die
not. You depart, but you depart to fire that never shall be
quenched. I will not dwell upon the topic. I return again to
ask the question—"Who among us shall dwell with the devouring fire? Who among us shall dwell with everlasting burnings?"
Who here is prepared to make his bed in hell? Who shall lie down
and rest forever in that lake of fire? You must, my hearers, if
you are ungodly, except you repent. Are there none of you behind
me there, who have been living without Christ, and without hope
in the world? Are there none of you? Surely there are some such.
I beseech you, think of your destiny—death and after death the
judgment. The wind, and after the wind the whirlwind, and after
the whirlwind the fire, and after the fire—forever, forever lost,
cast away, where ray of hope can never come; where eye of mercy
can never look upon you, and hand of grace can never reach you.
I beseech you, oh, I beseech you, by the living God, before whom
you stand this day, tremble and repent. "Kiss the Son, lest he be
angry, and ye perish from the way, when his wrath is kindled
but a little." "Tophet is ordained of old; yea, for the king it
is prepared; he hath made it deep and large: the pile thereof is
fire and much wood; the breath of the Lord, like a stream of

brimstone, doth kindle it." "Turn ye, turn ye, why will ye die, O house of Israel?" "Let the wicked forsake his way, and the unrighteous man his thoughts: and let him return unto the Lord, and he will have mercy upon him; and to our God, for he will abundantly pardon."

I pray God, the Holy Spirit, to touch some ungodly hearts now. Remember, my dear hearers, if there be in your bosoms this morning one desire toward Christ, cherish it—blow the little spark till it comes to a flame. If your heart melts ever so little this morning, I beseech you resist not—quench not the heavenly influence. Yield up yourselves, and remember the sweet text of last Sunday morning, "Whosoever will, let him come and take the water of life freely." Oh that you would but come to him! Oh that ye knew how to weep for yourselves! Oh that ye knew what a fearful thing it will be to be cast away forever! Why will ye die? Is there anything pleasing in destruction? Is sin so luscious to you that you will burn in hell forever for it? Is Christ so hard a master that you will not love him? Is his cross so ugly that ye will not look towards it? I beseech you by him whose heart is love, the crucified Redeemer, who now speaks, look to him and be saved, for he came into the world to seek and to save that which was lost, and him that cometh to him he will in no wise cast out, for "he is able also to save them to the uttermost that come unto God by him."

Today, O Spirit, bring sinners to thyself. I exhort you, sinners, lay hold on Christ. Touch the hem of his garment now. Behold, he hangs before you on the cross. As Moses lifted up the serpent in the wilderness, even so is Jesus lifted up. Look, I beseech you, look and live. Believe on the Lord Jesus Christ and you shall be saved. As though God did beseech you by me, I pray you in Christ's stead, be ye reconciled to God. And O may the Spirit make my appeal effectual! May angels rejoice this day over sinners saved and brought to know the Lord! AMEN.